AF697382

Criminal Deterrence Theory

Criminal Deterrence Theory

The History, Myths & Realities

David J. Cornwell

eleven
international publishing

Published, sold and distributed by Eleven International Publishing
P.O. Box 85576
2508 CG The Hague
The Netherlands
Tel.: +31 70 33 070 33
Fax: +31 70 33 070 30
e-mail: sales@elevenpub.nl
www.elevenpub.com

Sold and distributed in USA and Canada
International Specialized Book Services
920 NE 58th Avenue, Suite 300
Portland, OR 97213-3786, USA
Tel.: 1-800-944-6190 (toll-free)
Fax: +1 503 280-8832
orders@isbs.com
www.isbs.com

Eleven International Publishing is an imprint of Boom uitgevers Den Haag.

ISBN 978-94-6236-815-6
ISBN 978-94-6274-807-1 (e-book)

© 2018 David J. Cornwell | Eleven International Publishing

This publication is protected by international copyright law.
All rights reserved. No part of this publication may be reproduced, stored in a retrieval system, or transmitted in any form or by any means, electronic, mechanical, photocopying, recording or otherwise, without the prior permission of the publisher.

Printed in The Netherlands

Table of Contents

By the Same Author

Criminal Punishment and Restorative Justice, Waterside Press, 2006

Doing Justice Better: The Politics of Restorative Justice, Waterside Press, 2007

The Penal Crisis and the Clapham Omnibus, Waterside Press, 2009

Civilising Criminal Justice, [Edited with John Blad and Martin Wright], Waterside Press, 2013

Mercy: A Restorative Philosophy, Waterside Press, 2014

Desert in a Reparative Frame, Eleven International Publishing, 2016

Acknowledgements

As this work goes into print there are a number of people whom I would like to thank for making this entire endeavour possible, and without whose encouragement and support it might never have reached completion. Indeed, at the conception stage, some colleagues with whom the idea was discussed expressed quite reasonable reservations about its ultimate usefulness in the present climate of penal politics and sentencing practices that prevail in a number of contemporary democracies in Western Europe and elsewhere worldwide, but most particularly within the United Kingdom. I hope that at least to some extent their misgivings may have been allayed by the outcome.

To Selma Hoedt, Jolien Suurmond, Jesse Meindertsma, Melanie Boote and their Graphic Design Department colleagues at Eleven International Publishing at The Hague in the Netherlands I owe an immense debt of gratitude for their friendly and efficient handling and editing of the manuscript and its ultimate presentation. Their advice and professional expertise has been greatly appreciated.

I am also extremely grateful to Professor Bas van Stokkom of Radboud University, Nijmegen, for his comments on the draft manuscript, and for finding the time within a busy work schedule to write the Foreword for this work. His insights as both a criminologist and a philosopher have proved a source of inspiration and challenge as this work neared completion.

As ever, my friend and colleague Dr John Blad – recently retired from Erasmus University, Rotterdam – has been supportive and always constructive as work on this book progressed. Our frequent e-mail conversations have proved a sustaining influence over recent years on a number of journeys through the criminological wilderness. His infectious enthusiasm, intellectual honesty and width of vision will be much missed by his many former students and professional admirers.

Finally, every journey has a beginning. Mine was at York University in 1979 following some twenty-three years of military service, and under the supervision of Dr Tony Fowles and the late Professor Kathleen (Kay) Jones who steered my path through both Master's and Doctoral studies with endless patience. Tony has remained a valued friend over the ensuing almost forty years, and I acknowledge with admiration and many thanks his contribution to what has proved to be an eventful and challenging second career.

About the Author

Dr David J. Cornwell is a semi-retired consultant criminologist and author who now works from his home near Tewkesbury, Gloucestershire in the United Kingdom. He is a former soldier, prison governor and academic researcher with considerable experience as a criminal justice practitioner in both the public and private sectors of correctional services in the United Kingdom, in several overseas countries in Western Europe, and in the Republic of South Africa.

He is the author of six previous books focused predominantly upon criminal punishment and restorative justice, and of numerous journal articles and conference papers published over the past thirty years in the United Kingdom and elsewhere. Most recently, the main emphasis of his work has been devoted to the urgent need for penal reform in England and Wales, and the advancement of mediation and reparative justice within the criminal justice processes of contemporary Western-style democracies worldwide.

David Cornwell was educated at Christ's Hospital School, Horsham, the Royal Military Academy Sandhurst, and the University of York which awarded his Master's and Doctoral degrees. He was also a former Tutor at HM Prison Service College, Wakefield, West Yorkshire between 1989 and 1994, and served as a governor grade manager in various grades and prisons between 1982 and 1997. He was subsequently employed by Group 4 Prison and Court Services in the private sector management of prisons in the United Kingdom and at Bloemfontein in South Africa. His final post in HM Prison Service was as Head of Security Audit in the Standards Audit Unit, in which capacity he visited and audited the security of some eighty prisons in England and Wales between 1995 and 1997. His other interests lie in rugby football, cricket, and a lifetime of participating in choral music.

The Author of the Foreword

Professor Bas van Stokkom is a philosopher and criminologist from the Netherlands. He has worked at the Centre for Ethics, Faculty of Philosophy, Radboud University Nijmegen, and is also Assistant Professor at the Criminological Institute of that university and Lecturer at the Faculty of Social Sciences, Free University, Amsterdam. His research has focused on the fields of freedom of speech, deliberative democracy, restorative justice, and punishment ethics. He is the Chief Editor of the Dutch-Flemish *Tijdschrift voor Herstelrecht*

(Journal of Restorative Justice), and co-editor of the studies *Images of Restorative Justice Theory* (2008), *Reflections on Reassurance Policing in the Low Countries* (2008), and *Public Forgiveness in Post-Conflict Contexts* (2011).

Among other more recent publications, Bas van Stokkom notably contributed a chapter entitled 'Tempering Justice with Compassion: Rationales of Personal Mitigation in Sentencing' to the collection of international essays in *Civilising Criminal Justice*, D.J. Cornwell, J.R. Blad and M. Wright (Eds.), Hook, Hampshire, Waterside Press, 2013, pp.255-286, which received wide recognition for furthering the cause of restorative justice worldwide. There are few colleagues of my acquaintance across the world better placed to provide the Foreword for this work, and I am greatly indebted to him for sparing the time from a busy workload to do so.

Author's Preface

During the almost two year period spent considering and researching the material for this book, the criminal justice process of England and Wales, like those of a number of other democratic nations worldwide, has plunged further into chaos. As a former practitioner in that process, and as a criminologist over some forty years past by academic inclination, I, like many of my professional colleagues past and present, search persistently for the root causes of this deplorable situation.

Crises in democratic state organisations and services very rarely occur accidentally or suddenly, but are more frequently the result of systemic misdirection, of political indecision and vacillation, and, ultimately, of professional frustration and abandonment or neglect of fundamental operational principles and practices. Consider one very basic question: how has the situation arisen in which our prisons have increasingly become more dangerous and violent places for staff and prisoners alike; in which a culture of illicit and even psychotropic drug-taking has become endemic; and in which detection of forbidden mobile phones in the possession of prisoners has become a commonplace occurrence?

Another question arises from the situation just described. How can it 'accidentally' have become the case that the prison population of England and Wales rose from 41,500 (40,300 males and 1,200 females) in 1976, to 52,000 (50,300 males and 1,700 females) in 1996, and then to 84,300 (80,500 males and 3,800 females) in 2016? What drove this sudden escalation as the new millennium began, if not a deliberate attempt to deter and control crime through policies of mass incarceration and incapacitation in which politicians and the judiciary were complicit, and which were inspired by the mass media. For as Michael Tonry astutely observed: 'the bottom line is that current policies, political rhetoric and punishment patterns are as they are because politicians, however motivated, wished it so' (2003:6).[1]

This book is about the origins and impact of the deterrence doctrine in criminal justice, the claims made for and against it, and the extent to which it has influenced the development of penal policies and practices particularly since World War 2. That it is based primarily upon the criminal justice processes of England and Wales provides only an exemplary context, since it is evident that many of the aspects of deterrence discussed within its chapters are, to some or another extent, replicated in other jurisdictions worldwide.

1 M. Tonry (Ed.), *Confronting Crime: Crime Control Policy Under New Labour*, Cullompton, Devon, UK: Willan Publishing, 2003.

There is little doubt that the concept of deterrence has enjoyed a widely taken-for-granted acceptance over centuries past, but the extent to which it has penetrated contemporary penal policies and practices is distinctly questionable both conceptually and operationally. This book was conceived to explore the extent to which deterrence theory is an acceptable basis upon which to promote policy and practice, having due regard to some of its evidently dysfunctional effects upon the lives of offenders, would-be offenders, victims of crime and communities in particular.

It must also remain a matter of concern that at the political level, and particularly since the closing decades of the previous century, the notion of deterrence in combination with retribution and incapacitation has heavily influenced sentencing policies to the extent of driving the custodial penal population of England and Wales to unprecedented levels in this new millennium. During this same period, rates of post-sentence recidivism have also escalated, making the deterrent effect of imprisonment similarly questionable – particularly in an era in which both overall crime and victimisation rates across Western Europe have shown consistent decreases since the mid-1990s. These trends have also detracted from serious consideration of alternative policies based upon concepts of reparative and restorative justice as a means towards reducing crime.

The deterrence doctrine is, without doubt, the most complex of the four traditionally accepted grand theories of punishment, and also the most evasive of rational justification. This fact has made a book of this nature the more difficult to write, though it has been a stimulating endeavour designed to fill an important gap in the contemporary criminological literature. For in spite of the prevalence, and continuing (though somewhat uncritical) acceptance of the status of deterrence as a cardinal purpose of criminal punishment, it displays, on careful examination, a fragility that should alarm the discerning reader.

Few people, other than possibly Jack Gibbs (1975), Daniel Nagin (1998 and 2001) and Raymond Paternoster (2010)[2], have produced convincing and substantial analyses of the specific effects of deterrence theory upon penal policy making since the 1970s. The latter in particular, in concluding his assessment of the operant effect of deterrent measures on rational actor offenders, contended that this effect was significantly affected by their perceptions of evading apprehension and, if apprehended, the temporal lapse before punishment is imposed (pp.818-823). If this reasoning is as convincing as many may find it to be, it casts considerable doubt upon the contemporary prevalence of sentencing practices

2 See here the relevant bibliographical entries at the end of this work and subsequent references to their contributions to the deterrence debate in the main chapters.

that increase the severity of sanctions for deterrent purposes rather than reducing the time taken to bring offenders to justice.

These and many other considerations related to deterrence theory emerge within this book which, it is hoped, will provide some clarification of the extent to which the taken-for-granted status of deterrence within contemporary criminal punishment theory and practice has become distinctly questionable and even counter-productive.

Finalisation of the manuscript of this work has taken place at a time in which a majority of the citizens within the United Kingdom have clearly signalled their wish to leave the European Union (EU) and its ever-increasing incursions into the economic and social affairs of sovereign member states. The process of negotiating the terms of what has come to be described as 'Brexit' is under way, and should be completed during 2019. Once this separation has been achieved, an opportunity will arise to significantly reform and re-shape the criminal justice processes of the United Kingdom – a reform which is long overdue and urgently necessary.

These processes, though procedurally different within England and Wales, Scotland and Northern Ireland respectively, differ in many historical and traditional respects from those of the nations of continental Europe. While few would deny that the criminal justice process of England and Wales, upon which this book is based, is in almost chaotic disarray, the measures necessary to reform it effectively are not amenable to increasing 'pan-Europeanism', even though the causes and symptoms of the contemporary crisis may be similar to many being experienced in several Western European and other democracies at the present time.

For many of the reasons identified within this work, the English criminal justice process has, for some decades past, sleep-walked into a paralysis of its own making. Unquestioned acceptance of, and adherence to deterrence-based policies, resulting in ill-conceived sentencing legislation, has contributed significantly to this *malaise*. This book, in many respects a companion work to its predecessor *Desert in a Reparative Frame* (2016), is designed to propose how the present un-sustainable situation could be resolved to a significant extent. It is a timely 'call to arms' to all concerned in 'doing justice better' to unite and seize the opportunity to do just that.

On a sombre but realistic note, however, it is an undeniable fact that urgently necessary as it may be, far-reaching and effective penal reform is an unwelcome enterprise for risk-averse politicians and jurists alike to contemplate. To the former it poses a risk to their electoral credibility; to the latter, interference with their traditionally cherished independence. To overcome this difficulty it might be suggested that the time has arrived for a truly independent Royal Commission on the Penal System of England and Wales, drawing on the extensive wisdom and professional experience of all the participants in criminal justice administration and operation, academic research, penal reform organisations and the media. Unless and until there is a consensus for reform, the existing penal system will remain a seriously neglected and pathogenic threat, and unfit for purpose within a civilised democracy.

David J. Cornwell
Conderton, Tewkesbury, United Kingdom
October 2017

Foreword

Bas van Stokkom

In the author's preface David Cornwell suggests that the deterrence doctrine is the most complex of the four 'grand theories of punishment' and 'the most evasive of rational justification'. 'It displays a fragility that should alarm the discerning reader'. The author examines the emotional attractiveness of this doctrine and criticises its speculative and untestable claims. He argues that deterrence has always been a vague and unmeasurable construct. The efficacy of deterrent measures within penal policies remains an intuitive construct rather than a theory based on empirical evidence. 'The attractiveness of deterrence theory lies in its seductive appeal to intuition as a means of crime control rather than crime reduction' (p. 45).

This book deals mainly with the alleged deterrent effect of imprisonment on individual offenders; it does not extensively discuss the role of penalties in reinforcing the law abiding behaviour of the general public. This book is essentially focused on specific deterrence: using punishment, and especially imprisonment, to discourage a person from re-offending.

Cornwell's assessment of specific deterrence is crystal clear: imprisonment fails to deter ex-convicts and contributes to re-offending. Why then, he asks, has the deterrence doctrine survived as a cornerstone of the penal process? Why is imprisonment still – and increasingly – used as a bulk punitive measure? The answer is that the crime control version of deterrence became the predominant strategy. The current crime control agenda encourages the use of disproportionate sentencing to create a new form of exclusive 'outlawry'.

Clearly, the concept of deterrence can be used rhetorically. It is often linked to the fantasy that punishment 'will' work or 'must' work. Politicians who want to promote an image of decisiveness have always been fond of this rhetoric. David Cornwell refers to the 'hawkish' Home Secretary Michael Howard, who stated in 1993: 'Let us be clear. Prison works. It ensures that we are protected from murderers, robbers and rapists – and it makes many who are tempted to commit crime think twice' (p. 67). In the Netherlands, ex-minister of Justice Ivo Opstelten and associated politicians were also eager to demonstrate that deterrence 'must work'. They introduced a *bonus malus* system which put an end to 'all kinds of privileges' that would be available in prison. Only detainees who 'behave' may participate in education, activities and have access to temporary release. Thereby they simply ignored the mass of research findings about defiance and its contribution to recidivism.

Behind the deterrence rhetoric, atavistic 'control' intuitions play a role, such as 'breaking the will of the villain', 'showing who's the boss' and 'intimidate the convict into law abiding behaviour'. Of course, these impulses cannot be expressed too loudly in an era of human rights sensitivities, but they continuously surface in the political arena and obstruct attempts to understand what is needed to get perpetrators back on track. At worst a zero sum populist rhetoric is put to the test: if you pay attention to the criminal, you let the victim down. Victims are injured again when the evil-minded receive support.

In Belgium and the Netherlands, after the First and Second World Wars, substantial reforms to the prison system took place. An important reason for this was the fact that social and political leaders had been taken captive during the war. They had experienced the hard prison life themselves and became convinced that change in the penitentiary regime was necessary. In the Netherlands, the tolerant post-war penal climate has often been associated with the concentration camp experiences of the elites, including criminal justice scholars and criminologists. For example, Dutch criminologist Herman Bianchi spent several months in prison in 1944. The relationship between his life-long battle for the reform of criminal law and his own detention was evident. In his words: 'I know what it's like to be locked up. It's the worst that you can do to a human being. It's a goddamn shame to detain people. It is a crime to respond with a crime.'[1]

Today's elites and middle classes do not seem to worry much about the impact of imprisonment. There is a deep gap between the prison population of marginalised people and the wealthy echelons of the population. Considering all this may illustrate why David Cornwell speaks about a 'prison crisis' and the '*malaise*' in the present criminal justice system. The expansion of the penal system in England and Wales 'reveals a deep seated crisis of legitimacy' (Introduction p. 5). Moreover, there is a 'crisis of numbers'. In 1990 the prison population in England and Wales reached 50,000. In spite of decreasing crime figures since the nineties, this growth has continued. In early 2017, the prison population had reached 85,000. The government – in the White Paper *Prison Safety and Reform* (2016) – heralded 'a further wave of new prisons'. Although the author mainly describes penal developments in England and Wales, this growth is characteristic of many countries. For example, Belgium also shows this paradoxical trend of decreasing crime figures but

1 Cited in Jacques Claessen, Straffen en herstellen in bijbels perspectief: de geestelijke erfenis van Herman Bianchi, *Tijdschrift voor Filosofie* 2017, 78 (4): p.844.

increased custodial sentences. By contrast, the Netherlands shows a positive development: its prison population dropped from 17,000 in 2005 to about 11,000 in 2016.

There is a recurring critique of the penal system in Cornwell's *oeuvre* and a recurring plea for profound penal reform. In this book he sketches the contours of this reform agenda and pleads for true crime reduction and an inclusive strategy within the consequentialist logic: maximising the potential of sanctions to have beneficial outcomes and minimising disadvantageous outcomes of exclusion, recidivism and enhanced criminality (p. 77). He realises that crime reduction strategies imply a wide range of reforms and involve considerable investment costs, but he also makes it clear that these changes can be accomplished. He argues that short prison sentences are considerably less effective than community sanctions in reducing recidivism. For this reason he proposes that all sentences of four years imprisonment or less[2] be replaced by community sanctions. 'Such an initiative would immediately reduce the prison population by some 27,000 places, while at the same time eliminating prison overcrowding' (p. 124).

Furthermore, the author argues that reparative justice is the potential key to desistance from crime: making offenders responsible for their wrongful actions, enabling them to make amends for the harm they caused, and giving positive incentives to change their behaviour. The main task for criminal justice policy makers is to facilitate desistance. It requires an investment in time and resources to equip offenders with the ability to self-reform and make reparation. The financial costs of this investment have to be balanced against the excessive costs of re-offending within the current crime control model.

Is this a revolutionary vision? No, it is realism! This realism – as Cornwell emphasises – was clearly evident in some White papers. The New Labour government – see *Justice for All* (2002) – acknowledged that short prison sentences of twelve months or less were not only 'usually ineffective' but also 'increase chances of reoffending'. In another White Paper, published in 1990 under the aegis of the conservative government, it was acknowledged that 'imprisonment is an expensive way of making bad people worse' (p. 76). Importantly, this realism seems to be gaining greater influence. In America, a remarkable consensus has been established regarding the harm of mass incarceration among the political left and right.[3] In the words of criminologist Shadd Maruna: 'it's now or never! The moment has

2 Under present rules (Criminal Justice Act 1991), such sentences are effectively two years or less in custody, the remaining half of the sentence being served in the community

3 See, T. Clear & N. Frost, *The Punishment Imperative: The Rise and Failure of Mass Incarceration in America*, New York: University Press, 2015.

never been better for a reparation based justice model that can counter the demonizing forces of the worldwide 'just us' and 'my country first' populist movements.'[4]

There is no utopianism in David Cornwell's vision, nor does he demonstrate abolitionist ambitions. He realises that prisons contain hard-to-change repeat offenders who are not suitable for reparative regimes. At the same time he is an engaged thinker, always reasoning from an enlightened perspective, avoiding abstract and reductionist language; an independent spirit, who feels at home in many disciplines and knows the classics.

Cornwell could be viewed as an author of 'grand narratives', not worrying much about constructing a systematic model or theory. He dares to write 'entire elephant' stories from a wide range of perspectives: historical, social sciences and philosophical. In academic *milieus* this is generally discouraged. Probably, the gathered specialists in leading peer-reviewed journals would oppose the publication of a text with such all-encompassing views. The question is whether current academics *could* compose a thorough justice narrative *überhaupt*. I think most would lack a solid philosophical overview of punishment justifications and lack the abilities to put the criminal justice system in an accurate historical frame. Luckily, David Cornwell displays these skills from the outset.

He is also an innovative thinker. In his study *Desert in a Reparative Frame* (2016) he argued that the retrospective perspective of the 'just deserts' theory largely denies legitimate desert-claims of both victims and offenders and therefore presents only a limited and 'negative' interpretation of the importance of desert. The author demonstrated that the retrospective notion of deserved punishment is only one component of a much more comprehensive interpretation of desert. In the present book he focuses once again on philosophical core concepts. The author gives a positive interpretation of consequentialism and actually intends to safeguard crime reduction from the logic of deterrence. In this sense, he is a real philosopher: he tries to rethink and refresh the stiffened concepts that have dominated punishment theory for a long time.

David Cornwell elucidates alternatives for the failing crime control policies and sketches a constructive justice perspective that would be very helpful for all the parties involved.

4 See: S. Maruna, 'Desistance and Restorative Justice: It's Now or Never', in *Restorative Justice: An International Journal*, 4 (3), 2017, pp.289-301.

This book deserves widespread attention and readers who are prepared to take the time to consider this well-thought-through reform perspective.

Bas van Stokkom
Criminologist and Philosopher, Radboud University Nijmegen, The Netherlands.

List of Abbreviations Used in This Book

ACPS	Advisory Council on the Penal System
AFSC	American Friends Service Committee
AMTBF	Average Mean Time Between Failures
CBC	Cannabicyclohexanol (aka 'Spice')
CCCCJS	Cabinet Committee on Crime and the Criminal Justice System
CCTV	Closed Circuit Television
CICA	Criminal Injuries Compensation Authority
CJA	Criminal Justice Act
CJF	Community Justice Forum
CNA	Certified Normal Accommodation
CSO	Community Service Order
ECHR	European Court of Human Rights
ESPP	Extended Sentence for Public Protection
EU	European Union
FGC	Family Group Conference
GBP	Pounds Sterling (£) British Currency
HMCIP	HM Chief Inspector of Prisons
HORU	Home Office Research Unit
ISPP	Indeterminate Sentence for Public Protection
LRC	Local Review Committee
MoJ	Ministry of Justice
MTBF	Mean Time Between Failures
MTBF(AL)	Mean Time Between Failures (At Large)
NAO	National Audit Office
NAPO	National Association of Probation Officers
NOMS	National Offender Management Service
PA-PPAG	Parliamentary All-Party Penal Affairs Group
PCC	Police and Crime Commissioner
PD	Preventive Detention
PFI	Private Finance Initiative
PGA	Prison Governors Association
POA	Prison Officers Association
ROTL	Release on Temporary Licence
SI	Statutory Instrument
SSU	Special Secure Unit

TTAL	Total Time At Large
TTIC	Total Time in Custody
VIS	Victim Impact Statement
VOM	Victim Offender Mediation
VPS	Victim Personal Statement
VWGF	Victim and Witness General Fund
VW&CF	Victim Welfare & Compensation Fund (Replacement for VWGF)

Part I
Descent into Chaos

INTRODUCTION

The primary focus of this book is on what is often referred to within the criminological literature as the second of the grand theories of criminal punishment, namely deterrence. It is also, as Philip Bean suggested some thirty-five years ago, the most complex of the four grand theories of punishment originally expressed as retribution, deterrence, rehabilitation and reform as its central purposes (Bean, 1981:29).

However, as Bean further pointed out:

> while at one level it is reasonably clear what deterrence is supposed to mean, at another it is not at all certain if deterrence is a psychological theory based on threats, or a sociological theory based on social control, or perhaps both (*Ibid.*).

As will subsequently become evident within this work, the difference between these explanations or, alternatively, the relationship between them is more than just a matter of semantics.

What certainly is clear is that the concept of deterrence has, since its earliest expression in the works of philosophers such as Hugo Grotius (1583-1645), Thomas Hobbes (1588-1679), John Locke (1632-1704), Samuel von Pufendorf (1632-1694), and later of Cesare Bonesana-Beccaria (1738-1794), Jeremy Bentham (1748-1832) and John Stuart Mill (1806-1873) exerted a strong – if largely intuitive – influence on the subsequent development of punishment theories and practices. Later we shall examine the extent to which the ideology of deterrence as a principle of punishment brought it into conflict with the other grand theories previously mentioned during the nineteenth century and onwards to the present day.

Criminal punishment is, or should be, a means towards the moral, just and socially acceptable resolution of the harm caused by the illegal or negligent actions of offenders. But herein lies a paradox that has to be confronted in determining the essential nature and purpose of punishment processes. Crimes of whatever form or extent of seriousness which are brought to justice are defined from past acts or omissions that caused harm which cannot be undone: resolution of the harm occasioned by a crime is a prospective activity that should have a beneficial effect in reducing both the harm and the likelihood of future similar offending. Thus, punishing the harm retrospectively and retributively as the dominant purpose of punishment runs counter to the concept of reducing the harm caused and the likelihood of offending (or re-offending) which is the essence of individual (or specific) deterrence.

At the strategic and political level the paradoxical situation described above compels policy-makers and politicians to make a deliberate choice between crime control or crime reduction as the dominant purpose of criminal justice processes. Unfortunately, both criminological and sociological history serves to remind us that crime within societies both past and present is, by its very nature, endemic and largely un-amenable to control even within the most totalitarian of regimes due to its opportunistic and spontaneous unpredictability. Thus, efforts and resources devoted to attempting crime control result almost inevitably in an ever-increasing escalation in sentencing severity and the size of custodial penal populations, both of which are socially undesirable and economically counter-productive in humanitarian terms.

This much stated, of the two strategic options cited previously, crime reduction is the more realisable, if less spectacular, purpose of criminal justice administration. It does, however, require a morally re-educative rather than an essentially punitive approach, and one that is focused upon the preferable nature of a law-abiding lifestyle rather than a criminal one.

The second strand of deterrence theory is that widely referred to within criminological discourse as general deterrence. Stated briefly, it is based on the assumption that the penalties imposed on individual offenders for their offences will, if of sufficiently unpleasant severity, deter others who might consider offending in a similar manner from doing so. The American criminologists Franklin Zimring and Gordon Hawkins (1973) described such an approach as 'the legal threat in crime control',[1] and in spite of its intuitive appeal it is not without its own criticisms and detractors.

At first sight the proposition may seem entirely reasonable and even attractive as a means of crime control, and there is a considerable research literature on the general deterrent effectiveness of various penalties. However, while this research tends to indicate an inverse relationship between various crimes and the probability of arrest and conviction, it fails to confirm any direct relationship between crime and the severity of penalties. The inverse relationship also cannot be conclusively interpreted as deterrence evidence since negative

1 Here see: Zimring, F.E. & Hawkins, G., *Deterrence: The Legal Threat in Crime Control*, Chicago ILL: University of Chicago Press, 1973.

correlations between crime and arrest probabilities are compatible with other hypotheses that cannot be discounted.[2]

All of this leads inevitably to some discussion of the nature of criminal offending itself, and the circumstances in which it is committed. Some reputable theorists have put forward accounts based predominantly upon offenders perceived as 'rational actors' who calculate the likelihood or otherwise of evading detection and arrest, while others favour accounts suggesting that the majority are impulsive and/or opportunistic in committing offences, discounting or ignoring the chances of being brought to account for them.[3] Clearly, such theories have significant implications for the entire concept of deterrence, and in particular for the crime prevention *versus* crime control considerations indicated previously. We shall return to both aspects later within this work.

Meanwhile, no account of the nature of deterrence to be found in this book would be complete without two essential dimensions. The first involves a survey of the development of deterrence theory from the sixteenth century up to the present day, and of the principal participants whose works have influenced that development. The second dimension must be a contextual analysis of the philosophical and political effects of adopting deterrent policies within contemporary criminal justice processes. The prevailing penal situation in England and Wales will be discussed as an exemplar of such policies and their operational outcomes. It is to these important dimensions that the first three chapters of this work are devoted.

In Chapter 3 we shall, in particular, trace the effects of implementing penal policies predicated upon retribution and deterrence which precipitated the now long-running penal crisis within England and Wales as a specific example. Though superficially it has taken the form of a crisis of 'numbers', viewed more analytically it reveals a much more deep-seated crisis of legitimacy, political manipulation and confused thinking by successive governments since the early 1990s and into the present millennium. What was initially a manageable crisis with recognisable antecedent causes has now become a *malaise* in which the penal process has become pathogenically infected on a multi-virus basis.

2 For a more detailed analysis of this situation see: Byleveld, D., *A Bibliography on General Deterrence Research*, Berkhamstead, UK: Saxon House, 1980.

3 Such offenders also include those whose crimes are committed under the influence of alcohol or drugs, and whose behaviour may be temporarily or permanently impaired as a result of substance abuse or dependence. See, for example, Christopher Mumola, *Substance Abuse and Treatment, State and Federal Prisons 1997*, US Bureau of Justice Statistics Special Report, 1999, quoted in V. Wright, *Deterrence in Criminal Justice: Evaluating Certainty vs. Severity of Punishment*, Washington DC: The Sentencing Project, 2010, p.2.

The focus in Chapter 4 is upon the need to determine whether crime control or crime reduction strategies best meet the requirement for law observance and social order within contemporary democracies, and the implications of both for the formulation of penal policies. It follows from the discussion in Chapter 3 that if crime control (whether achievable or not) is to determine the basis of penal policies, and uncritical belief in the efficacy of general deterrence is to remain unchallenged, then rates of imprisonment will continue to escalate as sentencing becomes ever more severe in pursuit of deterrence. If, on the other hand, crime reduction is to dominate the policy agenda, then increased emphasis has to be placed upon understanding and reducing the causative social factors that encourage criminality within democracies in which disparities in affluence, opportunity and eligibility have become widespread. Individual or specific deterrence from crime can only become a reality when the perceived need to offend or the encouragement to do so is significantly diminished, and the risk: gain calculus of offending is re-balanced in favour of law-abiding behaviour.

The case for and against deterrence in criminal justice (in both its specific and general forms) is also examined from two ethical standpoints or approaches – those of the consequentialist and deontological explanations respectively. The purpose of this analysis is to determine which, or whether either, offers sufficient justification for incorporating deterrence-based components within punishment and sentencing practices. Here it will be noted that in the British tradition of sentencing it has for some decades past been seen as necessary to express the extent of sentencing in terms of the appropriateness of sanctions – and in particular imprisonment – in 'meeting the requirements of retribution and deterrence'. If, therefore, there is a 'deterrence premium' included explicitly or implicitly within sentencing practices, it is important to know the basis on which this is calculated and how it is justified.

It remains a paradoxical situation that in most of the democracies of Western Europe overall rates of recorded crime have decreased consistently since the mid-1990s, as has the likelihood of the average citizen becoming a victim of crime. And yet in some of these countries, including England and Wales in particular, over the same period, average daily prison populations have continued to rise year on year. In Chapter 5 this curious situation is examined and the necessity for its existence is challenged from the differing perspectives of victims and offenders, and the effects upon both in delaying necessary penal reform.

In the light of the discussion in the foregoing chapters it will have become evident that the undiscriminating acceptance of deterrence theory and practices has, over the decades since the end of World War 2, exercised a predominantly malign influence in the criminal justice processes of a number of democracies worldwide. In Chapter 6 we consider how this situation might be reversed, and how a more enlightened penal strategy might be envisaged for this new millennium and onwards. A case will be made for a more inclusive penology involving all the stakeholders in criminal justice – states, offenders, victims of crime and communities – with a greater emphasis on mediation, reconciliation, reparation and restoration within its processes. In so doing it might be possible to free justice from its pre-occupation with punitive incarceration and segregation and towards a more prospective and logical approach to correctional policy-making and its delivery.

In Chapter 7 the focus of attention is devoted to the contemporary situation in which the penal process of England and Wales is constrained to operate, and a comparison of this situation with other nations of Western Europe in particular. It also then becomes appropriate to explore the considerable differences in the rates of imprisonment that exist between those countries that use imprisonment the most and those the least in an attempt to discover whether or not cultural and social traditions and conditions might be seen to account for these disparities. Within this chapter we shall also explore how dependence upon prisons and imprisonment might be reduced without a significant increase in public risk, and with the potential to reduce current high rates of recidivism. This discussion will also consider the urgent need for the reform of sentencing practices and the consequent need for increased emphasis on effective non-custodial penalties including, where appropriate, the incorporation of reparative justice practices.

The final chapters of this work (Chapters 8 and 9) look towards a new criminal justice paradigm for the future. We return to Philip Bean's assertion mentioned earlier concerning the essential nature of deterrence theory, and draw some conclusions about this and the implications that it has for the criminology of the future. Few modern democracies facing the straitened fiscal and social circumstances of the contemporary situation in Europe and elsewhere can afford to be profligate with the burgeoning costs of unnecessary and ineffective imprisonment. That some of the more enlightened nations of Western Europe have deliberately chosen not to do so, particularly when other means of dealing effectively with low and medium risk offenders are available, is a matter of record worthy of serious consideration.

In Chapter 8 emphasis is placed on the potential for mediation and reparation to provide a platform for reducing short-term prison populations and increasing community participation in justice processes. Drawing on the experience of the Scandinavian nations, it becomes possible to envisage a more enlightened approach towards achieving these objectives within a unified structure of correctional services delivery involving the courts, prosecution authorities, mediation services, prisons and probation services.

The final chapter draws together the various strands of discussion throughout this work including learning from past failures, deciding upon the future direction of criminal justice strategy, and the measures of reform necessary to deliver a justice system that meets the needs of contemporary democracies in a coherent and more effective manner than present practices permit.

The full title of this work reflects its purpose: to explore, examine and evaluate the way in which unchallenging acceptance and adoption of the deterrence doctrine has influenced the stagnation of penal policies within many present day democracies. For however emotionally attractive deterrence theory may be, it remains a predominantly speculative, untestable and even illusory phenomenon that has, for too long, occupied a largely uncontested place within the philosophy and practices of criminal punishment.

Excessive or unnecessary use of imprisonment may be imagined to have a protective motive in a sociological context, but in the hard reality of our contemporary world it is actually a means of placing criminal offenders beyond the reach of the realities that govern functional citizenship on a day to day basis. Whether or not such exclusion from making life-changing choices is desirable socially or psychologically beneficial, the reader must decide.

1 Deterrence Theory C16-20

In this chapter we shall survey the works and ideas of a number of writers who are widely accepted as being the founding fathers of deterrence theory from the sixteenth century up to the present era. That these people were all citizens of European countries is no accident, since it was within the northern hemisphere that philosophical enquiry into crime causation originally became widespread in universities and theological circles, and the subject of serious academic analysis and discourse. Much earlier than this, however, traces of interest in the treatment of crime within societies are to be found most notably in the works of Socrates, Plato, Aristotle, Saint Augustine, Saint Thomas Aquinas, and a number of others whose interest focused primarily upon the nature of laws, rights and obligations within societies.

Natural law, as distinct from divine law, can be discovered from reason alone and applies to all people everywhere, whereas divine law derives from the revelation of spiritual and moral truths, most of which might be described as 'god-given' as expounded by religious leaders of many different denominations and traditions. However, natural law defines the nature of duties and obligations of citizens as members of societies, whereas natural rights usually relate to privileges or claims to which citizens become entitled in societies in return for their contribution to social well-being and law-abiding behaviour. Thus, within the scholarly discourses that we shall subsequently examine here, we shall also discover differences of view as to which, if either, of the two is the dominant consideration, or rather whether they are to a significant extent inter-dependent.

The writers and works described here are dealt with in the date order of their lives and without any necessary prior suggestion of congruence in their beliefs and approaches. In certain instances, however, areas of an overlapping philosophical nature will become evident in their works as might be expected since the span of their active adult lives similarly overlapped.

Hugo Grotius (1583-1654)

It seems altogether fitting that this account of the evolution of deterrence theory should start with a most unusual scholar – a philosopher, lawyer, theologian, diplomat, and escapee from persecution. Huig van Groot, subsequently better known as Hugo Grotius and of Dutch nationality, was born in Delft to parents of distinguished ancestry. His father Jan was a former curator of the University of Leiden and Burgomaster of Delft, and his mother was from a long-established and respected family.

By the age of seven Hugo was familiar with Latin and Greek, and at fourteen he obtained his first degree from the University of Leiden in history, philosophy, astronomy, theology and law. Aged fifteen he accompanied a Dutch mission to the court of Henry IV of France to secure that nation's continued support for the war against Spain. He went as a companion to the son of Jan van Olden Barneveldt, one of the leading Dutch officials, and his brilliance so impressed their hosts that he was awarded the honorary degree of Doctor of Laws by the University of Orleans. In 1599, at the age of seventeen he was sworn in as a lawyer and his legal career began.

In 1608 Hugo married Maria van Reigersberg who was of aristocratic descent and evidently a very resourceful lady. At this time he had already published a Latin tragedy in verse (*Adamus Exil – Exile of Adam*) and had started in 1604 on a major work (*De Jure Praedae-Concerning the Law of Prizes*) which advocated freedom of the seas.[1] After his marriage, he embarked on a political career, and, with Barneveldt's sponsorship, rose to a high position, being involved in a number of important international missions. However, through his friendship with Barneveldt he had joined a religious faction called the Remonstrants (or Arminians after one of their leaders Jacob Arminius) who were opposed to another group known as the Calvinists (or Contra-Remonstrants) when the Protestant Dutch Reformed Church split into two major groups following a schism. The latter were headed by Prince Maurice who in 1618 moved troops against the Arminians, occupied the main cities, and arrested Barneveldt and Grotius. After a summary trial Barneveldt was executed and Grotius was sentenced to imprisonment for life, with his property confiscated, in the fortress prison of Louvestein on the River Meuse.

After two years in captivity there, accompanied by his wife Maria who with their maid Elsje planned and executed it, Grotius was enabled to escape in a wooden chest that had been used to bring him books to aid his studies, and was moved by sea to Gorcum where he emerged weak from exposure and lack of air, and was welcomed by Louis XIII in France where he settled in Paris, continued his writing, and was later joined by his faithful wife. In Paris he completed his most notable work *De Jure Belli et Pacis- The Law of War and Peace* which achieved considerable fame and was widely read by statesmen in many different

1 The original manuscript of this work subsequently became lost and was not rediscovered until 1865, but its central ideas appeared in other of his published books and treatises.

countries.[2] This success enabled him to contemplate a return to Holland which he undertook in 1626, but after six months his re-arrest was ordered under the old charges plus that of escaping, and he fled to Sweden where he subsequently became an ambassador to France from 1635 to 1645. On 25th August 1645, while travelling from Stockholm to Lubeck, he was shipwrecked and died from exposure shortly after being taken ashore near Rostock, Mecklenbrg-Schwerin. His body was recovered to his home city of Delft where his memorial remains to this day.

This astonishing life story apart, Hugo Grotius was a scholar of massive intellect and breadth of understanding. His vision for international order and peaceful political relationships was almost revolutionary in a world dominated by the religious feuds, colonial aspirations and shifting national alliances that emerged during the Thirty Years War between 1618 and 1648, in which almost the whole of Europe ultimately became actively involved to a greater or lesser extent.[3]

In *The Law of War and Peace* Grotius dealt with the punishment of both offending nations and individuals in terms of deterrence from an almost utilitarian perspective. In Book 2 at Chapter 20 'On Punishments' of this work he included (at section IX) the following observation:

---

2 See: Hugo Grotius, *De Jure Belli et Pacis*, originally published by Buon in Paris in 1625 and re-published by Liberty Fund, Indianapolis, 2005 in three volumes. It was in Book 2 of this work at Chapter 20 'On Punishments' that Grotius set out his analysis of the purpose of deterrence in criminal justice.

3 The Thirty Years War 1618-48 was precipitated by an event known as the (Second) Defenestration of Prague on 23rd May 1618, in which the religious differences between the Catholic and Protestant elements of the Bohemian kingdom came to a head. The incident of defenestration occurred when envoys of King Ferdinand of Styria and King of Bohemia were sent to Prague to arbitrate in a dispute that had arisen over the curtailment of building Protestant churches on royal land. The freedom of Protestants to follow their own religion in Bohemia had been assured by a *Letter of Majesty* issued by a former Emperor, Rudolf II, in 1609 who was succeeded by King Matthias who had died childless and nominated his cousin Ferdinand as his successor. Matthias had been sympathetic to the cause of the Bohemian Protestants, but Ferdinand was an adherent of the Catholic Counter-Reformation and was less well-disposed to Protestantism and Bohemian freedoms. The Bohemian Protestants had interpreted the letter written by King Rudolf to extend not only to the lands controlled by the nobility of self-governing towns, but also to the King's own lands. When they protested against the curtailment, Ferdinand had their assembly dissolved and their powers nullified. The four Catholic envoys of Ferdinand, styled as Lords Regent, arrived at the Bohemian Chancellery and were met by met by members of the dissolved assembly who demanded to know whether any or all of them had been party to the order of King Mathias for the cessation, had recommended it, or had approved it. The Lords Regent asked for an adjournment of the meeting in order to consult their superior Adam von Waldstein who was not present, but the Protestants demanded an immediate answer. Subsequently, two of the envoys were declared innocent of any responsibility, and were removed from the meeting room, but the remaining two and their secretary admitted responsibility, assuming that they would be merely arrested and possibly punished by the Protestants. In the event, they were thrown from the third storey window of the meeting room (defenestrated), but somehow survived the seventy foot fall to the ground below and left Prague bruised but alive.

> The good of mankind in general, which was the third object of punishment, involves the same problems as the good of one who has been wronged. For in this case the punishment may be inflicted to prevent the man who has injured one person from injuring others, which is accomplished by removing him or weakening him or restraining him so that he cannot do harm, or by reforming him. Or the punishment may be inflicted to prevent others from being induced by a feeling of security to annoy any person whatsoever. This is attained by the infliction of outstanding penalties, which the Greeks call *paradeigmata*, the Romans *exempla*, or 'examples'. These exemplary punishments so that the punishment of one may cause many to fear, and that others may be frightened by the nature of the punishment, as the laws say, or according to Demosthenes, 'that others may learn wisdom and be afraid'. (Grotius, 1625:2, 20, IX).[4]

The passage above is illustrative of Grotius' familiarity with the philosophical discourses of the early classical eras of Greece and Rome that are evident throughout his writings. It is in this particular sense that his works bridge the void between the ancient and the emerging Enlightenment worlds of the eighteenth century and onwards in the spheres of law, politics and philosophy.

Thomas Hobbes (1588-1679)

Like Grotius, Hobbes was a precocious youngster schooled in the classical importance of Greek and Latin. He graduated from Magdalen Hall in Oxford in 1608 at the age of 20. His views on punishment were, however, quite different from those of Grotius, especially in relation to the preventive nature of deterrence as a principle and purpose of punishment. Hobbes saw the actions of human beings as motivated by causes – either just or unjust – and therefore determined as acts of will rather than predetermined. Such an approach differs from that of the doctrine of free will in an important respect insofar as, in the case of illegal or criminal acts, the motivations to act wrongfully may stem from causes such as avarice, passion, lust or envy as contributory factors (causes) within each person. However, if the act is committed knowing that it is illegal, that punishment will result from its discovery, and the threat of punishment is insufficiently strong to dissuade its commission, then it is wilfully responsible and therefore justifiably punishable. For as Hobbes said:

---

4 The extract quoted here is from Hugo Grotius, *The Law of War and Peace*, re-published by the Liberty Fund, Indianapolis, 2005, Book 2, Chapter 20, pages un-numbered. For further commentary on Grotius' work see: R. Tuck (Ed.), *The Rights of War and Peace: Political Thought From Grotius to Kant*, Oxford University Press, 1990, especially Chapter 3.

> ... what necessary cause soever precede an action, yet if the action is forbidden, he that does it willingly may justly be punished. For instance, suppose that a man who by the strength of temptation is necessitated to steal and is thereupon put to death; does not this punishment deter others? Is it not a cause that others steal not? Does it not frame and make their wills to justice? To make the law is therefore to make a cause of justice and to necessitate justice; and consequently it is no injustice to make such a law (Hobbes, 1645:24-5).[5]

Thus, for Hobbes, the main purpose of punishment is the deterrence of future crime, not retribution for past acts. Freedom of will, as Yates (2012:18) has pointed out, is, in the Hobbesian analysis, not pertinent to punishment, but protection of society is. And, further, enforcing justice becomes part of the web of causes necessitating human action. For the sake of society, justice must be caused through the use of punishment (*Ibid.*). This mechanistic and political view of legality is quite different from Grotius' natural law concept of justice. However, as Hobbes was aware, punishment is of limited effectiveness in enforcing law observance: in order to necessitate justice, the desire to obey the law must exceed the effect of antisocial motivations in the public perception. However, the same interpretation of punishment imposed to secure future good rather than requiting past evil recurs in Hobbes' *Leviathan* where punishment as deterrence is defined as a law of nature (Hobbes, 1651 and 1991:106-7).[6]

Even at this early stage we can perceive the emergence of differing justifications of punishment as deterrence, and, indeed, some of the limitations that reliance upon its effectiveness implies. There is, though, perhaps a more profound observation that derives from these early considerations of punishment philosophy: it is that the exercise of state power to deal with wrongdoing began, during the sixteenth century, to shift away from absolute monarchical rule and towards sovereign parliamentary authority in the making and enforcement of justice. Put another way, perhaps, the 'divine' right of kings to define and impose laws demanding observance and obedience by their subjects deriving from 'natural' law became openly questionable, and the seeds of a more democratic mode of law enforcement for the protection and preservation of society were beginning to germinate. It is in this sense that we may perceive the beginnings of a politicisation of justice administration.

---

5 This quotation is from Hobbes' *Of Liberty and Necessity*, Vere Chappell (Ed.), Cambridge: Cambridge University Press, 1999, also quoted in Arthur L. Yates. *Thomas Hobbes on Punishment*, Ph.D Thesis, Canada: University of Western Ontario, 2012, p.18, available at: <http://ir.lib.uwo.ca/cgi/view.content.cgi?article=1651&context-etd> [accessed on 18 November 2016].

6 See: Thomas Hobbes, *Leviathan*, Richard Tuck (Ed.), Cambridge: Cambridge University Press, 1991, pp.106-7.

SAMUEL VON PUFENDORF (1632-1694)

Samuel Pufendorf as he was known until shortly before his death when he was ennobled by King Charles Gustavus X of Sweden, was by birth a German jurist, political philosopher, economist, historian and statesman of considerable international repute. The son of a Lutheran pastor, his early education destined him for the ministry, and following his school studies he was admitted to the University of Leipzig to study theology. While there he abandoned the narrow and dogmatic teaching of theology for the study of public law, having moved to the University of Jena where he studied the works of Grotius, Hobbes and Descartes in particular. On graduation in 1658 with the help of his brother, a diplomat in the Swedish service, he became a tutor in the family of Petrus Coyet, one of the resident ministers of the Swedish king in Copenhagen. At the time, Charles Gustavus was attempting to impose an unwanted alliance on Denmark, and during the negotiations he opened hostilities on that country. This move angered the Danes who turned against the Swedish envoys and although Coyet escaped, the remainder of the Swedish mission were arrested and imprisoned.

After eight months in prison during which he meditated on the works of Grotius and Hobbes, he was released and moved with Coyet's sons to the University of Leiden where he was allowed to publish his reflections in his *Elements of Universal Jusisprudence* (Pufendorf, 1660) dedicated to Charles Louis the Elector Palatine who created a chair of the Law of Nature and Nations for him at the University of Heidelburg.[7] There he met and married the widow of a colleague Elizabeth von Palthen in 1665, but had to leave in 1668 having had his chair withdrawn due to his opposition to a new tax on official documents. In 1670 Pufendorf was called to the University of Lund where in 1672 he published his major work *On the Law of Nature and of Nations* and in 1675 a résumé of the same work *On the Duty of Man and Citizen* describing his analysis of just war theory.[8] Between 1677 and 1688 Pufendorf filled the post of Historiographer Royal in Stockholm where he continued to publish extensively before moving once again to the service of Friedrich Wilhelm of Brandenburg. Shortly after his arrival the Elector died and his son Frederick instructed Pufendorf as historiographer and privy councillor to write a history of his father's life which was published under the title *De Rebus Gestis Frederici Wilhemi Magni* (1695). Finally, in 1694 -the year of his death- the King of Sweden conferred a barony on him, though he suffered a stroke shortly thereafter and died in Berlin.

---

7 This chair was the first of its kind in the world, indicating the confidence Charles Louis had in the potential of Pufendorf's work to become influential in a global dimension.

8 In compiling this outline of Pufendorf's life I am indebted to the account provided by the New World Encyclopedia contributors and those of the Wikimedia Foundation to be found at: <www.newworldencyclopedia.org/entry/Special:Cite?> [accessed on 17 November 2016].

How best can we summarise Pufendorf's considerable contribution to the advancement of moral and political philosophy during his lifetime and thereafter? Firstly, having been influenced by the work of Grotius and Hobbes early in his career, he subsequently (in *De Jure Naturae et Gentium, 1672*) developed their theories of natural law and societies to make a clear distinction and reconciliation between the differing authorities of the church and the state which had precipitated the Thirty Years War that had torn Europe apart during the first half of the seventeenth century. Secondly, and in contrast to Hobbes, he insisted (in *De Officio Hominis et Civis*, 1673) that it was the essential nature of man to live sociably in peace, and that war was justified only if it was necessary to establish or maintain that peace. Thirdly, (in *De Habitu Religionis Christianae ad Vitam Civilem*, 1687) Pufendorf set the limits between civil and ecclesiastical power through his 'collegiate' concept of church government which, when subsequently developed by the Lutheran theologian Christoph Pfaff, formed the basis of the relationship between church and state in Germany, and opened up the prospect of official tolerance of religious differences by other European governments. Fourthly, and although his writings on crime and punishment were limited in extent, in *De Jure (supra)* he set out, in broad terms, his concept of punishment and the purposes of deterrence as a prospective rather than a retrospective and retributive means of furthering and facilitating justice and social well-being.[9]

John Locke (1632-1704)

Locke was born in the English West Country village of Wrington, Somerset, the son of a small landowner and legal clerk who had seen military service with the Parliamentary forces during the English Civil Wars of 1642-1651. He was educated as a teenager at Westminster School in London, and subsequently at Christ Church in Oxford where he graduated in Medicine and Natural Philosophy (Science) and remained as a tutor from 1652 until 1677.

On leaving Oxford, Locke was attached to the household of Lord Anthony Ashley Cooper (later the Earl of Shaftesbury) as a tutor and personal physician, and became a member of the recently formed Royal Society in 1688. From 1675 he travelled extensively in France and Western Europe gaining insight into comparative forms of government, and apparently became a proponent of the Natural Law approach to political rule, much in line with the thinking of Pufendorf who was a contemporary. However, as a member of a family who had originally taken up arms against the sovereign (Charles I), and who had espoused the

9 And here see also: D. Hűning (Ed.), 'Souveränität und Strafgewalt: Die Begrűnding des *Jus Puniedi* bei Samuel Pufendorf' in *Naturrecht und Staatstheorie bei Samuel Pufendorf*, Baden-Baden, Nomos, 2009, pp.71-93.

Cromwellian cause between 1649 and 1660, he was tainted by his association with Shaftesbury whose own political life had been highly ambivalent in his support for, and subsequently against the monarchy, and his own survival was truly remarkable. Eventually, just before his death, Shaftsbury fled to Holland against which country Charles II had declared war on religious grounds, and where he became ill and died in 1683.

Shaftesbury, as a deposed Lord Chancellor of England under Charles II, had been a leading critic of monarchical rule, an anti-Catholic, and a delegate early on in the lengthy and covert process of negotiating the invitation of the protestant William of Orange to accept the English throne in the Glorious Revolution of 1688-89. Locke as his adherent, fled to Holland on Shaftesbury's death in fear of religious persecution for his known tolerance of religious diversity. It was there that his major political work entitled *Two Treatises Concerning Government* (Volumes I and II) were published anonymously in 1689.[10] In the second Treatise he set out his ideas on the natural rights of citizens, and a version of social contract theory and religious toleration, claiming that it was not the business of the state to dictate in matters of religion. He opposed Catholicism on the basis that involved allegiance 'to a foreign prince' – the Roman Pope – and was thus a threat to civil government and peace. He also denounced atheism on the grounds that such persons had no belief in the after-life, and therefore could be trusted neither to behave morally nor maintain their part in the social contract.

Scholars interpretive of Locke's works have disagreed to a marked extent about the relationship between natural law and natural rights in his analysis. Leo Strauss (1953) and some others believe that he saw natural rights as the dominant issue, as did Thomas Hobbes, since these emphasised the privileges or claims to which an individual was entitled. On the other hand, natural law as Richard Ashcraft (1987) and others have contended, emphasised the duties of men in society, and that when he maintained the right to life, liberty and property Locke was indicating the duty not to kill, enslave or steal. These commentators maintained that duties became the dominant issues in Locke because rights exist to ensure that men are able to fulfil their duties. Some such as Simmons (1992; 1993) have further suggested that rights are not just the 'flip side' of duties in Locke, nor merely a means to performing duties, but that, instead, rights protect our ability to make choices. While these choices cannot violate natural law, they are not a mere means to fulfilling natural law either.[11]

10 Locke, J., *Two Treatises Concerning Government*, [Volumes I & 2], 1689, P. Laslett (Ed.), Cambridge: Cambridge University Press, 1988.

11 Here see: Strauss, L. *Natural Rights and History*, Chicago, ILL: University of Chicago Press, 1953: Richard Ashcraft, *Locke's Two Treatises of Government*, London: Unwin Hymen Ltd., 1987; A. John Simmons, *The*

All of this speculation apart, there are areas of ambivalence in Locke's work in relation to natural law that remain unresolved or at least open to differences of scholarly interpretation. The same is, to an extent, true of his writings on punishment. Locke defined political power in his Second Treatise as 'a *Right* of making laws with Penalties of Death and consequently all less Penalties' (*Two Treatises*, 2.3). As Alex Tuckness (2016:11) points out, Locke's theory of punishment is central to his political philosophy, but he also referred to his account of punishment as a 'very strange doctrine' (2.9) presumably because it ran counter to the assumption that only political sovereigns could punish (*Ibid.*). Locke evidently believed that there could be no punishment without a law, but that since the state of nature has the law of nature to govern it, it is possible to describe one person as punishing another in that state. This is so, according to Locke, because the fundamental law of nature is that mankind be preserved, and since that law would be 'in vain' without human power to enforce it, it must therefore have been legitimate for individuals to punish one another even before government existed. Such a concept was at odds with that of Pufendorf who had insisted that the idea of punishment made no sense in the absence of an established legal structure.

Such a stance was, for Locke, to say the least problematic. He realised that allowing people the power to act as judges with the power to punish in the state of nature was such as to result in their becoming judges in their own cause, and that this transgressed the laws of natural justice. According to Tuckness, he admitted that this was a serious inconvenience, and a primary reason for leaving the state of nature (2.13, and see Tuckness, *op. cit.*:11). However, Locke maintained this position since it served to explain the transition into civil society in which the power to seek one's own preservation is limited by the law, and the power to punish is transferred to government. Thus, the power to punish in the state of nature becomes the right of government to use coercive force.

Locke's writings on criminal punishment and its rationales also display some ambivalence in relation to the purposes of retribution, deterrence and reparation as the following passage from *Two Treatises* demonstrates:

> And thus in the State of Nature, *one Man comes by a Power over another*; but yet no Absolute or Arbitrary Power, to use a Criminal when he has got him in his hands, according to the passionate heats, or boundless extravagancy of his own Will, but only to retribute him, so far as calm reason and conscience dictates, what is proportionate to his Transgression, which is so much as may

Lockean Theory of Rights, Princeton: Princeton University Press, 1992; and, *On the Edge of Anarchy: Locke, Consent and the Limits of Society*, Princeton: Princeton University Press, 1993.

> serve for *Reparation* and *Restraint*. For these two are the only reasons, why one Man may do harm to another, which is that [which] we call punishment (2.8, quoted also in Tuckness, 2016:11).

Here, Locke seems to be attempting, in a single definition, to establish a bridge between the natural law concept of punishment and that of legitimate state punishment. In the former sense, punishment was seen to meet the positive purposes of preserving human life and property, while in the latter sense it was perceived as a means of visiting retributive censure (and pain) upon the perpetrators of criminal acts. However in some writings in the era of Locke's deliberations, the term 'retribute' also occurred in theories of punishment that refuted the notion as primarily and essentially retributive. It is interesting, however, that Locke's concept was apparently both backward and forward looking insofar as it was intended to involve not only censure, but also reparation to those offended against.

Locke's work and approach to political philosophy has attracted the analytical attention of many scholars during the twentieth century in particular, perhaps because it was completed in the very turbulent pre-Enlightenment era of the seventeenth century in Europe. In many respects it established a connection between the earlier writings of Grotius, Hobbes and Pufendorf, and the later works of Beccaria, Bentham and, to a lesser extent, of Mill as will subsequently become clear.[12] However, as Peter Laslett (1988) pointed out so wisely, perhaps Locke the philosopher and Locke the political writer should be kept very separate.[13]

CESARE BONESANA-BECCARIA (1738-1794)

The eighteenth century was notable, with respect to deterrence theory evolution, for the works of two particular philosophers: Beccaria the Milanese nobleman in Italy, and Jeremy Bentham (1748-1832) the English penal reformer to whom we shall turn subsequently. Marchese Cesare Beccaria was the eldest son of an aristocratic family, educated by Jesuit teachers, and destined for a career in politics and government. There seems to be no record of his scholastic abilities in particular, or of his having had a university education, but it appears that he was influenced in his thinking by the works of Hobbes and Montesquieu (1689-1755) and of other social contract theorists of the Enlightenment era. He focused upon the cost: benefit calculus of rationally self-interested actors in relation to criminal

---

12 In this assessment of John Locke's works I am indebted to the scholarly commentary provided by Alex Tuckness (2016) in 'Locke's Political Philosophy', set out in the *Stanford Encyclopedia of Philosophy*, (Spring 2016 Edition), Edward N. Zolta (Ed.), at: <http://plato.stanford.edu/archives/spr2016/entries/locke-political/> [accessed on 17 November 2016].

13 Peter Laslett (Ed.), *Locke: Two Treatises on Government*, Cambridge Texts in the History of Political Thought, Cambridge: Cambridge University Press [Revised Edition], 1988.

offending to assert that they will refrain from crime if the cost (pain) of committing it exceeds the benefits that might accrue from doing so. In a rational and hedonistic world, Beccaria argued in his only enduring work *Dei Delitte e delle Pene* published in 1764, that general deterrence was of greater importance than specific deterrence since, viewed in utilitarian terms, both laws and the punishment of crime should result in the 'greatest good of the greatest number of citizens' (1764:Ch.XII, p.20). Thus, the focus of penal measures should be upon the preservation of social well-being rather than upon the individual offender whose wrongdoing could not be undone.

Close reading of *Dei Delitte* reveals that Beccaria's thinking was strikingly innovative in an era in which the public witnessing of barbaric forms of criminal punishment was still widespread in Europe.[14] In prisons, people either convicted or un-convicted were held in squalid, insanitary and vermin-infested conditions with minimal food and water, and charged money for the privilege which was pocketed by the warders responsible for their secure keeping (Walker, 1972:82-4).[15] Beccaria insisted that laws including the specification of crimes and the penalties for law-breaking should be made known to the public in the vernacular language, proclaiming: 'happy the nation where the knowledge of laws is not a science'! (1764:Ch.XIV, pp.21-23).

As important, perhaps, in Chapter XIX of *Dei Delitte*, we find the following comment on the advantages of immediate punishment following the commission of offences: 'The degree and the consequences of the crime ought to be so contrived as to have the greatest possible effect on others, with the least possible pain to the delinquent'. Furthermore, Beccaria argued that if the sole purpose of sanctions is to prevent crime in society, 'punishments are unjust when their severity exceeds what is necessary to achieve deterrence' (1764:Ch.XXVII, pp.36-37). In the same Chapter he stated that in addition to considerations of certainty of detection and the swiftness of punishment, 'if laws be too cruel, they must be altered, or anarchy and impunity will succeed'. This reference may be understood as Beccaria's belief that laws of an excessive nature will eventually be rejected (probably forcibly) by those governed, while just judges will simply refrain from enforcing them, or impose them with lesser severity on the more privileged sectors of society.

14 In the forms of public hangings, the drawing and quartering of treasonous offenders, gibbeting, flogging, and even the burning of witches that lasted until 1790 in Britain (Walker, 1972:79).

15 In Newgate Prison in London, prisoners confined in irons to prevent their escape were charged a fee for the loan of their irons, and those admitted a fee of three guineas for entry to the prison, half a guinea per week for a bed, and further fees for candles, eating utensils and fuel (Walker, 1972: *Ibid.*). Those who could not pay the fees were kept in prison until they could do so or someone else paid for them. In the early eighteenth century a man could pay as much as £5,000 for the privilege of being a prison warder at Fleet Prison in London; he could sell his post for the same amount, and make a massive profit in the meantime (*Ibid.*).

Further, stated Beccaria, 'In proportion as punishments become more cruel,[16] the minds of men as a fluid rises to the same height as that which surrounds it, grow hardened and insensible. If punishments be very severe, men are naturally led to the perpetration of other crimes to avoid the punishment due to the first' (*Ibid.*).

There are two further aspects of Beccaria's enlightened thinking that should be noted here. The first is his firm belief that all forms of torture and capital punishment should be abolished in favour of imprisonment, and that all punishments should be proportionate to the seriousness of the crime committed and the extent of harm thereby caused to society. Second, moreover, judges should confine themselves to determining guilt and the application of the law, rather than interpretation of the spirit of the law. To this end, legislators should pass laws that define crimes precisely, and provide specific punishments for each crime. To have a deterrent value Beccaria insisted, in addition to swiftness and certainty of discovery of crimes, the celerity of appropriate punishment must be manifestly evident (1764, *passim*).[17]

Translation of *Dei Delitte* into a number of European languages followed quickly after its publication in 1764, and had a profound impact upon post-Enlightenment thinking in many countries at the time. Though not of voluminous length, many other aspects of jurisprudence were discussed – some more briefly than others – within the treatise. As will be seen later, it was to influence the works of Jeremy Bentham and Immanuel Kant, both contemporaries of Beccaria, and subsequently of John Stuart Mill to a discernible extent. What was, however, evidently unusual in Beccaria's considerably utilitarian approach to criminal punishment was the fact that, as an aristocrat, he displayed a rare concern for limiting the barbarity and public mortification of penalties to the minimum consistent with the reformed conduct of the offender, which he saw as being in the interest of the wider society. This was, perhaps, the first published elaboration of the principle of parsimony in punishment, expressed in an age in which few limits (if any) were placed upon the physical pains, deprivations and humiliation visited upon criminal offenders.

16 Here, I interpret Beccaria as meaning 'draconian' as opposed to mentally or physically intense or barbaric.

17 Throughout this discussion I refer to the translation of *Dei Delitte e delle Pene* (On Crimes and Punishments) as translated and provided at: <www.thefederalistpapers.org/wp.../Cesare-Beccaria-On-Crimes-And-Punishments.pdf>. The document makes no reference to the translator by name or date [accessed on 29 November 2016].

Jeremy Bentham (1748-1832)

According to the edited compilation of Jay Greene (1967),[18] Jeremy Bentham was sent by his father to Oxford University at the age of twelve in preparation for a career in the law. Admission to such studies at that time was contingent upon the participant student signing the Thirty-nine Articles of the Church of England which, since the sixteenth century, had expressed the official doctrine of the church. Bentham had considerable reservations about this requirement, but he was persuaded to comply and never forgot that experience.

It seems to be the case that Bentham was more a great theorist of penal reform than an actual reformer in practice. He became, through his studies, an acute critic of existing institutions, and devoted his life to devising efficient and reasonable ways of improving practices that were performed poorly or not at all (*Ibid.*:309). After leaving Oxford he had a brief and somewhat reluctant career as a lawyer, being stridently critical of the existing legal procedures and judicial behaviours which he perceived as being largely self-seeking at the expense of those who appeared before the courts on trial.

Though naturally an eccentric individual, he became a singular reformer who contested the received wisdoms of the era such as the doctrine of natural rights and the theory of the social contract, but he embraced wholeheartedly what he termed 'the greatest happiness principle' or the principle of utility. Happiness in Bentham's terms was defined in terms of pleasures and pains, by the presence of the former and the absence of other. Though this concept predated Bentham, he set about making it a guiding principle by devising ways of making institutions of government work operationally, and more effectively and efficiently than current practices allowed.

Bentham's eventual pre-occupation with prison reform was the product of a complex and diffuse range of influences – religious, economic, political, humanitarian, philanthropic and legal. He was considerably concerned by John Howard's (1777) book *The State of the Prisons in England and Wales* which gave a graphic account of the disgracefully squalid conditions of prison life, the brutality and self-seeking behaviour of prison staff, and the 'fee system' under which they made a handsome living at the expense of those in their charge. Following on from Howard's evidence given to a House of Commons Committee in 1774, two parliamentary Acts were passed: the first to release immediately every prisoner against whom a grand jury failed to find a true bill (or indictment) and abolishing the fee system in favour of remunerating gaolers from the county rate; the second requiring Justices

18 Here see: Jay E. Greene (ed.), *100 Great Thinkers*, Simon & Schuster Inc. New York: Washington Square Press, Two Volumes, 1967, at Volume 2, pp.209-213.

of the Peace to undertake annual inspections of prisons and the conditions provided therein.

Howard had promoted a reform of prison practices based upon enforceable rules and behavioural requirements applicable to both inmates and staff and aimed at the elimination of *ad hoc* practices, exploitation and abusive conduct. Proponents of prison reform emerged from a wide range of interests, religious and secular, industrial and professional across all sectors of the population. These were augmented by an increasing 'charitable' interest in the poor and destitute portion of the population in both the streets of cities and in prisons themselves.[19]

During the 1770s the prisons in London and the provinces were plunged into crisis. The outbreak of the American War and the sudden suspension of transportation of convicted felons to the colonies of the British empire resulted in massive overcrowding, outbreaks of disease, and riotous behaviour in prisons. As Michael Ignatieff (1978) recalls, the Penitentiary Act of 1779 drafted by John Howard and some others recommended the creation of a whole network of 'hard labour houses' or penitentiaries[20] either by converting existing prisons or building new ones at the national expense. As it transpired, however, the plan was scaled down in scope, and the Act provided for only two penitentiaries to be constructed in the London area: one to hold six hundred males, and the other to hold three hundred females (*Ibid.*:93). The regime in these places was to be one of solitary confinement by night and hard labour of the most menial type by day. Prisoners were, however, to be provided with a meagre diet and uniform clothing, and the supervisory staff were to be, like the police, salaried employees of local government subject to codes of conduct, thus abolishing dependence on fees and charges.

At the same time, Bentham was also pre-occupied with prison design. In terms of the structural reform of prisons, he became almost obsessed by the radial design for a new generation of prisons which became known as the 'panopticon', functioning on what he termed the 'inspection principle'. It was modelled on a factory built by his brother Samuel

19 This 'charitable' interest, became evident during the closing decades of the eighteenth century in the work of groups such as The Society for Bettering the Condition of the Poor led by reformers such as the philanthropist Thomas Bernard. However, in Bernard's mind, as Michael Ignatieff (1978:76-7) has pointed out, this meant replacing indiscriminate almsgiving with a systematic attempt to distinguish between the deserving and the undeserving (or feckless) poor.

20 The term 'penitentiary' originally derived from the use of 'houses of correction' for offences against the rules of the Roman Catholic Church from the fifteenth century onwards. In such places offenders were secluded as a form of penance and self-examination in isolation and silence with a view to repentance under the supervision of religious orders. More recently in continental Europe, these places were replaced by 'hard labour houses', examples of which were visited by John Howard in the course of his travels in Holland, France, Italy and elsewhere.

in Russia for Catherine the Great, and comprised a circular, tiered honeycomb of open cells ranged round a central tower, into which the prisoners could not see, but from which the supervisors or keepers had a clear view of each cell (*Ibid.*:110). Not only would such a design permit constant surveillance of the inhabitants, but the conduct and efficiency of staff could also be monitored. The design was later revised to separate groups of cells in the form of 'halls' or wings radiating from the central tower, confining specific numbers of inmates on two or three levels or 'landings' for ease of supervision and control. It remains visible in many of the Victorian prisons still in use in Britain to this day.

In the panoptican model, convict labour was to be provided and used by merchant contractors under prevailing market conditions, but had to be of a hard and menial nature with products that could be sold as a form of revenue.[21] In the event, Bentham's design failed to impress the House of Commons committee to whom it was presented in 1790 for adoption as a vision for the future of prisons and effective imprisonment devoted to the reform of criminals through arduous labour and self-examination in silent seclusion.[22] The Committee made no haste to adopt the model, citing as its reason for delay doubts within its membership about the contractual arrangements for convict employment. The Committee were dubious that such an innovative reform might open up opportunities for corruption and unlawful discretion, and also that it would change the relationship between state and prisoner by replacing it with one of employer and worker. It did, however, take the Committee twenty years to come to a final deliberation in the matter. In disgust Bentham abandoned the project, though after his death it was to be resurrected, modified and adopted during the nineteenth century in the building of many Victorian era prisons in Britain.

Somewhere at the core of Bentham's reforming ideas was the desire to make government and its outcomes more effective in delivering conditions that would improve the daily lives of citizens and reduce the dysfunctional effects of poverty, disease and social deprivation. Later in his life he realised that those in authority were not particularly interested in reform or concerned with the welfare of the governed, but only with their own welfare and positions of power. In relation to the penal system of the era in particular, he regarded its brutality and squalid conditions as entirely detrimental to the task of deterring and reducing crime,

21 Such products included marble sawing, oakum picking, grinding plaster of Paris, logwood chopping, weaving, shoemaking and the like. Market gardens were also established within or close to gaols to provide the prison with vegetables and fruit to supplement the meagre dietary allowance.

22 It took the House of Commons Committee until 1810 to finally reject Bentham's panoptican design, but its underlying purpose of regulation and surveillance of prisoners and their keepers, and the elimination of brutality and *ad hoc* practices remained central to the reformist agenda into the Victorian era.

and set himself to instigate reforms which those in power were indifferent about undertaking. As Greene concluded in assessing Bentham's legacy:

> [T]hat he was not completely successful does not detract from the fact that he provided the impetus to lead others to carry on the work. The reforms that have been accomplished in England and elsewhere all rest partly on his work (Greene, 1967 *op. cit.*:312).

John Stuart Mill (1806-1873)

In Mill we find yet another highly unusual character for the age into which he was born and in which his personality developed. His father, James Mill, was a friend of Jeremy Bentham, and as such an adherent of the 'philosophical radical' or utilitarian political persuasion. James Mill decided to privately educate his son John himself rather than send him to school, since the schools of the time merely indoctrinated their pupils into acceptance of the social *status quo*, and John would learn a pattern of thinking that would hold him back from innovative self-expression and inquiry through the prevailing emphasis on conformity. Instead, from an early age he learned Greek and Latin, studied literature, history, mathematics and science, and later in his early teenage years, philosophy and economics. He spent a year in France at the age of fourteen, learning French and absorbing the post-Revolution culture, and returned to study under his father's guidance rather than attend either of the major universities (Oxford and Cambridge) which were under ecclesiastical control.

At the age of eighteen Mill was set to editing Bentham's work on judicial evidence which was subsequently published in five volumes as his *Rationale of Judicial Evidence* in 1827, and from which task he emerged exhausted and in a state of what he described as 'a crisis in my mental life' or depression. He overcame this situation with the help and influence of his friend Harriet Taylor whom he subsequently married, and found employment as an examiner of correspondence for the East India Company – a *quasi*-civil service position which he held until his retirement to a life of writing and travel. Aside from his formal employment, however, Mill wrote in his spare time and on vacations a large number of newspaper and magazine articles, and books on many subjects including economics and political thought, assisted by his wife Harriet. Thus his reputation as a reforming commentator and philosopher in the field of social science and political economy became established. His earliest work *The Principles of Political Economy* (1848) updated the theories of taxation, wages, rents, wealth and production pioneered by Adam Smith (1723-1790) and David Riccardo (1772-1823). He also served as an independent Member of Parliament for

Westminster between 1865 and 1868 at the invitation of the local citizenry, but was not re-elected largely due to his reforming ideas which were considerably ahead of his time.

The French Revolution of 1789 and its gruesome outcomes[23] had considerably affected British political thinking and created an aversion to change amongst those in positions of power and government to the extent of hindering the reforms necessary to capitalise on the changes brought about by the industrial revolution. The factory system which led to the rise of many industrial towns and cities also led to abuses of labour and considerable suffering. Mill perceived this development as one that required a radical and purposeful reform of Parliament and its practices. The outcome of his deliberations led him to advocate a more democratic and representative form of government guided by the wisdom of men of knowledge and practical experience rather than the traditionally powerful and elitist political figures of the time. His major work *Considerations on Representative Government* published in 1861 drew on his father's (and Bentham's) philosophy of government in the utilitarian tradition.

Perhaps Mill's most influential contribution to the political philosophy of his lifetime and subsequently, lies in an entirely separate study that he undertook during the 1850s on individual freedoms and social relationships within democratic national life. His *On Liberty* published in 1859 became a classic text, though it was subjected to some fiercely critical responses from the rich and powerful traditionalist elite of the period.[24] He did, however, establish the vital moral link between wrongdoing and punishment through his insistence that an act should not be declared wrong unless it is implicit that a person ought to be punished in some way for doing it: if not by law, then by the disapprobation of his fellow men (Cf. e.g. Bean, 1981:70-71). Mill developed this concept of moral wrong and the correlative requirement for justice at some length in his treatise *Utilitarianism* (1863 and 1964).[25] He did, however, go further to insist that there was a sentiment of justice which involved two essential ingredients: the desire to punish a person who has done harm, and the knowledge or belief that there is some identifiable person or persons to whom harm has been done (1964:306). Thus, punishment occurs when a wrong occurs, and a wrong is a moral term. Justice exists to determine the nature of that punishment within a moral

23 In the vengeance taken by the Republicans against the aristocracy of France with a view to their elimination as a ruling class through humiliation, torture, imprisonment and public execution at the guillotine.

24 Here see, for instance, Sir James Fitzjames Stephen's '*Liberty, Equality, Fraternity*' (1873), which was a direct response to Mill's *On Liberty* when the author, who subsequently became a High Court Judge, was a regular contributor to the influential Cornhill Magazine. It can be found in Louis Blom-Cooper and Gavin Drewry's edited volume *Law and Morality: A Reader*, London: Duckworth, 1976, at pp.13-18.

25 Especially in Chapter 5 – 'On the Connection between Justice and Utility', but see also: J.S. Mill, *Utilitarianism*, (Ed. M. Warnock), London: Collins Fontana, also at Chapter 5.

framework. And this is so whether the wrong is legal or otherwise, and whether the punishment is legal or otherwise (Bean, 1981 *op. cit.*:72).

Though Mill was not exactly a giant in criminological terms, his contribution to the philosophical and socio-economic development of his period was immense. If he was a 'hedonist' in the strict sense of the term, it was his belief in the right of all men to freedom of thought and discussion, of tastes and pursuits, and of association that characterised his considerable breadth of writing. These liberties he saw as essential to the maximisation of the wellbeing and happiness of all people in his attempt to answer the question: 'What is the good?' which is a central, and one of the oldest, questions of philosophy. Above all else, perhaps, it was Mill's conviction that liberty in a modern world is threatened not so much by government as by that form of society in which custom and the power to preserve it can suppress individuality. This much stated, however, truly representative and progressive government relies (in Mill's terms) less upon tradition than upon meeting the reasonable expectations of those who are prepared to meet its obligations of morality and responsible citizenship.

The larger question for the purposes of this work is that of when, and to what extent in Mill's thesis, the state is justified in intervening in the lives of citizens to preserve both morality and utility. Further, I should venture to question, if by 'utility' defined as Mill seems to insist in *Utilitarianism* (1863) as 'the greatest reasonable happiness of the greatest number of citizens, happiness being defined in terms of a preponderance of pleasure and the absence of pain', does this state of happiness necessarily presuppose a state of equality as between citizens, and if so, to what measurable extent? Mill's theory that state intervention is justifiable only when there is an injury (or the danger of it) to utility interests may be seen, as Ted Honderich (1976:202-6) has pointed out, to be closely related to the deterrence theory of punishment. Put another way, perhaps, that it is a necessary condition of justified punishment that a harm has been caused, and that supposed immorality is, by itself, neither a sufficient nor a necessary condition of that intervention or punishment. Such an approach evidently precludes the possibility of combination with most forms of traditional retribution theory.[26]

Mill's thesis does, however, combine with deterrence doctrine insofar as the necessary condition of justified punishment is consistent with the sufficient condition of deterrence theory. Thus intervention *via* punishment is justifiable, the necessary condition being met, if the behavioural harm does infringe utility interests. Therefore, punishment is justified

26 If only because the harm may be evident and provable, but the immorality of its causation may be a question of dispute as to motivation and intention (*mens rea*) which would render it a guilty act.

in deterrence terms if this condition is satisfied and it is also true that the punishment is economical.[27] There are, notwithstanding, further problems inherent in a thesis such as Mill's which relate to equality between citizens. It is possible that the intervention mentioned earlier as justifiable could cause or perpetuate existing inequalities of utility which, in Mill's terms would, of course, be unacceptable even if justifiable in deterrence terms. We shall return to discussion of this situation in Chapter 3 of this work.

Into the Twentieth Century

If the Enlightenment years of the eighteenth century had resulted in increasing public and political disillusionment with the more barbaric forms of punishment, the growth of the reformist movements of the nineteenth century had awakened, at least in the dominant political conversations, an awareness of the need for radical penal reform. In Britain this reform was addressed by the building of a large number of new generation prisons during the Victorian era, many of which were designed on Bentham's panoptican model of segregation, silence and self-contemplation combined with hard labour and harshly disciplined regulation of daily routines. The principal architect in this development was one Joshua Jebb (1793-1863) who in 1837 was appointed technical adviser to the Home Office, and who designed and built the new model convict prison at Pentonville in London (opened in 1842), and subsequently in the following six years fifty-four new cellular prisons on much the same model in the provinces. These prisons were almost fortress-like in design, the outward aspect of each being of an intimidating nature with high stone walls and castellated gatehouses preventing any public view of the interior. There seems no doubt that such places were intended, by their bleak and imposing facades, to deter the populace from criminal acts out of fear of being interned within their walls. This extensive building programme led, in turn, to the establishment of the Directorate of Convict Prisons in 1850, of which Jebb became the first Chairman, a position that he held until his death.

In 1863, Edmond DuCane (1830-1903) was appointed to the Directorate, and became Chairman in Jebb's place in 1869. In 1877 when prisons were 'nationalised', he became the first Chairman of the newly formed Prison Commission. He was succeeded by Evelyn Ruggles-Brise (1857-1935) who remained in that post from 1895 until 1921. DuCane's impersonal and strictly disciplined concept of prison régimes became the subject of considerable criticism and attack during the 1890s, by William Morrison the chaplain at Wandsworth prison in particular. Morrison insisted that there had been an increase in crime as a result of the manner in which prisoners were treated, and not the decrease that

27 The term 'economical' as used here implies that the punishment is not excessive, and that it is, in some way, proportionate to the extent of the harm occasioned.

had been expected. His attack on Du Cane lead directly to the setting up of the Gladstone Committee in 1895, and the appointment of Ruggles-Brise in the same year. As a result, sweeping changes were made towards a more paternalistic approach to the management of prisoners, the abolition of hard labour machines such as the treadmill and the crank, and their replacement by programmes of education, moral training and welfare in terms of diet, hygiene, medical care, and preparation for discharge and resettlement. These reforms were continued by Alexander Paterson (1884-1947) who succeeded Ruggles-Brise in 1922, and implemented the system of Borstal Training for young prisoners initiated by his predecessor on a 'boarding school' model of education and training. Paterson remained Director of Convict Prisons and a Prison Commissioner until 1947, and it was he who insisted that 'men are sent to prison as a punishment, not for punishment'. He also introduced open prisons for those inmates selected for such an environment and who could be trusted to abide by the more relaxed rules of their regimes.[28]

THE ORIGINS OF PROBATION

A significant development in the non-custodial treatment of offenders occurred in 1907 with the Probation of Offenders Act in Britain, and more or less simultaneously in Boston, Massachusetts in the USA. The British model can, however, be traced back to the Justices of the Peace Act of 1361, allowing magistrates to 'bind over' individuals to be of good behaviour and keep the peace. Those being bound over originally had to enter into a *recognizance* – a sum of money forfeitable to the Crown in breach of a Binding-Over Order. Probation Orders became widely used, after the Criminal Justice Act of 1948, as an alternative to custodial sentences, and subsequently after 1974, also Community Service Orders (later re-named Community Orders), suspended sentences, and deferred sentences. Latterly, in 1998, the Anti-Social Behaviour Order (ASBO) was devised in the Crime and Disorder Act of that year, but was a measure applied by the civil courts on application by the police and local authorities. Breach of (or non-compliance with) an ASBO becomes a criminal offence punishable with a custodial sentence in serious instances.[29] All of these measures became the task of the Probation Service to supervise, and, in default, to apply to the court for a Revocation Order currently provided for in Part 32 of the Criminal Procedure Rules 2015 and previous legislation. We shall return to a discussion of the history and changing role of the Probation Service in Chapter 6.

---

28 Here see, for instance, S.K. Ruck (Ed.), *Paterson on Prisons: The Collected Papers of Sir Alexander Paterson*, London: Frederick Muller, 1951, and M. Fitzgerald and J. Sim, *British Prisons*, [Second Edition], Oxford: Basil Blackwell, 1982.

29 For a more detailed explanation of these measures see Bryan Gibson's account in *The Pocket A-Z of Criminal Justice*, Hook, Hampshire: Waterside Press 2009, pp.23, 31 and 41 respectively.

The 'Naissance' of Criminology in the Twentieth Century

If the Probation of Offenders Act 1907 signalled an increasing political awareness of the need to reduce the use of imprisonment by measures dealing with less serious offenders within the community, what has to be questioned is how the willingness to consider alternative strategies for crime control or reduction actually arose within governmental circles in Britain and elsewhere. Certainly, the increasing influence of penal reform groups, of the more enlightened penal administrators such as Ruggles-Brise, and the Report of the Gladstone Committee of 1895, had raised awareness of the need for a revised approach to the purposes of imprisonment as the twentieth century opened. The latter Report, in particular, sowed the seeds of a radical re-appraisal of the purposes of imprisonment which, though slow to germinate, provided an impetus for statements such as that of Paterson quoted previously. Indeed, at the commencement of the Report we find the following: 'We start from the principle that Prison treatment should have, as its primary and concurrent objects, deterrence and reformation' (Departmental Committee on Prisons, [The Gladstone Report], *Parliamentary Papers*, Vol.lvi, 25, London: Home Office, 1895).

Here, suddenly, we find no mention of retribution, but rather a clear indication of a changing perception of the use of prisons which was to be accompanied by a re-modelling of regimes abandoning the former 'separate' system, hard labour, and a move towards the more liberal concept of purposeful work and training, freedom of prisoner association, and the role of prison staff in the encouragement of prisoners to lead law-abiding lives on release.

Despite the intervention of World War 1 (1914-1918), the first half of the twentieth century witnessed a significant expansion of academic interest in the study of crime and punishment as social phenomena throughout Europe and in North America. I believe it to be true to assert that the origins of this interest are to be found in the field of ethics and moral philosophy, and in particular in the early works of writers such as A.C. Ewing in Britain,[30] Edwin Sutherland in America,[31] and a number of others whom we shall consider subsequently. Though much of this original academic study was discursive in its approach, it had been suggested earlier that crime might be amenable to study on a scientific basis,[32] even though punishment and its outcomes might be stubbornly resistant to such treatment.

---

30 A.C. Ewing, *The Morality of Punishment*, London: Kegan Paul, Trench & Trubner, 1929.

31 E.H. Sutherland, *Criminology*, [First Edition], Chicago, ILL: J.B. Lippincott Company, 1924.

32 As had earlier been suggested and attempted by Cesare Lomboroso (1835-1909), and subsequently his students Raffaele Garofalo (1851-1934) and Enrico Ferri (1856-1929) of what came to be known as the Italian Positive School. Lomboroso was a Professor of Forensic Medicine at Turin, and with Garofalo and Ferri became known as the 'fathers' of modern criminology for their *quasi*-scientific approach to the diagnosis and explanation of criminality within societies.

It was not until the cessation of hostilities in World War 2 (1939-45) that serious consideration of a scientific approach to criminology could be undertaken in Europe and elsewhere. That this became a reality was (at least in Britain) largely due to the influence of one Leon Radzinowicz (1906-1999), a Polish immigrant who had studied under Enrico Ferri in Rome,[33] read law in Paris and Geneva, and subsequently was a doctoral candidate in Cracow in Poland. He moved to England in 1938 funded by the Polish Ministry of Justice to study the English legal system, and then pursued an academic career at Cambridge University where, from 1949-1959, he was Director of the Department of Criminal Science. In 1959 he founded the Institute of Criminology and became the first Wolfson Professor of Criminology. He was knighted in 1970, and elected a Fellow of the British Academy in 1973.[34]

Radzinowicz and those working with him believed that given sufficient reliable data on crime committed and the outcomes of attempts to deal with it in the form of treatment programmes and therapeutic interventions applied as elements of the sanctioning process,[35] it would become possible, using scientific research principles and protocols, to transform criminology into a verifiable academic discipline. The same form of approach was also being adopted in leading universities in Western Europe, North America, and elsewhere worldwide, since it suggested a scientific interpretation of Edwin Sutherland's widely accepted definition of criminology expressed in the following terms:

> Criminology is the body of knowledge regarding crime as a social phenomenon. It includes within its scope the processes of making laws, of breaking laws, and of reacting toward the breaking of laws. These processes are three aspects of a somewhat unified sequence of interactions. Certain acts which are regarded as undesirable are defined by the political society as crimes. In spite of this definition some people persist in the behaviour and thus commit crimes; the political society reacts with punishment, treatment or prevention. This sequence of interactions is the object-matter of criminology (Sutherland, 1924; 1955:3).

While Sutherland's definition has stood the test of time, it has to be stated that in parallel with efforts to establish a science of criminology, the academic study of sociology had dominated what came to be known as the Social Sciences since the late 1890s and particu-

33 See fn.32 above.

34 For a history of Sir Leon Radzinowicz's life see: R. Hood (Ed.), *Crime, Criminology and Public Policy: Essays in Honour of Sir Leon Radzinowicz*, London: Heinemann, 1974.

35 Such was to infer that given access to such data, it would be possible to measure the extent to which the processes of criminal punishment actually deterred crime (both individual / specific and general deterrence), and recidivism as an outcome of evaluated treatment programmes experienced by offenders as part of the punitive process either in custody or in the community.

larly in the years pre- and post-World War 1 in America and mainland Europe. The 'Sociological School', as it became known, refuted the biological theories of Lomboroso and his followers of the Positivist School, perceiving the causes of crime as located within the social structure rather than in individual pathology. This, in turn, resulted in the establishment of what was termed 'The American School' during the early 1900s,[36] which focused its studies of crime, to a considerable extent, upon the social environments in which it was committed.

In Europe, sociology owes perhaps its greatest debt to the French philosopher Émile Durkheim (1858-1917) who pioneered its study as a scientific discipline separate from both philosophy and the positivist tradition of Lomborosian thinking about crime from an anthropological perspective. Durkheim located the causes of crime and the treatment of it within the social structure as 'measurable' entities rather than as philosophical constructs, and as potentially amenable to a separate methodological discipline.[37] This discipline subsequently became adopted within the 'Sociological School' as a basis for criminological studies, and may also be seen to have paved the way for the establishment of criminology as a discrete social science as envisaged and set in place by Leon Radzinowicz and his followers.

Deterrence Theory in Its Modern Perspective

The second half of the twentieth century viewed in a criminological context presents a confusing and somewhat ambivalent approach to deterrence studies and research methodologies. Immediately post-World War 2, the deterrence hypothesis within the emerging social science of criminology relied heavily upon philosophical interpretations of deterrence as a key intellectual foundation of Western criminal law and penology. The deterrence literature from Andenaes (1952)[38] to Zimring (and Hawkins) (1973)[39] is replete with debates as to the morality and operational effectiveness of its doctrinal prescriptions, and almost none is conclusively convincing.

36 See here, for example, the works of Carroll Wright (1899); Frank Tolman (1902:1903), Maurice Parmelee (1908); Phillip Parsons (1909); and John Gillin (1914), all quoted in Sutherland (1924, 1955:57 at fn. 9, 10 and 11).

37 Durkheim's major work in this field is evident in his *The Rules of Sociological Method and Selected Texts on Sociology and Its Method*, [Tr. W.D. Halls; S. Lukes (Ed.)], New York: The Free Press, 1982. But see also: Steven Lukes, *Émile Durkheim: His Life and Works*, Harmondsworth, Middlesex: Penguin Books, 1973.

38 Johs Andenaes, 'General Prevention – Illusion or Reality?' in *Journal of Criminal Law, Criminology and Police Science*, 43, July – August, 1952, pp.176-198.

39 Zimring, F.E. & Hawkins, G.J., *Deterrence: The Legal Threat in Crime Control*, Chicago, ILL: University of Chicago Press.

Even before this, as our survey of the foundational thinkers about crime from the pre-Enlightenment through to the modern eras has shown, though each in turn considered deterrence within criminal justice to a greater or lesser extent, every one of them without exception seemed to accept it on an intuitive *a priori* basis as an indisputable component of criminal punishment. That it took until the advent of the more rigorous criminological research methodologies of the post-World War 2 era to cast doubt on the efficacy of deterrence as a largely unmeasurable construct remains quite remarkable.

And yet, even at the present time and on a worldwide basis, penal policies and political punishment rhetoric persist in the apparent belief that increasingly punitive sentencing in pursuit of crime control will deliver both specific (individual) and general deterrence. How, other than through incapacitation, this *mantra* is to become manifestly verifiable is left largely unanswered, and will, in all probability, remain so. In Chapters 2 and 3 we shall examine how this situation contributed to recurring conditions of penal crisis in Britain during the closing decades of the twentieth century.

2 Deterrence Doctrine C20-21

Overview

In the course of this chapter we shall trace the transition during the twentieth century of the largely philosophical discourses on deterrence theory into an attempt to develop deterrence doctrine as an empirical academic component of criminological science. Such an inquiry may shed some light upon the nature of Philip Bean's (1981, *op. cit.*) assertion (see *supra*) of uncertainty between the psychological and the sociological bases of deterrence theory in terms of its underlying purposes: crime prevention or crime control.

Let us start with a relatively simple syllogistic example of deductive inference relating to the perceived effectiveness of deterrence within criminal justice policies and practices in both the modern and post-modern eras of our experience. This may be set out as follows:
- all 'p' are 'd' (all punishments are a deterrent);
- all 's' are 'p' (all sentences are punishments);
- therefore, all 's' are 'd' (all sentences are a deterrent).

Which conclusion is logically consistent, provided only that the first premise is, in fact, true. It may be true that the *intention* is that all punishments and sentences should act as deterrents to further offending, but in practice it is evident that this is clearly not the case.

In criminal justice terms there are some difficulties inherent in the consistency of this logic, simply because most of the evidence about the functionality of the penal systems and processes discussed in the previous chapter makes the reliability of the first premise, and therefore of the conclusion extremely questionable.[1] Moreover, as we shall subsequently see in Chapter 3, the extended period over which episodes of concerted disorder, criminal damage to prison premises, and overcrowding of penal establishments resulting from increasing numbers of offenders being sentenced to imprisonment, make the deterrent effectiveness of custodial sentences open to serious questioning.

1 Recidivism statistics for England and Wales published in 2016 indicate that 46% of all adults released from prisons during 2013-4 were reconvicted within one year, and that for those serving sentences of less than twelve months this increases to 60% (Ministry of Justice, 2016; Prison Reform Trust, 2016:4). Further, 48% of women leaving prison were similarly reconvicted, and the figure for those (males and females) less than 18 years old was 68% (*Ibid.*).

And, yet, as we shall also see in Chapter 3, and particularly since the early 1990s, the entire sentencing rationale in England and Wales and elsewhere in Europe and North America has been predicated on penal policies of an increasingly punitive nature based upon retribution, deterrence and incapacitation in pursuit of social control. Of these purposes, there is little doubt that implicit acceptance of the deterrence doctrine has played a major and, indeed, an increasing part in the escalation of prison populations.

The main reason for the latter assertion requires a brief explanation. The nature of the most frequently punished offences (e.g. robbery, burglary, assaults, thefts, frauds and deceptions) differs only marginally in seriousness and culpability from year to year.[2] What can and often does change is the 'prevalence' (or volume) of certain offences which can be affected by actual rates of detection and prosecution, and also the perceived likelihood of evading it.[3] Thus, in order to make sentences deterrent, more frequent use has been made of imprisonment, and for increasing periods to be spent in prison custody.

The search for increased effectiveness of deterrence has also resulted in expanded use of indeterminate sentences such as those up to life imprisonment or what in England and Wales has been termed 'imprisonment for public protection' (IPP).[4] In addition, prisoners serving life sentences currently spend an average of 17 years in prison, up from 13 years in 2001. The proportion of persons serving indeterminate sentences in England and Wales is now 13.5% of the prison population (Ministry of Justice, 2016; Prison Reform Trust,

2 The general exception to this situation lies in the range of 'aggravated' offences in which the use of weapons is threatened or involved. Though the 'volume' of some offences committed can change from time to time, rates of detection and prosecution being also subject to change, the generic nature of offences and culpability for the commission of them, remains relatively stable year on year.

3 For example, rates of domestic burglary have generally decreased over recent years due to increased use of surveillance methods (CCTVs and alarm systems), while those of fraud and deception have increased with the widespread availability (and misuse) of credit cards. Motor theft has similarly decreased due to the development of increasingly sophisticated alarm and immobilisation devices. The prevalence of drug-related offences has increased due to wider availability and the manufacture of synthetic narcotic substances on private premises evading detection.

4 The IPP sentence was enacted in the Criminal Justice Act 2003 in two different forms; the Indeterminate Sentence for Public Protection (ISPP) and the Extended Sentence for Public Protection (ESPP). The former sentence was given to offenders convicted of sexual or violent sentences carrying a maximum sentence of ten years imprisonment or more, and the latter sentence was given to similar offenders convicted of offences carrying a maximum penalty of at least two years and up to ten years imprisonment. In both cases, the court would set a 'tariff' period for punishment and retribution, after which release would be at the discretion of the Parole Board. However, in the case of the ISPP, the period of licence supervision in the community would be indefinite, whereas in ESPP cases the custodial period would be of at least twelve months in duration, followed by an extended licence period of up to eight years. For a further description of these provisions, see Gibson, 2009 *op. cit.*:87. These measures have since been repealed by subsequent legislation in the Legal Aid, Sentencing and Punishment of Offenders Act 2012, though not retrospectively. Thus many ISPP prisoners are still in custody and beyond their tariff dates. In the Summer of 2016, 4,133 such prisoners were still serving IPP sentences, 81% of whom (3,347) were beyond their tariff periods.

2016 *op. cit.*:2).[5] In summary, increased use of long (four years or longer) prison sentences since 1993 has accounted for 66% of the increase in the average daily prison population of England and Wales, and at the present time, such people represent almost three in five of those held in prisons (*Ibid.*:2).

Philosophical Developments of Deterrence Doctrine

Where did this pre-occupation with deterrence begin? A survey of the literature, though extensive over time if not altogether convincing in substance, provides some measure of understanding.[6] It will be recalled from the previous discussion that, as Bean has hinted, and particularly in the pre-criminological era, explanations of deterrence were based predominantly within the discourses of the psychological, philosophical and sociological schools of academia. These different explanations require some attention.

As early as 1924, Edwin Sutherland produced a seminal work on crime and its causation in which the following passage occurs:

> Among those who advocate punishment because of its social utility, some claim that the infliction of pain upon those convicted of crime serves to deter others from crime, and that it has great value for that reason, even if some individuals are not deterred. Generally, the notion that punishment reduces crime is based on the hedonistic assumption that people regulate their behaviour by calculation of pleasure and pains. In the recent period this assumption has been seriously challenged.
> Many criminals never consider the penalty. Sometimes this is because they are psychopathic or feebleminded or acting under the stress of a great emotion. Sometimes the penalty merely makes the prohibited act more alluring. Many prisoners have describes their psychological reactions while in the process of violation of law, and it appears that few of them give much consideration to the penalty.

5 According to Council of Europe statistics in 2014, England and Wales have more than twice as many prisoners serving indeterminate sentences as France, Germany and Italy combined – the highest number in Europe (11,505) by a significant margin (Prison Reform Trust, 2016 *op. cit.*:3; Council of Europe, 2014: Table 7).

6 The reader must understand that I make no claim that what follows amounts to an exhaustive literature review of deterrence theory or its genesis. Rather, that the sources alluded to represent as balanced an attempt as possible to trace the development of deterrence doctrine as it progressed through the twentieth century and into the present millennium across the nations of the northern hemisphere in which notable contributions to its accretion were made.

> However, a refutation of hedonistic psychology and its conceptions is probably not sufficient to justify the rejection of the broader aspects of the deterrence argument. In a broader perspective, the criminal law and its application by police and courts probably have great effects upon public morality. Whenever the fiction that is known as a 'crime-wave' is heralded, a demand for an increase in the severity of the penalties arises, based on the assumption that the more severe the penalty, the more effectively it will deter others from similar crimes. These demands ordinarily are based on a confusion of penal sanctions as general expressions of hostility to crime on the one hand, and severe punishments as deterrents of specific persons who are contemplating prohibited acts on the other hand (Sutherland, 1924/1955 *op. cit*:288-90).

Moving on slightly in time, we find in the writings of the British philosopher Alfred Ewing an extensive dissertation on the morality of punishment in which he, as an early proponent of a deontological approach to the explanation of its social necessity, expressed some considerable misgivings concerning the social and moral disadvantages of imposing excessive or disproportionate penalties for criminal acts. His major contribution to this debate and the efficacy of deterrence lies in his *The Morality of Punishment* (1929 *op. cit.*) which was remarkably similar to the explanations of Sutherland noted previously. This much stated, within his analysis we find the following observation:

> [W]hile it must be admitted that, in general, other things being equal, a severe punishment will deter more than a milder one, it is very easy to exaggerate both the extent to which deterrence is possible at all and the extent to which it can be made more effective by greater severity. [T]he bad moral effects on society of a very severe penal system have to be considered. It would be quite wrong to suppose that the deterrent effect increases in the same degree as the severity of the punishment. Any sentence of imprisonment appeals to the imagination of most men as a fairly formidable deterrent, but this effect is not likely to be very much increased by even doubling the sentence. An additional length of time in prison will probably make little impression on the mind beforehand compared to the prospect of being imprisoned at all, especially as any addition to the usual sentence will not have to be served immediately after conviction, but will be further away in time and therefore less terrifying. Provided a punishment is sufficient to give a potential offender the general sense that it would be a very serious misfortune to incur it, it is doubtful how far its deterrent effect will be increased by any addition to its severity (*Ibid.*:56-7).

This brief quotation from Ewing's much lengthier analysis of deterrence doctrine reveals some doubt as to the operational effectiveness of deterrence theory *per se*, and also the moral implications for society of increasing the severity of sentences disproportionately.

Ewing, as H.B. Acton (1969:14) rightly pointed out, clearly did not think that either reform or deterrence could provide the main justification for criminal punishment, but equally, he had reservations about the retributive justification of punishment as well. This somewhat equivocal approach to his analysis is interesting if only for the fact that it left the philosophical explanations of the morality and probity of punishment in general, and of deterrence in particular, in some disarray. The moral philosophical debates about the actual justifications of punishment that ensued during the pre- and post-World War 2 period, though extensive, failed to resolve this anomalous situation satisfactorily, leaving those of a primarily retributive disposition at odds with those of a reformatory or rehabilitative persuasion.[7]

Towards Empirical Explanations of Crime and Punishment

In the Fifth Edition of *The Principles of Criminology* (Sutherland & Cressey, 1955), the emphasis on predominantly moral philosophical explanations of crime and punishment was, to a considerable extent, displaced by the more contemporary pre-occupation within academic research in America (and subsequently in Northern Europe) with sociological explanations of crime causation and control post-World War 2.[8] Here it will be noted, however, that the traditional differences of approach of the nineteenth century 'Positivist' and 'Classical' Schools mentioned in Chapter 1 showed signs of re-emergence in the American 'Behaviourist' School of the mid-twentieth century, though in a considerably more empirical manner.[9]

Post-War societies in many of the northern hemisphere countries, focused upon recovery from and reconstruction following the conflict, became increasingly aware of the disruptive effects of deviant and criminal behaviour within their populations, and of the need to control it. The rehabilitative 'ethic' with its emphasis on treatment and 'cure' of criminality

---

7 Here, see the excellent collection of papers collated by H.B. Acton in his *The Philosophy of Punishment*, London: Macmillan, (1969). This volume included contributions from some of the foremost moral philosophers of the period including J.D. Mabbott (1939 and 1955), A.M. Quinton (1954), John Rawls (19550, Antony Flew (1967), and K.G. Armstrong (1961) among others.

8 See here, for example, Sutherland's own theory of 'differential association' set out in Chapter Four of the Fifth Edition (Sutherland and Cressey, *op. cit.*, 1955:74-80), and the work of Robert Merton on 'anomie' (Merton, 1938:677-682) and Sheldon Glueck on 'crime causation' (Glueck, 1941:86-108).

9 Particularly in the work of sociologists such as Howard Becker (1963 and 1964), Emile Durkheim (1958), Talcott Parsons (1951), and Kai T. Erickson (1964).

may be seen (with hindsight) to have emerged from a neo-positivist *quasi*-medical approach to crime causation which, while to a certain extent derived from almost philanthropic motivations, was ultimately a crude means of social control. It was, however, in humanitarian terms perceived as preferable to the predominantly retributive approach to criminal punishment that had preceded it. When its demise became almost inevitable during the 1970s, a penological vacuum occurred into which the apparently 'firm but fair' prescriptions of the 'justice model' fitted with some evident attraction (Cf. Hudson, 1987:37-8).

With the justice model came also a realisation that its tenets of proportionality, strictly determinate sentencing, and reduction of administrative discretion, yielded a punishment agenda based on deterrence and desert that was at least potentially measurable. Yet it was also a utilitarian model in its conception that would seek to restore the balance of advantage and disadvantage, pleasure and pain, and demonstrate the disapprobation of societies towards criminal acts. This prospect alone gave birth to a range of studies into deterrence, bolstered by its linkage to desert as a means of making deterrent measures justifiable (*Ibid.*: 40-41).

But the justice model was also predicated on the notion that the specification of offences, the punishments applicable to the relative seriousness of each, and the degree of culpability of offenders, would effectively deter the commission of crimes. Such a concept would, of course, depend considerably upon wide public knowledge and understanding of the extent of the penalties prescribed for each offence type, whether would-be or actual offenders had internalised the pleasure: gain calculus involved, or whether they chose to discount the risk on a possibility/probability of not being apprehended.[10]

That the justice model was beset with problems of explanation and interpretation in terms of criminal justice policy formulation soon became undeniable. When the difficulties of quantification and specification of deterrence theory and its outcomes on an empirical basis are added to this situation, it was bound to become untenable. However much it held appeal for a wide range of interests in criminal justice and reform, it also became a divisive concept born more out of frustration with the indeterminacy of the rehabilitative ethic than a realistic appraisal of 'deliverable' justice. Perhaps the most comprehensive analysis of this situation lay in a seminal work by Jack Gibbs (1975) in which, in his Overview, the following opening statement appears :

10 A further problem for deterrence theorists lay in the spontaneous or opportunistic nature of the circumstances in which many crimes were committed, and whether or not those committing them were or were not aware of the penalties involved. Some studies conducted in America (e.g. California Assembly Committee on Criminal Procedure, 1968; Jeffery, 1965, Gibbs, 1975, and later, Paternoster, 1987) concluded that such was not generally the case.

> This book is a continuous denial of immediate prospects for satisfactory answers to questions about crime, punishment and deterrence. Critics may be sorely disappointed by such an inconclusive stance, but horrendous problems preclude a categorical rejection or acceptance of deterrence doctrine (*Ibid.*:1).

After an exhaustive description of deterrence theory and the methodological issues involved in its evaluation, the work ends on this sombre note:

> It would be questionable to call for more conventional research on the deterrence question. A sophisticated theory will not be realized without exploratory research to answer several empirical questions about the relation between properties of punishment and crime rates, but the research and the interpretation of findings will have to be quite different from those in the past.
> Whatever strategy is eventually adopted to take into account extralegal conditions and preventive consequences of punishment other than deterrence, defensible tests of the deterrence doctrine are precluded until that doctrine is stated as a systematic theory. Such a statement is not feasible without extensive exploratory research and the assessment of alternative methods. The methodological problems are not limited to numerical representations of properties of punishment; additionally, special crime rates are needed because there is every reason to believe that conventional crime rates are unsatisfactory for deterrence research.
> For reasons just suggested, there is no immediate prospect of deterrence research having an impact on penal policy. All social scientists can do at present is emphasize the difficulties in assessing evidence for or against deterrence doctrine. Legislators undoubtedly want more than a litany of difficulties, but the only alternative to recognizing the difficulties is a penal policy based on comfortable ignorance or a concealed yearning for retribution (*Ibid.*:237-8).

If Gibbs' down-beat assessment of the prospects of making deterrence theory an empirical reality was somewhat subdued, it was in fact also under-stated. His own research into the deterrent effect of the death penalty upon homicide rates in three American states cited within his 1975 work provided a striking example of how properly structured deterrence research could become reliable (*Ibid.*:153-157). It was, in fact, a further development of the discussion in an earlier journal article published in 1968[11] which, when viewed alongside

11 See: J.P. Gibbs, 'Crime, Punishment and Deterrence', in *Social Science Quarterly*, Vol., No.4, 1968 (March), pp.515-530, available at: <www.jstor.org/stable/42867909?seq=1#page_scan_tab_content> [accessed on 18 January 2017].

another article by Gary Becker[12] published in the same year, triggered a renewed interest in empirical deterrence research in America.

The interesting feature of these two articles was that Gibbs' contribution was, as Paternoster (2010:777-824) has recorded, that of a positivist sociologist in the Beccarian tradition, while that of Becker was of a utilitarian economist of the Benthamite persuasion replete with formulaic presentation. Both, however, from differing directions, agreed that criminal behaviour required no special motivation, but was ultimately a product of an assessment of the net utility of the action in terms of benefits and costs to the actor him- or her-self. Gibbs' article, while presented in less scientific but logically argued form accompanied by reliable statistical data, was based on the premise that states in which the certainty and severity of punishment were higher would display lower homicide rates. This was precisely what his research proved unequivocally, providing empirical evidence that, at least in terms of homicides and the death penalty, punishment (or the threat of it) can be effective in securing compliance with laws.

These articles were followed by the widely read work of Frank Zimring and Gordon Hawkins (1973, *op. cit.*), and by Jack Gibbs' expanded explanation of deterrence research limitations previously mentioned (Gibbs, 1975, *supra*) which served at least to revive interest in empirical deterrence research which continued into the 1980s and beyond in both the sociological and criminological fields of academic study.

All of this stated, however, there are and will remain considerable problems with empirical research into deterrence in the context of criminal justice. With wide acceptance of the 'rational actor' concept of criminal behaviour comes the difficulty of devising law-enforcement measures that are neither disproportionately punitive nor uneconomical in resource expenditure terms to implement. Further, if, as seems likely, many criminal offenders do, to whatever extent, internalise the hedonistic gain: cost calculus, while others commit offences spontaneously as a result of opportunities or situations[13] occurring, are the same threatened punitive responses liable to deter them or others who might behave similarly? Daniel Nagin raised this same important reservation concerning the potential boundaries and limitations of deterrence research at the turn of the previous century (Nagin, 1998:35-36), and to date it seems to have remained largely unanswered.

12 G.S. Becker, 'Crime and Punishment: An Economic Approach', in *Journal of Political Economy*, Vol.76, No.2, (Mar.-Apr.), 1968, pp.169-217, available at: <http://jstor.org/sci=0022-3808%29196803%2796%C169%ACAPAEA%E2.0.CO%3B2-1> [accessed on 18 January 2017].

13 Here, by 'situations' I wish to imply circumstances in which responses to provocation or perceived threat trigger criminal acts, and also situations in which offences are committed under the influence of substances such as drugs or alcohol causing temporary impairment of judgement. See, e.g. Wright, 2010:2 and *passim*.

It is also seems true to assert, as Michael Tonry (2008) has suggested, that the implications and, indeed, the impact of new research findings and data – whether derived from meta-analyses or more nuanced single study conclusions – are 'unlikely to have much relevance for the development of policies at either governmental (legal) or criminal justice operational (organisational) levels' (*Ibid.*:301). The reasons for this are complex, having to take account of the inevitable influences exerted by political expediency, traditional reluctance to embrace reformative change, media attitudes and editorial stances, and the concern of politicians to maintain electoral credibility among their constituencies. As Tonry pointed out earlier: 'the bottom line is that current policies, political rhetoric and punishment patterns are as they are because politicians, however motivated, wished it so.' (Tonry, 2003:6).

There is, in addition, some compelling evidence to indicate that the differing routes of approach towards the nature and effects of deterrence doctrine and its research adopted by sociologists, economists and criminologists have resulted more in confusion than enlightenment over the past thirty years or so. That each tells the story differently, and from divergent baselines of academic training, understanding and methodological criteria, is not altogether surprising given the 'vacuum-packed' nature of their professional agendas and motivations. Sometimes such differences, when accepted and shared, can be revealing and mutually advantageous: at other times they can be divisive and largely unhelpful to the interests of progress. Tonry, aptly as ever, summarises the situation thus:

> It is unclear to me which is more surprising: that so little credible evidence exists that criminal behaviour is much affected by changes in punishment policies or that policy makers continue to believe that policy changes significantly affect behaviour and that research continues to test for their crime-preventive effects. Although I have observed in this essay that understanding of deterrent effects has changed little over the past thirty years, it can also be said that understanding has changed little over the past two centuries (Tonry, 2008, *op. cit.*:301-2).

Taken together, the various strands of this discussion so far indicate that over the period surveyed we may detect at least four quite separate lines of approach to the explanation of deterrence doctrine: the moral philosophical, the sociological, that based in economic research, and the criminological. The first is founded in logical reasoning and deduction;[14] the second in the reasons for functional and dysfunctional behaviours of people within

14 Such is to suggest the moral 'rightness and wrongness' of deterrence doctrine in the regulation of the relationships between citizens and the state, and between citizens and each other.

modern and post-modern societies;[15] the third in fiscal assessments of the cost: benefit calculus of deterrence policies in operation;[16] and the fourth in attempts to construct a scientifically tenable explanation of how deterrence (in its specific and general forms) does or does not work in practice, through the accumulation and evaluation of empirical research data.[17]

Now, as we have seen in the foregoing discussion, interest in the first line of approach (the moral-philosophical enquiry) appeared to flourish until the appearance of the 'justice model' of the 1970s and 1980s, and decreased relatively rapidly thereafter. As Hudson (1987, *op. cit.*) and others have pointed out, critiques of the model came from a number of different directions, the more cogent of which concerned its 'taken-for-granted' liberalism at a time of economic recession and considerably increasing crime rates, and the reaction to this situation voiced loudly by right-wing' law and order' lobbies in Britain and America (*Ibid.*:164-5) which coincided with the demise of the rehabilitative ethic (see also, Paternoster & Bynum, 1982:18). This same reaction as Hudson further suggested, provided a legitimising rhetoric for attempts by right-wing political groups to pass off dilemmas of unemployment, poverty and inequality as crime problems, and to control by wider and severe punishment what they were not prepared to cure by radical social change (*Ibid.*:164). In this manner, uncritical faith in the potential of deterrence to reduce crime made deterrence policies attractive as a means of crime control and, the rhetoric argued, their effectiveness would be assured by increased severity of sentencing.

Strangely, the same critique was co-opted by left-wing critics in the sociological discourse of the time, though in a different manner. In times of economic decline, the crimes of the disaffected poor as a reaction to their deteriorating conditions and widespread unemployment can be identified as the cause of increased lawlessness due to their own fecklessness rather than government neglect, and thus the government can justify itself in doing nothing to alleviate inequality, decline and decay. As Hudson also reminds us, at such times 'it is not merely that the state *does* select the crimes of the disadvantaged as those to be taken seriously, it is that it *must* do so' (*Ibid.*:165, emphasis in the original).[18]

---

15 This implies a 'structuralist' account of the causative aspects of criminal behaviour, and how these may or may not be affected by deterrence aimed at promoting social cohesion.

16 Strictly expressed, assessments based upon the laws of economics concerning the social utility of deterrence-based policies measured against the competing social welfare demands for other goods and services within modern democratic economies.

17 Primarily through the correlation of reliable statistical data on, for example, post-sentence reconviction rates within specified time periods against other variables that can be kept sufficiently stable for the purposes of comparison and evaluation.

18 For a further elaboration of this situation, see generally: Steven Box. *Recession, Crime and Punishment*, Basingstoke, Hampshire: Macmillan Education Limited, 1987, and especially Chapter 2, pp.28-68.

As to the third (econometric) line of approach noted above, and the demise of the 'justice model' in favour of penal policies based on the increased severity of sanctions and the potential efficacy of deterrence, the argument becomes more complex. For if, after implementing such policies it were to be established that crime rates had decreased, then it would be attractive in policy terms for governments to claim a 'cause and effect' relationship, citing the decrease and its 'associated' fiscal savings (if any) as the outcomes of the implementation. However, if crime had *decreased* to a measurable extent and penal system costs had *increased*, then it would be necessary to be able to calculate precisely the net utility or disutility of the policy change in economic terms. It seems that such a calculation routinely evades the ability of statisticians to compute, possibly because the cost bases of the comparison are mutually incompatible in correlative terms.

Much the same problematic situation attends the accumulation and correlation of criminological data relating to the outcomes of changes in sentencing patterns. Recidivism rates from different forms of sanction over specified time frames can be ascertained, but it is altogether unknowable with any certainty why some individuals desist from re-offending, or indeed, why others who do re-offend (similarly or differently) were not deterred from doing so by the nature of the sentences previously imposed upon them. Thus, reliance upon the efficacy of deterrent measures within penal policies for reducing crime is at best speculative, or worse still, a matter of complete supposition in criminological terms.

Where, then, does all this discussion leave us in relation to Bean's assertion (p. 3 *supra*), and what are the implications for the deterrence doctrine in the future? The evidence surveyed so far seems to enable us to reach some tentative conclusions which I summarise as follows:

- if deterrence doctrine is a psychological theory based on threats, then the evidence from recidivism statistics indicates that it fails to deliver substantial crime reduction or control;
- if it is a sociological theory based on social control in general and crime control in particular, then expanded use of imprisonment and longer sentences do not achieve its objectives;
- if punitive and deterrent penal policies are predicated on the belief that economic savings will result from their implementation, combined with crime reduction, then reliable longitudinal statistical information has yet to be made available; and,
- from an entirely criminological perspective, the efficacy of deterrence as a principle and purpose of criminal punishment remains an intuitive philosophical construct rather than a theory based on empirical statistical evidence.

These conclusions, if substantially correct, leave deterrence doctrine, as presently conceived, in a parlous state. Part of the reason for this situation is, I venture to suggest, due to a confusion of purposes and motivations in the formulation of criminal justice policies for reasons that deserve exploration. In the last part of this chapter I shall attempt to explain how and why I believe this confusion has arisen.

Deterrence Doctrine: A Confusion of Aims

The reader will recall from Chapter 1 the brief discussion of the motivations that inspired the works of Jeremy Bentham and John Stuart Mill in a utilitarian context. Both were liberal thinkers of their periods whose philosophies were not only utilitarian in nature, but also had a consequentialist ethical motivation.[19] Thus, in both the utilitarian and consequentialist concepts of criminal justice, deterrence doctrine would be acceptable if, and only if it could be shown convincingly to reduce crime while at the same time increasing the likelihood that criminal offenders would subsequently lead law-abiding lifestyles.

Chapter 1 might also have included a discussion of the work of Immanuel Kant (1724-1804) the German philosopher, notable in two different respects for our purposes here. The first of these was his contention that the actions of mankind as a sentient being are those of a reasoning free-will actor; the second was his insistence in the form of a categorical imperative that human beings should 'so act as to treat humanity, whether in thine own person or that of any other, in every case as an end withal, never as a means only' (1785/1996:429).[20] This imperative, if acceptable in moral philosophical terms as many would claim, clearly has implications for the operational pursuit of general deterrence.

Given the tentative conclusions indicated above, and Bean's assertion discussed earlier, it has to be questioned why contemporary penal policies continue to be designed to deliver both retribution and deterrence as the foundation of their operational purposes. It could with some force be argued that increasing the severity of sentencing beyond levels proportionate to the gravity of offences, the culpability of offenders and the extent of harm occasioned, lies outside the bounds of moral behaviour. In essence, it implies that retribution

19 In this sense, utilitarianism is devoted to securing a situation in which actions are governed by the extent to which they maximise the good or benefit of the greatest number within societies, while minimising their dysfunctional or non-beneficial outcomes. Consequentialism is largely concerned with the moral and social outcomes of actions that contribute positively to state welfare and order (state consequentialism) and promote harmonious conditions within societies.

20 See: Kant, I., 'Groundwork of the Metaphysics of Morals', in *Practical Philosophy*, [Tr. Mary McGregor], Cambridge: Cambridge University Press, 1996, p.429, and generally also: Kant, I., *Critique of Practical Reason: A Critical Guide*, [Tr. A. Reath & J. Timmermann], Cambridge: Cambridge University Press, 2010.

is an entirely retrospective punitive response focused on past actions, the harm of which cannot be undone by punishment – whether excessive or not.[21] To compound this already dubious practice, by augmenting it with an additional 'premium' supposed to deliver the operationally flawed and prospective concept of deterrence, becomes extremely questionable. This is, of course, ultimately part of the argument for parsimony in the use of punishment.[22]

Kant's imperative, taken to its logical conclusion, implies that the use of prospective general deterrence for the purposes of social control and crime prevention is morally unacceptable. This is so because it uses persons who may not or who have never offended as means rather than ends under the duress of threats. It is, therefore, both a psychological theory based on threats and a sociological theory based on social control. Thus, though the use of punishment for specific or individual deterrence may have some merit in securing or at least encouraging the future compliance of those who *have* committed offences, it should be confined to that purpose alone and not used for the purpose of increasing sentencing severity.

The attractiveness of deterrence theory to the minds of some policy makers, politicians and members of the general public alike lies in its seductive appeal to intuition as a means of crime control rather than, necessarily, of crime reduction. However, as we have seen earlier in this discussion, many criminal offences are committed on an opportunistic or spontaneous basis in circumstances in which the perpetrator assesses neither the gain: pain calculus, nor the nature and extent of the punishment prescribed for each form of offence.[23]

If, therefore, specific deterrence is to be retained as a purpose of criminal punishment, it has to be validated through the use of sophisticated longitudinal research into the post-sentence careers of ex-offenders over a significant number of years following the expiry of sentences.

---

21 This also brings with it questions about the status of the concept of desert and the extent to which it is calculable. For while it is possible to insist that certain offences are more blameworthy (or harmful) than others, measurement of the extent to which this is true becomes a subjective issue, and crudely variable depending upon the sociological factors selected for the purpose.

22 On the basis that no system of criminal punishment will be logically flawless however socially necessary it may be as a response to crime, and that therefore the extent of punishment should be set at the minimum level consistent with the gravity of the offence to reduce arbitrariness as far as possible.

23 This may be due to the mental process known as 'discounting' in the criminological literature in which the sanctions for offending are ignored at the time of offence commission, or due to ignorance of, or discounting the extent of penalties if found guilty. See, generally, Erlich (1972:259-276); Dean *et al.*, 1996; and Mastrobuoni & Rivers (2016 *passim*) for further elaboration of this concept.

Figure 2.1 Illustration of Criminal Offence Pattern Plotting Technique to Reveal the Frequency of Offences, Punishments and Average Mean Time Between Failure (MTBF) Rates

Year	2000	2001	2002	2003	2004	2005	2006	2007	2008	2009	2010	2011	2012	2013	2014	2015	2016
Age	16	17	18	19	20	21	22	23	24	25	26	27	28	29	30	31	32
Convictions and Dates	TWOC x 2 (18/7)		AOABH x 1 Burg x 2 (5/5)	Burg x 3 HSG x 2 (30/11)				Robbery x 3 Poss F/A W/I x 1 (1/6)					Rape x 1 AOABH W/I x 1 (10/1)				
Sentences	Fine £50		Det 12 mos	Imp 3 yrs				Imp 4 yrs					Imp 6 yrs ESPP*				
Time in Custody (Mos)			6		181				24					40			
Time at Large (Mos)		29		11			23				30						18

Source: After Cornwell, 1989 *op. cit.*

OFFENCE PATTERN SUMMARY

Total time in custody (TTIC) = 88 Months

Total time at Large (TTAL) = 104 Months (since first conviction)

Average Mean Time Between Failures (AMTBF) = 104÷5= 20.8 Months

KEY TO OFFENCE & SENTENCE ABBREVIATIONS

TWOC = Taking Vehicle Without Owner's Consent; AOABH = Assault Occasioning Actual Bodily Harm; HSG = Handling Stolen Goods; Burg = Burglary; Poss F/A W/I = Possession of Firearm With Intent to Commit a Criminal Offence. Note: ESPP * indicates an Extended Sentence of Imprisonment for Public Protection; Det = Detention; Imp = Imprisonment.

In England and Wales at the present time, reconviction statistics are largely confined to a period of two subsequent years, and are calculated using relatively unrefined criteria[24] which have doubtful reliability. In view of the time required to compute individual career patterns of criminal offending – approximately thirty minutes for each case – it is recommended that use of this offence pattern analysis should be confined to those offenders who have already served one or more custodial sentences. An illustrative example of a technique for plotting criminal career offence patterns is shown at *Figure* 2:1 based on an empirical research study of a sample of 250 individual cases completed by the author in 1989 with a follow-up comparative evaluation in 1994-5 (Cornwell, 1989).

At best, and for specific deterrence purposes, reliable career pattern information on criminal offenders can only indicate – based on past events – an informed statistical forecast of likely future individual offending activity and the nature of offences which might recur. It is worth noting, however, that the criminal him/herself provides us with the basis for this analysis in criminal records which are also available to the courts in making sentencing decisions. Though this may be useful in terms of specific deterrence it is only an indication, and should not be used as a consideration upon which criminal justice policies are formulated in pursuit of general deterrence or crime control.

The technique described here does, however, indicate very clearly the extent to which deterrent measures have not prevented recidivism, the frequency with which further offences are committed, and the intervals of time between the offences when the offender is at large in the community to commit them. This information is reliable and based upon evidence that is irrefutable. Those who sentence repetitive offenders should, therefore, be aware of such information which, although available from criminal records in the form of listed previous convictions, can too easily be overlooked. The protocol is also indicative of the sentencing measures that have not proved successful in the past in persuading the offender to desist from further criminal offending.

24 In order to ascertain the criminal career pattern of serious and/or repetitive offenders who have been sentenced to prison custody on one or more occasions, it is necessary to plot in a linear format over time (using their record of previous convictions), each occasion upon which they have been convicted in the courts, the sentences imposed, and the offences for which they were convicted. Further refinement of this methodological technique can be obtained by indicating the periods actually spent in custody, and thus the intervals between custodial periods in which the individual was actually at large and able to commit further offences. The periods at large, when aggregated and compared with the duration of the entire offence pattern also yield a statistical index (the average Mean Time Between Failure – MTBF rate) which will provide an indication (based on past offending history) of when further offences might be anticipated to occur. Supervision periods or sanctions within the community should extend at least to accommodate the MTBF period. Here see: Cornwell, D.J., *Criminal Dangerousness and Its Punishment: Beyond the Phenomenological Illusion*, D. Phil. Thesis, York, UK: University of York, 1989.

Here we may perceive how deterrence doctrine has contributed to a confusion of aims within contemporary penology. Reliance upon retributive measures is inevitably a backward-looking concept even though it may, in some individual instances, result in specific deterrence through future crime desistance. This cannot, however, be known with any certainty, and there is no justifiable reason to believe that any greater certainty will result from increasing sentencing severity. Punishment with the purpose of general deterrence is entirely a prospective concept of dubious morality as we have seen, is unquantifiable in its outcomes, and the more severe it becomes the greater the injustice that it creates. So if deterrence doctrine has any usefulness, it does not reside in the way it is articulated at the present time. It is at best an appeal to intuition, and at worst an appeal to vicarious vindictiveness.

Arguably the time has come to re-appraise completely whether or not deterrence theory has anything beyond its intuitive appeal to offer to a re-shaped conception of criminal punishment. If this is the case, then critical decisions have to be made as to whether criminal punishment is primarily to be administered on a predominantly retrospective deontological basis which might accommodate retribution to an extent, or on a predominantly forward-looking consequentialist basis which might seek to maximise the potential likelihood of crime desistance in general and reduce recidivism in particular.

The Spiral into Penal Crisis – The 1970s and Onwards

It is fitting that this chapter should conclude by suggesting that the contemporary penal crisis in England and Wales has an antecedent causal history reaching back over more than half a century. In the next chapter we shall assess the turbulent history of that penal system and the extent to which deterrence theories and practices contributed to the shaping of its legacy. Excessive penal populations do not happen accidentally, but rather as a result of the penal policies adopted by successive governments, and their political agendas in relation to criminal justice.

Though, as we shall see in the chapter that follows, the most remarkable acceleration in the expansion of the custodial sector of corrections in England and Wales occurred during the decade between 1997 and 2008, the reasons for this situation lie in the confused nature of penal policy-making and prisons administration dating back to the 1970s and thereafter. Most politicians and many of their advisers do not have the background knowledge of criminological science and its development over the years since the post-World War 2 period. More significantly, perhaps, they became increasingly reluctant to seek the advice and expertise that was available within universities in which criminology as a mature social science was rapidly expanding during the same period – a time which was also marked by the emergence of vociferous 'law and order' lobbies within many of the countries of Western Europe and North America. Such lobbies attract media attention as a focus for political action, and thus also the attention of parliamentarians anxious to retain their electoral credibility.

3 Penal Crisis or Business as Usual?

The Genesis of the 'Penal Problem' Post-World War 2

After the cessation of hostilities in Europe and South-East Asia in 1945, the average daily prison population of England and Wales stood at around 17,500 persons held in custody, the majority of them for relatively short periods of time.[1] Thereafter, this population increased steadily at an annual average rate of 2.5 *per cent* until 1990 when it reached 50,000. Between 1993 and 2012 there occurred a sharp average increase to 3.4 *per cent* annually, and by 2010 the population had reached 82,000. It was to reach a peak in 2012 at over 84,500 before declining slightly in 2013 and 2014, and then rising again to 85,583 in early 2017 (see *Figure* 3:1).[2]

In the years immediately following 1945, the dominant penal agenda changed from the pre-War emphasis on retribution and desert towards a post-War welfarism model based upon the classical notions of reform and deterrence, but with an increasing emphasis on the 'socialisation' of offenders in prison custody and their purposeful employment. Such a concept became enshrined in the re-drafting of the Prison Rules 1964[3] which stated: 'The purpose of the training and treatment of convicted prisoners shall be to encourage them to lead a good and useful life.'

The Criminal Justice Act 1948 established Detention Centres for young adult offenders modelled to a considerable extent on a 'military discipline' regime with education and routine work, and also the Probation Order as an alternative to custodial sentencing – principally for non-repetitive offenders of all age groups who might otherwise have attracted a short prison sentence. The Act also modified the rules for sentencing serious adult recidivists over 30 years of age to Preventive Detention.[4]

---

1 The average length of custodial sentences during the early post-War years is difficult to establish with accuracy, such statistics being unavailable from archival records of the (then) Prison Commission or the Home Office. With the exception of those sentenced to life imprisonment (then less than 3 per cent of the prison population), or exceptional determinate sentences, the majority of prisoners during the later years of the 1940s were sentenced to three years or less in prison custody.

2 See: House of Commons Library, *Prison Population Statistics [England and Wales]*, Standard Note SN/SG/4334, G. Berman (Author), 28 June 2013, London: House of Commons, 2013, p.2. And also: Ministry of Justice, *Prison Population Statistics – Population Bulletin 16 December 2016*, London: National Offender Management Service, 2016a.

3 Statutory Instrument (SI) 1964/388 at Rule 1.

4 Preventive Detention (PD) was introduced in the Prevention of Crime Act 1908, modified by the Criminal Justice Act 1948, and repealed by the Criminal Justice Act 1967. It was designed to deal with serious

Figure 3.1 Total Prison Population – England and Wales from 30 June 1945 - to june 2017 (rounded to nearest 500)

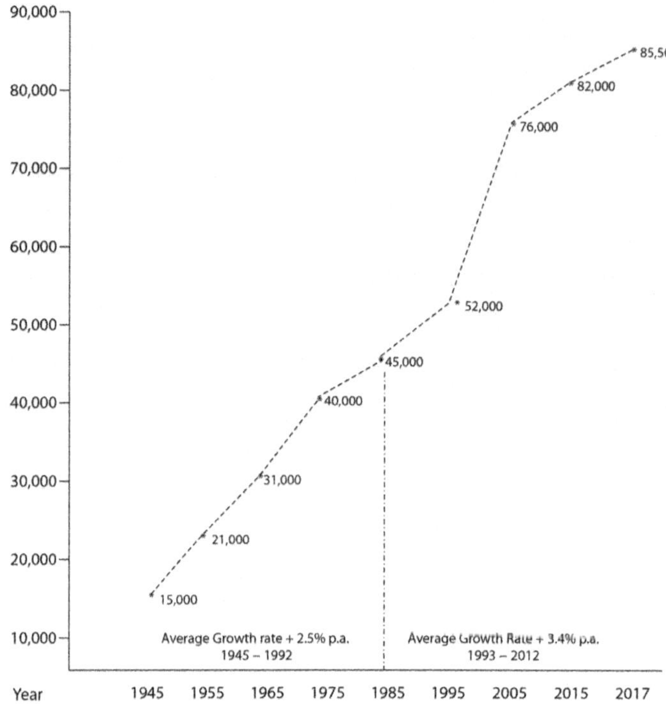

Source: Extracted from Ministry of Justice, 2016:3 updated.

TREATMENT AND TRAINING

These developments notwithstanding, further significant change was to follow without any marked decrease in the prison population. The late-1950s saw a move away from the

recidivist offenders over thirty years of age convicted of an offence punishable with at least two years imprisonment, and who had been similarly convicted on at least three occasions since the age of seventeen and similarly sentenced. The length of the PD sentence was between five and fourteen years (and thus indeterminate), and related more to an offender's past crimes than the present one for which he was being sentenced. After 1963, offenders serving PD were eligible for one third remission, and could be released on licence to a Probation Officer for the period of the sentence up to its expiry date. Any breach of the licence conditions made the offender liable to recall to prison for the entire unexpired portion of the sentence period. Though the PD sentence was designed primarily for public protection, in actual fact it became misused as a means of dealing with persistent petty offenders with long records of crime, rather than the serious offenders for whom it was intended, and was in no sense a deterrent. Following its abandonment in 1967, it was ultimately replaced by the Extended Sentence in the Criminal Justice Act of that year (s.37), and subsequently re-enacted by the Powers of Criminal Courts Act 1973 (s.28).

'penal welfarism' model towards what was to be a neo-Positivist and '*quasi*-Medical' approach involving 'treatment' and training in pursuit of reducing recidivism, and an increasing use of indeterminate sentences. This particular development mirrored one of a similar nature in America based on sociological research founded in a belief that criminals could be 'cured' with the use of psycho-therapeutic programmes administered by a new generation of professionals drawn from the disciplines of psychiatry and psychology. Release from custodial sentences was to be open-ended and dependent upon the individual offender showing some evidence of changed attitudinal behaviour towards a crime-free lifestyle. It did, however, place very considerable discretion in the hands of professionals – both medical and psychological – and those in an administrative capacity responsible for interpreting release criteria and authorising parole conditions.[5]

This change of emphasis took some years to develop, and in England and Wales it was not until the mid-1960s that it became government policy in a White Paper *The Adult Offender* published in 1965,[6] and implemented in the Criminal Justice Act 1967. The Act established the legislative framework for the parole system including Local Review Committees (LRCs) at prisons which were to assess cases recommended (or otherwise) by prison governor grades, and refer their findings to the Home Office Parole Unit which in turn would refer them to the Parole Board, with the Home Secretary having the final right of veto.[7]

The new initiative away from retribution and towards rehabilitation and reduced recidivism left the status of deterrence within the purposes of criminal punishment in a somewhat ambivalent state. For while, with retribution, it remained central to the traditionalist and philosophical backward-looking explanations of punishment, in an operational sense it could only, at best, retain a prospective orientation if the rehabilitative ethic could be evidently effective in terms of an empirically proven reduction in both crime rates and recidivism. What was certain in the late 1960s amounted to an increasing awareness that retributive punishment alone achieved neither of the latter outcomes, since rates of recorded

5 Such as members of Parole Boards drawn from the judiciary, psychiatry, psychology, academic social scientists, and the civil servants who administered their decision-making meetings.

6 See: Home Office, *The Adult Offender*, Cmnd.2852, London: HMSO, 1965, and for further detail, the account of Dermot Walsh in *A Dictionary of Criminology*, London: Routledge & Kegan Paul, 1983, pp.154-5.

7 Parole eligibility applied to prisoners serving sentences of more than eighteen months who had served one-third of their total sentence period or longer. Thus, a prisoner serving a six year sentence could benefit from remission of one-third of his sentence (twenty-four months), but become parole-eligible after eighteen months and, if successful, be released on parole licence to a Probation Officer after some two years. He would subsequently serve a licence period of two further years up to the two-thirds point of sentence (four years) and subject to recall to prison in breach, and the final two years on unconditional release.

crime were rising in increasingly more affluent democratic societies, and methodologically reliable longitudinal research studies into the extent of recidivism were almost non-existent.[8]

THE YEARS OF DOUBT AND UNCERTAINTY

In the early 1970s, serious doubts began to emerge in America and Western Europe about the effectiveness of the rehabilitative ideal, its sentencing implications, and its outcomes. Indeterminate sentencing and a growing risk-aversion within 'penal politics' resulted in prisoners spending increasing periods in custody, and this in turn drove an increase in average daily prison populations year on year. In England and Wales, the provisions enacted in the Criminal Justice Act 1967 for both Suspended[9] and Extended Sentences became, in effect, mutually exclusive. The former measure was designed to decrease reliance upon immediate imprisonment, while the latter was, as previously mentioned, a deliberate attempt to punish serious and repetitive offenders more harshly through incapacitation for public protection. This 'push – pull' effect upon the prison population was both unfortunate and ultimately counter-productive.

Though the death penalty had been abolished in Britain on a five year trial basis in the Murder (Abolition of Death Penalty) Act 1965, and subsequently on an indefinite basis in the Murder Act 1969, the accretion of a sizeable prison population of life sentence inmates was gradual but inevitable. This much stated, however, the sentence of life imprisonment has been expanded in its use in England and Wales, as will be apparent in the subsequent discussion in this chapter. It should be noted here, however, that the considerable body of research devoted in following years to the effectiveness of the death penalty as a deterrent to murder proved very far from conclusive.

8 This was largely due, at least in England and Wales, to the increasingly restrictive approach of the Home Office Research Unit (HORU) established in 1957 to commission academic research studies in conjunction with universities and allocate funding. During the 1970s in particular, the HORU became increasingly reliant upon its own 'in house' studies to inform government policy development, since Social Science researchers in universities could not be relied upon to deliver research outcomes that were consistent with the preferred approaches of politicians and ministers towards criminal justice policies and legislation. Here, see: Cornwell, 2016:72-76.

9 Suspended sentences were a measure widely used in European countries, particularly in Belgium and France since the 1890s. Normally of a fixed duration for one or two years, and used in conjunction with fines or other non-custodial sanctions, such sentences could be activated by further offending and conviction. In England and Wales the sentence was introduced in the Criminal Justice Act 1967, allowing the courts discretion to use it in place of any prison sentence of up to two years in duration, and mandatorily for sentences of six months or less. However, the measure was unpopular with sentencers and in particular with magistrates, and was subsequently repealed in the Criminal Justice Act 1972. There was some inferential evidence that the courts used it in place of Probation Orders and fines, rather than for the purpose for which it was intended (see: A.E.Bottoms, 'The Suspended Sentence in England and Wales 1967-1978', in *British Journal of Criminology*, 21(1), 1981, pp.1-26.

As the 1960s ended, the publication of a Home Office Report in Britain under the title *People in Prison* (Home Office, 1969)[10] was to signal yet another change of direction in penology and (with hindsight) the ultimate demise of the rehabilitative ideal. The Report acknowledged the unacceptable state of overcrowding in many prisons, and particularly in local prisons, and the effects of this on regime delivery to promote rehabilitation. If this situation were to be allowed to continue, the Report maintained, the ability of prison staff to maintain security, control and order in prisons would be threatened. This was a time at which significant doubts were being expressed in academic circles in Europe (including Britain) and North America as to both the practicality and the effectiveness of rehabilitative treatment programmes in prisons, and also, and equally significantly, about the extent of discretion that such programmes placed in the hands of therapeutic professionals and administrators within penal systems.

THE 1970S – WINDS OF CHANGE

Predictably, perhaps, these matters came to a head in the early 1970s, though from a number of different perspectives. In England and Wales, the Criminal Justice Act 1972 introduced the concept of Community Service Orders (CSOs) as a non-custodial sanction that was hoped would appeal to sentencing officials and the public alike. However, the same Act repealed the suspended sentence provisions of the 1967 Act, and replaced it with the Deferred Sentence.[11] Community Service Orders (CSOs) – currently and since 2003 Community Sentences[12] – retained their appeal to the courts and the public, and continue to do so.

10 Home Office, '*People in Prison: England and Wales*', Cmnd. 4714, London: HMSO, 1969.

11 The Deferred Sentence provided the courts with the power to defer sentence on conviction for a period of up to six months in order to take into account the offender's subsequent conduct (including the making of reparation) or changes of personal circumstances (i.e. in employment, accommodation or marital status, etc.). The offender had to consent to this if the court considered that such an outcome would be just. Any offence committed during the period of deferment would render him liable to be sentenced for the original and the subsequent offences. At the end of the period of deferment, the court (preferably as originally constituted) if satisfied as to the offender's conduct, might impose a non-custodial sentence or discharge him conditionally or absolutely. The measure proved quite popular with magistrates in particular, and was subsequently ratified in the Powers of the Criminal Courts Act 1973.

12 The Community Service concept originated in the Report of the Advisory Council on the Penal System (ACPS), *Non-Custodial and Semi-Custodial Penalties*, (1970), translated into legislation in the Criminal Justice Act 1972, and subsequently in The Powers of the Criminal Courts Act 1973. It empowered courts to sentence an offender aged over seventeen years convicted of an offence punishable by imprisonment and with his consent, to not less than 40 or more than 240 hours of unpaid work in the community supervised by the Probation Service. Failure to comply with the Order would result in his return to court which might revoke it and deal with him in any way appropriate to the original offence, or fine him leaving the Order in place. Since 2003, Community Sentences may include provisions to undergo supervision, unpaid work, specified activities, programmes to treat drug, alcohol or other addictions, or electronic monitoring and other restrictions as to residence, curfew compliance, travel abroad, or employment as elements of the

In spite of the innovative nature of the 1972 and 1973 Acts aimed at reducing dependence upon custodial sentences, during the ensuing years of the 1970s the prison population in England and Wales continued to rise, as did the volume of crime recorded by the police and the rates of post-release recidivism among those imprisoned. Similar patterns were also evident in the United States and within Western Europe, adding further fuel to the debates of disenchantment with the outcomes and ethical shortcomings of the rehabilitative ideal.

In 1972, the American Friends Service Committee (AFSC) published a report under the title *Struggle for Justice* which laid the foundations for what was later to become known as the 'justice model' of correctional punishment.[13] The report was particularly notable for its specification and elaboration of what it termed the 'presumptive sentence' which, in effect, recommended fixed penalties for certain crimes based predominantly on their relative seriousness. This much stated, however, the report provided latitude for the judiciary to lower the sentence in the case of mitigating circumstances, or raise it according to the circumstances of its commission and/or the previous criminal record of the offender (see, for instance, Bean, 1981:178-9; von Hirsch, 1976:84; and later, Cavender and Musheno, 1981, and Hudson, 1987:60-61).

The report was remarkable insofar as it formed a direct assault on the entire concept of indeterminate sentencing (with the exception of capital offences), and also because it suggested the notions of either providing sentencing officials with a range of options or sentence bands with maximum and minimum prescriptions for each offence type (a so-called definite scheme), or minimum sentences of a mandatory nature to which judiciaries must adhere. The latter subsequently paved the way for what became mandatory minimum sentences under, for instance, 'three strikes' legislative provisions (see: Gibson, 2009 *op. cit.*:225).[14]

The AFSC report was followed up by the publication of two further (and what were to prove to be landmark) documents in 1975 and 1976 respectively. The first of these was Robert Martinson's heavily suppressed account of the outcomes of a research study into the outcomes of prison-based programmes designed to reform offenders and reduce

supervision requirement. Failure to comply with the requirements of the Community Sentence may result in the offender being returned to court by the 'Responsible (Probation) Officer' and re-sentenced for the original offence.

13 American Friends Service Committee, *Struggle for Justice*, New York: Hill & Wang, 1972.

14 The term 'three strikes' is an allusion to the USA baseball rule in which the hitter is given 'out' after failing to hit the ball on three successive attempts. In justice terms, it implies the mandatory imposition of imprisonment on a third conviction for certain specified offences such as serious assaults, robbery, burglary, and the like.

recidivism (Martinson, 1975).[15] The research findings published in full in Lipton *et al.*, (1975) concluded that there was little evidence that prison programmes had any marked effect upon re-offending (see: Cornwell, 2006:45), though that was not to insist that these had no effect at all. Rather it was the case that 'such was not to say that we found no instances of success or partial success, but that such instances were isolated, producing no clear pattern to indicate the efficacy of any particular method of treatment' (Martinson, 1975:179).[16]

Martinson's pessimistic analysis was seized upon by those wishing to see the rehabilitative ideal abandoned, and was in some respects widely misinterpreted. In the idiom of the time it was hailed as the 'Nothing Works' thesis, but it did provide considerable ammunition for a study already in the later stages of preparation by the Committee for the Study of Incarceration whose report appeared as *Doing Justice* in 1976 (von Hirsch *op. cit.* 1976).

As I recorded in 2006, *Doing Justice* was an altogether different proposition. In effect it amounted to a full scale assault on the alleged cruelty and injustice of the rehabilitative model of criminal punishment, sentencing indeterminacy, the wide discretion exercised by professionals, and a number of other associated issues. The report urged a return to traditional retributive policies accompanied by a re-emphasis on general deterrence, denunciation and incapacitation (Haley, 1984:393; and see also Cornwell, 2006:46-7, and von Hirsch, 1976 *op. cit.*:xxxii-xxxix).[17]

But *Doing Justice* was not only concerned with the abandonment of the rehabilitative ethic: it was also to find, curiously, common cause with the emergence of a new radical criminology in North America and Britain during the late 1970s,[18] and with an increasingly vocif-

15 The research referred to here related to a five year study by Martinson and his colleagues which was completed in 1971 and funded by the New York State Governor's Special Committee on Criminal Offenders, based on the premise that offenders could be successfully rehabilitated, and that the prisons of the state were not making a serious enough attempt at rehabilitation. By 1972 it had not been published, and Martinson had been refused permission to publish its findings privately. It was only released following a court case in which (in 1975) it was subpoenaed from the state as evidence before the Bronx Supreme Court. Martinson published his version of the findings of the research outcomes in a journal *The Public Interest* in the Spring of 1975, and subsequently in J.A. Gardiner and M.A. Mulkey (Eds.), 'What Works? Questions and Answers About Prison Reform', in *Crime and Criminal Justice*, London and Lexington: D.C. Heath & Company, 1975, pp.155-87.

16 See: Lipton, D., Martinson, R. & Wilks, J., *The Effectiveness of Correctional Treatment*, London and New York, Praeger Publications, 1975.

17 The latter reference is to the Introduction to *Doing Justice* and the reasons advanced by the compilers of that report for abandonment of the rehabilitative ethic, and its replacement by a retributive model based on proportionality in sentencing, the assumed efficacy of general deterrence, the incapacitation of serious and repetitive offenders and strict limitations on judicial and administrative discretion.

18 See here, for instance, I. Taylor, P. Walton and J. Young (Eds.), *The New Criminology*, London: Routledge & Kegan Paul, (1975), particularly Chapter 1.

erous 'law and order' lobby urging a 'war on crime', and was expressive of considerable disenchantment with the probation and social work services in their dealing with offenders. We shall return to these developments in the subsequent discussion later in this chapter.

INCREASING PRISON UNREST IN THE 1970S – THE USA AND BRITAIN

Although prisons in the USA had been tormented by sporadic disturbances and prisoner militancy since the 1950s and even before (Adams,1982:46-79), most of these events were of a spontaneous or *ad hoc* nature against prison conditions, regimes, overcrowding and the injustices of the legal and penal processes as perceived by prisoners. The question of when a prison disturbance as a protest against local conditions becomes a riot designed to awaken public consciousness or awareness of crisis conditions and inhumane treatment has exercised observers of penal systems or processes for many decades past. The same may be claimed to be the case also in Britain, though until the 1970s on a considerably lesser scale.

As the American experience of the early 1950s indicates, with hindsight, concerted disorder by sizeable groups of prisoners becomes an infectious phenomenon within penal systems, spreading rapidly between prisons where opportunities for protest are presented by lapses in security and supervision by prison staff heavily outnumbered by those in their charge on a daily basis. This much is an almost universally acknowledged fact of prison life. It is, of course, also an undeniable fact that prisons operating in overcrowded conditions that prevent delivery of reasonable and constructive regimes and services become 'riot-prone' or at least vulnerable to concerted acts of indiscipline.

So-called 'crises' in prisons have many potential points of origin. These may be of 'numbers',[19] of conditions, of the perceived 'legitimacy' of the penal process, or even of the monopoly of power and influence arrogated by certain prisoner groupings in control of the illicit supply and distribution of contraband commodities within the inmate sub-culture. In some prisons, the presence of 'gangs' of geographic or ethnic origin can become a threatening and de-stabilising influence in the daily lives of those interned, and particularly the more vulnerable members of the inmate community.

The mid- to late-1970s in British and American prisons proved to be watershed years in which the always tenuous and fragile consensus between the guarded and the guards to

19 Such is to imply prisons required to accommodate inmate populations in excess of the normal operational capacity which the establishment was designed to hold in decent and secure conditions and deliver purposeful regimes.

maintain order and control began to show distinct signs of deterioration. Although there had been numerous yet sporadic demonstrations of increasing prisoner unrest (mainly related to prison conditions) in Britain during the 1960s, the major disturbance at Wormwood Scrubs Prison in London in November 1975 and the serious riot at Hull Prison in East Yorkshire in 1976 provided evidence (if it were needed) that the prison system in England and Wales was in considerable disarray. Prisoners climbing onto the roofs of prisons located in densely populated urban areas attract considerable local and media attention on the one hand, and the angry response of 'law and order' lobbies on the other. Even though there had been some thirty lesser incidents of concerted disorder during both 1975 and 1976, most were locally contained by prison staff using negotiation skills and with minimal resort to physical intervention and restraint.

The continuing escalation in the average daily prison population of England and Wales from some 32,500 in mid-1968 to over 41,000 in 1976/77 undoubtedly contributed to the growth of prisoner unrest in the local and training prisons of which only eleven had no disturbances between mid-May and early September 1976 (Adams, 1992 *op. cit.*:131). However, it became apparent that a sizeable element in the population growth was attributable to a significant increase in the number of young adult offenders serving longer than average sentences, and who were a disruptive influence upon the stability of prison regimes. The British Home Office, meanwhile, in its traditionally secretive and defensive approach to such matters, appeared to accept the situation with an apparent equanimity bordering on resignation.

Disquiet within wider governmental and opinion-forming circles in Britain was beginning to become manifest over the situation in prisons. The decline of the rehabilitative ethos with its 'treatment and training' emphasis created a penological 'vacuum' which, in both America and Britain, became filled by the so-called 'justice model' of correctional philosophy. That it embraced a neo-retributive rationale based on desert and proportionality in sentencing, combined with an implied if not explicit emphasis on deterrence, gave the model an appeal to a wide variety of interests in matters criminological. If *Doing Justice* was its *datum* point, it was also adjustable and amenable to co-option as a means of countering the perceived abuses of rehabilitationism.

1977 in Britain had seen the publication by the widely respected Church of England Board for Social Responsibility Working Party of its Report *Prisons and Prisoners in England Today* (CIO, 1977). In a Foreword by the Bishop of Truro its Chairman, the following statement appears:

> Uncertainty about the objectives which the prisons should be pursuing; an increasing feeling that offenders, particularly young people, should at all costs be kept out of prison; signs of a more militant attitude among both staff and prisoners – all these and other issues indicate the need for a radical re-examination of the place of prisons in the penal system of this country (*Ibid.*:v).

Whether as a response to the Report or for other reasons (of which there were many), rising internal and external criticism of the state of the prisons was becoming widespread in the media, and the Home Secretary Merlyn Rees decided to act by setting up a Committee of Inquiry into the United Kingdom Prison Services under the chairmanship of Mr. Justice May in November 1978. The May Committee reported in late 1979,[20] after having requested additional time to complete its task due to the complexity of the matters placed before it.

The May Committee Report, when it was eventually published, reflected the considerable breadth of investigative work demanded of its relatively small membership of ten persons and their support staff within a time frame of a single year. Its Terms of Reference identified four principal *foci* for investigation:

- the size and nature of the prison population, and the capacity of the prison services to accommodate it;
- the responsibilities of the prison services for the security, control and treatment of inmates;
- the need to recruit and train sufficient and suitable staff for the prison services; and,
- the need to secure the efficient use of manpower and financial resources in the prison services (Home Office, 1979:iii).

Faced with such a Herculean task, and given the background and extent of the contemporary prison unrest and discontent described in the foregoing analysis, it was scarcely surprising that the outcome deliberations of the Committee would be anything other than, at best, limited and in many respects superficial. Indeed, four separate committees of inquiry of a similar size of membership might have struggled to plumb the depths of the *malaise* within the prison services, and also penetrate the secretive culture of reluctance within the Home Office to being investigated, within the time constraints imposed.

As it transpired, the May Report failed to focus on the first and dominant issue within its Terms of Reference and emphatically propose political action to reduce the prison population to manageable proportions. Had it done so, the way would have become open to

20 See: Committee of Inquiry into the United Kingdom Prison Services, *Report*, Cmnd.7673, [The May Report] London: HMSO, 1979.

subsequently address the remaining issues within its remit in a deliberate and effective manner. It was an opportunity missed which was to have considerable repercussions in the following years during which crisis in the prisons and the wider processes of criminal justice became 'business as usual'.

Shortly after the publication of the May Report, the incumbent Labour government in Britain was defeated in the general election of May 1979 and replaced by a Conservative administration led by Margaret Thatcher as Prime Minister with William Whitelaw as her Home Secretary. The election manifesto of the new government had promised a considerably more 'right wing' approach to criminal justice based upon a return to penal policies designed to punish and deter offenders and would-be offenders, re-establish order in prisons, and outlaw militant trades unionism in the form of industrial action within essential public services which was threatening to de-stabilise the economy. Needless to say almost, such included action by prison officers limiting the full performance of their duties.

In 1980, a newly formed Parliamentary All-Party Penal Affairs Group (PA-PPAG)[21] published a Report under the title *Too Many Prisoners*[22] urging the Home Secretary to take urgent action to reduce the size of the prison population – advice which he appeared to have taken to heart very seriously as the following extract of his response to the Group indicated in a speech to the Conservative Central Council in Bournemouth on 21st March:

> It is no use continuing to over-burden the staff who have to run the [prison] system, too often in antiquated and inadequate buildings, with petty offenders who can be dealt with just as well in other ways… we must ensure that prison is reserved for those who we really need to contain in custody , and that sentences are no longer than necessary to achieve this objective… We shall need, and in this the courts have their part to play, to see that the prisons are not cluttered up with trivial and inadequate offenders who are no real threat to anyone, except possibly themselves, but whose presence helps to create the extremely acute pressures which afflict our prisons today and all who work in them (PA-PPAG, 1980:2).

Bold words, indeed, but the recourse adopted by the government was based not upon reducing the numbers unnecessarily sent to prison over which the courts declined to adopt

21 This Group effectively replaced the former ACPS which, since 1968, had been the principal source of governmental advice on penal policy. Here, see: Cornwell, 2016, p.79 at fn.15 for a further explanation.

22 See: PA-PPAG, *Too Many Prisoners: An Examination of Ways of Reducing the Prison Population*, (R. Kilroy-Silk Chair), Chichester and London: Barry Rose Publishers, 1980 (June).

control, but by expanding the prison building programme to accommodate more and more prisoners.[23]

THE 1980S – PLUS ÇA CHANGE ..

The Criminal Justice Act 1982 heralded a new approach by the Thatcher government to dealing with the problems of the criminal justice system. The sentencing of young offenders to Borstal training was abolished, and Detention Centre Orders were modified. A new sentence to Youth Custody was established, and the imprisonment of 18-21 year olds was also discontinued. A renewed interest in using partly suspended sentences previously provided in the 1967 Act and repealed in the 1972 Act was included on the advice of the Advisory Council on the Penal System (ACPS) in 1977.[24]

The drive to reduce prison numbers also brought the entire issue of parole release into a renewed focus during the early 1980s. It was precipitated by considerable disenchantment within the influential 'law and order' lobby of the Conservative Party with the workings of the parole system as it then operated, which was perceived as being too lenient – particularly in relation to the previously described and continuing incidences of disorder in prisons themselves.[25] It was this dissatisfaction that led to severe internal criticism of William Whitelaw at the 1981 Conservative Party conference as being 'soft on crime', and his swift replacement by Leon Brittan who, in 1984, introduced an entirely new policy for parole criteria and eligibility that was specifically 'tougher' in relation to more serious and 'dangerous' offenders.[26]

Apart from a major disturbance at Albany prison on the Isle of Wight in 1983 which caused extensive damage, the first half of the 1980s passed in an almost sullen, if uneasy, period of relative calm across the prisons estate of England and Wales. The problem of increasing

23 Here see my analysis in D.J.Cornwell, *The Penal Crisis and the Clapham Omnibus*, Hook, Hampshire: Waterside Press, 2009, p.99 and *passim*. By mid-March of the same year the average daily prison population had reached an all-time high of 44,800 housed in certified normal accommodation (CNA) of 38,500.

24 In fact, the advice was included in the ACPS Report *The Length of Prison Sentences*, London: HMSO, 1977, but held in abeyance pending the outcome of the May Report 1978 and subsequent parliamentary deliberations by the PA-PPAG in 1979-80.

25 The historical nature of this dissatisfaction went back to 1972 and concerned the nature of the relationship between the Home Secretary (and thus the Home Office) and the independent Parole Board over changes in the eligibility of prisoners for parole consideration and the criteria used to determine parole decisions. For those seeking a detailed account of this development and the tensions that it caused, see the admirable account provided by Michael Cavadino and James Dignan in *The Penal System: An Introduction*, [Second Edition], London: SAGE Publications, 1997, at Chapter 7, pp.181-203.

26 Specifically, those serving life sentences for certain types of murder, and those sentenced to five years or more for offences of drug trafficking, violence, and certain sexual offences (*Ibid.*:187).

numbers remained unresolved, and the atmosphere in many of the more overcrowded prisons remained potentially unstable with staff and prisoner relationships in a state of mutual distrust and uncertainty on a daily basis. Leon Brittan's revised parole criteria were deeply resented by many long-term prisoners, and viewed with considerable misgivings by the majority of prison governor and senior uniformed grades responsible for the day to day management and control of the prison population.

The winter months of 1985-6 resembled a period of pre-volcanic rumblings which, as the spring emerged, developed into an almost tangible atmosphere of potential eruption. As if almost on signal, widespread disturbances broke out in 46 English prisons between 29 April and 2 May, starting at Gloucester, and subsequently in more than twenty other prisons in which full scale riots took place and 45 prisoners escaped with many more injured, but amazingly no fatalities. The riot at Northeye Prison in Sussex resulted in the virtual destruction of the wartime hutted facility which was never subsequently to be re-used. The Report of the Chief Inspector of Prisons into the causes of these disturbances (The Hennessey Report 1987)[27] was greeted with considerable dismay and concern by penal reform organisations, and in particular by the influential Prison Reform Trust which commented: 'His report was subject to blatant (but highly effective) news manipulation by the Home Office which severely limited press coverage of his findings. Remarkably, his report was never debated in Parliament' (Prison Reform Trust, 1990:1 quoted in Adams, 1992 *op. cit.*:162).

After a lull in hostilities during 1987, rioting again broke out in the summer of 1988 at two relatively low security training prisons (Haverigg in Cumbria and Lindholme in South Yorkshire), and in the following year at Risley Remand Centre in Lancashire with a loss of more than 150 prison places (*Ibid.*:163).

As this brief summary of the turbulent years of the 1980s in the prisons clearly shows, the rise of militancy among the penal population was to a considerable extent a manifestation of discontent about conditions and treatment demonstrated in parallel with other issues of social *malaise* felt in wider British society of the era. Economic recession and industrial unrest were endemic features of the decade as witnessed by the widespread strikes in the steel production and coal-mining industries in particular. Such militancy also arose in the form of urban rioting and disturbances (some of a racial nature) in many of the larger

27 See: Hennessey, J., *Report of an Inquiry by HM Chief Inspector of Prisons for England and Wales, into the Disturbances in Prison Service Establishments in England between 29 April and 2 May 1986*, London: HMSO.

cities – London, Birmingham and Manchester most prominently – severely questioning policing policies and the exercise of authority by monolithic departments of state.[28]

STRANGEWAYS, APRIL 1990 – A WATERSHED EVENT

The riot at Strangeways Prison in Manchester from 1 -25 April 1990 was, by any standards, the most extensive, long-lasting and violent demonstration of destructive prisoner fury and frustration ever perpetrated in Britain or, indeed, worldwide.[29] Due to the urban proximity of the prison to Manchester city centre, resolution of the siege had to be conducted in the full glare of a worldwide media (TV and newspaper journalism), and the daily crowds of sightseers and prisoner families and supporters gathered in the streets and open spaces adjacent to the prison perimeter walls.

Within days of the riot starting, major disturbances of a 'copy-cat' nature broke out at a further five prisons during April 1990,[30] and to a lesser extent at some twenty other prison establishments in Britain. In his over-arching assessment of the cause of the Manchester riot and those that followed immediately after, Lord Justice Woolf identified three main and inter-related factors in the running of prisons – security, control and justice – which he concluded had become out of balance. There were failures in the maintenance of control; failures to achieve and maintain necessary standards of justice; and potentially (if not actually) failures to maintain necessary standards of security. It was, in Woolf's view, failures to maintain a just environment that fuelled prisoner grievances, and the other failures provided the opportunity for their exploitation. Woolf (and Tumim) concluded their two-volume Report with twelve main recommendations, among which was one that there should be a new Prison Rule that no establishment should exceed its certified normal accommodation (CNA), and that Parliament should be informed if, exceptionally, it did so. This, and a number of the other recommendations, involved significant resource

28 Such an explanation is to a considerable extent consistent with accounts such as that of Arthur Marwick (2003), a distinguished academic and social historian with extensive experience of the post-World War 2 era in both Britain and the USA. For his account see: Marwick, A., *British Society Since 1945*, [Fourth Edition], London: Penguin Books, 2003, Chapter 21, pp.275-298.

29 The author was present in the prison during all 25 days of the riot, having been summoned by the Prison Service HQ to coordinate and lead a team of prison staff trained in hostage negotiation techniques in persuading the rioting prisoners to abandon their violent protest and surrender to lawful custody. His account of the riot and the negotiation process (co-written with David Boag a psychologist colleague) was subsequently published following the official Inquiry conducted by Lord Justice Woolf and Judge Stephen Tumim during 1990/91 (Woolf & Tumim 1991) in HM Prison Service, *Proceedings of the Prison Service Psychology Conference 1991*, London: HM Prison Service, pp.104-124, under the title 'The Multi-Perpetrator Dimension in Prison Siege Negotiation: Psycho-Strategic Considerations (Cornwell & Boag, 1991).

30 These prisons included Glen Parva, Dartmoor, Cardiff, Bristol and Pucklechurch.

implications which evidently required time, structural, capital and political commitment to implement, and the determination of the Prison Service and Ministers to deliver.

The 1990s – A Decade of Reflection and Despair

In spite of the shock waves felt throughout the prisons of England and Wales during and after the Strangeways riot and its associated imitations in prisons elsewhere, sporadic disturbances continued to break out during 1991 which the Home Office Press Office attempted to down-play, or at least in one instance 'failed to report'.[31] The year also saw a return to urban rioting during the autumn months in Cardiff, Oxford, Newcastle and Birmingham. The causes of these riots were difficult to identify precisely, but appeared to be more in the form of conflicts between rival groupings of disaffected youth within downtown areas of the cities affected by poverty and considerable unemployment. In an attempt to allay public fears and bolster confidence in the police, the Criminal Justice Act 1991 was enacted in July by parliament, and expressed the government's intention to impose harsher sentencing powers in the courts as alternatives to imprisonment, combined with longer custodial sentences for serious offences.[32]

The 1991 Act indicated a significant 'shift' in government policy towards criminal offending, away from any post-rehabilitationist philosophy or even the proportionality concept implicit in the 'justice model', and towards a 'law and order' doctrinal model based upon incapacitation and deterrence. Community sanctions were re-termed 'punishment in the community' and reinforced by a new measure to be known as the Combination Order which gave the courts increased powers to impose restrictive provisions on offenders through what was, in effect, a combination of a Probation Order with a Community Service

31 The first of these was revealed by the Home Secretary Kenneth Baker in announcing, as reported in the *Guardian* newspaper of 17 July 1991, the escape of two IRA terrorist suspects from Brixton Prison in London ten days previously. The second concerned a 'secret riot', unreported by the Home Office, at Frankland Prison near Durham, but reported by the same newspaper on the same date as having involved 'IRA and Palestinian terrorists and a group of Mafia and London gangsters' in the destruction of a complete landing with £200,000 of damage as a protest against being 'ghosted' around the prison system (Adams *op. cit.*:1992:167). In actual fact, as the author found on being posted as Deputy Governor to the prison in 1992, the damage was considerably more extensive than the *Guardian* had claimed. The rioting prisoners had discovered that by using metal bed-frame components from their cells, the cell window frames could be levered outwards giving access to the surrounding area of the prison interior. This discovery resulted in the need to upgrade cell windows in all four wings within the prison on a two-year rolling programme, taking each wing out of use for some six months in succession, and decanting its prisoners elsewhere in the prison estate.

32 The offence of Prison Mutiny was created in the Prison Security Act 1992, carrying a sentence of up to ten years imprisonment to run consecutively to any other sentence passed on offenders for criminal offences committed in the course of prison disturbances.

Order: the former of up to three years in duration; the latter a specified number of hours of community work (to a maximum of 240 hours) to be completed within a specified time frame. The measure was specifically an alternative to a custodial sentence which could be imposed in breach of its requirements.

In mid-1990 the premiership of Margaret Thatcher had ended with her replacement by John Major, and the post of Home Secretary had passed from David Waddington to Kenneth Baker until 1992 and then on to Kenneth Clarke in 1992. By this time the average daily prison population of England and Wales had decreased marginally from 45,700 in 1988 to around 44,200 in 1993. One stated purpose of the 1991 Act was to reduce this population further, but as we shall see, events turned out otherwise. The reforms proposed by Woolf and Tumim moved very slowly, though without the changes advocated by reformers or the additional resources the Prison Officers Association (POA) considered necessary. Emphasis was, instead, 'placed on the imperative of maintaining control of an expanded prison system through improved security,[33] and lacked a clearly timetabled prior commitment to the resources required to benefit prisoners substantially' (Adams, 1992 *op. cit.*:169).

May 1993 saw the replacement of Kenneth Clarke as Home Secretary by Michael Howard, an infinitely more 'hawkish' politician and lawyer who almost immediately set about dismantling some of the central provisions of the Criminal Justice Act 1991. The 'just deserts' principle of proportionality in sentencing implicit in the 1991 Act and derived from the 'justice model' was a major casualty of the revised agenda, as was the provision for Unit Fines[34] related to an offenders daily disposable income previously favoured by both Kenneth Baker and Kenneth Clarke as a more just and equitable means of imposing financial penalties and of avoiding unnecessary use of prison custody in default of payment. At the same time, Michael Howard also had in mind changes to the rules concerning the disclosure of previous convictions by prosecutors, following a finding of guilt and prior to the determination of sentences in the court process.

33 To which end, £23 million was allocated by re-adjustment of the prisons budget priorities to allow immediate expenditure on enhanced security (*Ibid.*:169).

34 The Unit Fine concept is widely used in Scandinavian countries, and was originally pioneered in Finland in 1921. It is based on the daily disposable income of an offender, and set above the minimum fine level for each type of offence, and is thus based upon the principles of proportionality to the seriousness of the offence, and the ability of the offender to pay. In this respect it punishes offenders of different financial means proportionately, and is thus a measure aimed at diverting offenders from custody in default of payment due entirely to financial inability. The Unit Fine is normally set at a daily rate and expressed as a number of penalty days – hence the term also 'Day Fine', and the number of days for each offence type has a maximum level fixed, which courts may not exceed.

And so, from 1993 onwards, followed what Cavadino and Dignan (1997, *op. cit.*:5 and *passim*) aptly described as '*the law and order counter-revolution*' which was to alter the direction of the entire criminal justice discourse from the mid-1990s and into the present millennium with a revised Criminal Justice Act 1993. Howard's philosophy was to be encapsulated by the tenor of his (in)famous speech to the Conservative Party Conference in October 1993 in which he insisted: 'Let us be clear. Prison works. It ensures that we are protected from murderers, robbers and rapists – and it makes many who are tempted to commit crime think twice'. He went on to say that he did not flinch from measures that would increase the prison population.

The 'law and order' agenda adopted from 1993 onwards restored retributive incapacitation and deterrence to pride of place within the justifications of criminal punishment and penal policies, and almost immediately triggered a significant escalation in the average daily prison population of England and Wales, the impetus of which was to be maintained undiminished until 2010. From just below 50,000 in 1993 it reached 65,000 in 1998, and 82,000 in 2008 – an increase of 64%, or an average annual growth rate of 3.4%, sustained over 15 years.[35]

These population increases were met by an inevitable increase in prison overcrowding, the construction of additional houseblocks in prisons with available space to permit expansion, and by contracting out the design, construction, management and financing of new prisons to private sector consortia on a leasehold basis under what was termed by the government the Private Finance Initiative (PFI). This process was augmented by a strategy of 'market testing' a number of existing public sector prisons within the Prison Service estate on a competitive basis with bids from selected private sector contractors to provide the same (existing) or enhanced security, control and regime conditions.[36] The 'market testing' process caused considerable resentment within the Prison Service, although, ironically, it drove up standards of performance and management that met many of the improvements identified in the Woolf Report.[37]

35 These data are extracted from Ministry of Justice, *Story of the Prison Population 1993-2016 England and Wales*, London: Ministry of Justice, 2016b. (July).

36 The 'market testing' procedure explicitly included financial costing comparisons in the bidding process which, to an extent, favoured private sector contractors who could recruit staff at salary rates below the existing scales of remuneration of Prison Service grades.

37 Following the 1990 riot HMP Manchester was largely rebuilt and modernised. Management of the re-opened prison was put out to competitive tender and was retained by the Prison Service whose bid was successful in 1994, and has since been renewed three times under the same process.

1994/5 – THE ANNUS HORRIBILIS OF THE PRISON SERVICE

If the escape of the two IRA suspects Pearce Macauley and Nessan Quinliven from Brixton prison in the summer of 1991 had embarrassed the government sufficiently to publish a White Paper *Custody, Care and Justice* (Home Office 1991) setting out proposals for tightening security arrangements in prisons holding Category A prisoners,[38] worse by far was yet to come. The White Paper effectively ignored the advice of Woolf that excessive emphasis on security in prisons could be counter-productive by creating an oppressive environment that would fuel genuine grievances among prisoners which, in turn, would be reflected in violence and disorder.

In September 1994, a group of six armed prisoners escaped (albeit briefly) from the Special Security Unit (SSU) at Whitemoor prison in Cambridgeshire, a 'prison within a prison' at one of the eight maximum security 'dispersal' prisons in England and Wales. The escape was followed by the discovery of Semtex explosives and detonators within the prison, and, in the ensuing Enquiry headed by Sir John Woodcock, a former Chief Constable of North Yorkshire and Chief Inspector of Constabulary, of serious lapses in routine security procedures by the staff of the Unit. In his Report on the escape published in December 1994,[39] Woodcock described it as a 'disaster waiting to happen' in which 'so many things were wrong, so many procedures and policies totally ignored and with such regularity that the escape could have taken place on any day of the week with the same chance of success' (Woodcock, J., 1994: *passim*).

The Whitemoor 'fiasco' was followed on 3rd January 1995 by the escape of three life sentence prisoners from Parkhurst prison on the Isle of Wight – another of the 'dispersal' prisons. The prisoners were subsequently recaptured after some days at large on the island, but the political repercussions of the incident and the fury of the Home Secretary Michael Howard became a matter of national embarrassment. Although the Director General of the Prison Service Derek Lewis had acted swiftly to suspend the governor of the prison (John Marriott) from duty pending an investigation into the escape, he himself was subsequently dismissed in a spectacular manner by Michael Howard in the following October.

Derek Lewis' dismissal followed the publication of a highly critical Report by General Sir John Learmont into the Parkhurst escape, and a review of overall prison security in England

38 These were prisoners in the highest of the four security categories whose escape from custody would pose a serious risk to the public, the police and state security.

39 Woodcock, Sir J., *The Escape from Whitemoor Prison on Friday 9th September 1994*, [The Woodcock Enquiry], Cm 1456, London: HMSO, 1994 (December).

and Wales published in the autumn of 1995.[40] Lewis, much respected throughout the Prison Service for his leadership qualities and his approachable personality, was not one to 'go quietly'. In 1997, he published his own account of the events leading up to his dismissal, the difficulties of his relationship with Michael Howard, and the 'mandarin' behaviour of senior civil servants.[41] He subsequently issued a writ against Howard in October 1995 alleging repeated interference in operational matters in a claim for damages for wrongful dismissal which was eventually ruled in his favour, after much delay and prevarication on the part of the Home Office and its legal advisers, in the High Court in March 1996.

In pursuit of tougher sentencing policies, the Offensive Weapons Act 1996 and the Crime (Sentences) Act 1997 were the final salvoes of the Michael Howard era at the Home Office. The 1996 Act provided for increased sentences for carrying offensive weapons, while the 1997 Act introduced mandatory and minimum sentences for repeated drugs and burglary offences, and the mandatory life sentence on conviction for second or subsequent Serious List offences.[42] In May 1997 the Conservative government of John Major was replaced in the general election by the 'New Labour' administration led by Tony Blair, with Jack Straw appointed as Home Secretary.

The legacy of the Major government and of Michael Howard in particular was, by mid-1998, an all-time high average daily prison population of 65,300, an increase of almost 20,000 over the corresponding level a decade previously. The newly established 'war on crime' had become firmly entrenched on the basis of social protection and incapacitation, with the 'justice model' abandoned and a continuing belief in the deterrence doctrine underpinning the penal agenda as the new millennium approached.

At the same time, the Prison Service had little alternative but to concentrate its efforts on maintaining security and control of its expanding estate, and dealing with its charges in as humane a manner as its overcrowded conditions permitted. Emphasis on 'humane containment' precluded any revival of rehabilitative aspirations beyond the development of a limited range of 'treatment' programmes for sexual offenders and others who displayed

40 Here, see: Learmont, Gen. Sir J., *Review of Prison Service Security in England and Wales and the Escape from Parkhurst Prison on Tuesday 3rd January 1995*, Cm 3020, London: HMSO, 1995 (September).

41 Lewis, D., *Hidden Agendas: Politics, Law and Disorder*, London: Hamish Hamilton, 1997.

42 Serious List Offences include a number of indictable offences including murder, manslaughter, terrorism, aggravated robbery, rape, certain sexual offences against children and young persons, aggravated burglary, arson, and, by definition, certain serious fraud offences. These were eventually set out in schedules to the Serious Crime Act 2007, but were earlier considered serious in accordance with the degree of harm occasioned, the culpability of the offender, and the use of weapons in the commission of them. See also the Prevention of Terrorism Act 1996, the Sexual Offences (Conspiracy & Incitement) Act 1996, and the Sex Offenders Act 1997.

a potential for 'anger management' reductive interventions to reduce their aggressiveness. Pre-occupation with preventing further notorious escapes, and measures (inevitably intrusive) to improve surveillance of inmate behaviour to maintain control inevitably resulted in reduction of regimes and leisure activities which ran counter to the prescriptions of the Woolf Report which had, effectively, been overtaken by subsequent events.[43]

In view of all that has been recorded in the foregoing analysis, it seems altogether surprising that the term 'deterrence', in either of its accepted forms within the criminological literature, retained such a 'taken for granted' status within the political and penological discourses of the post-modern era. Evidently, crime prevention measures failed to deter increasing numbers of serious offenders; imprisonment failed to deter recidivism; and prison conditions failed to deter repetitive episodes of rioting and concerted disorder. Why, then, did the deterrence doctrine survive as a cornerstone of the penal process, and what evidential logic ensured its longevity? In the chapter that follows I shall endeavour to answer this intriguing question with reference to the literature on deterrence research, and the direction in which deterrence policies and political initiatives moved as the new millennium arrived.

43 Here see the comment of Roy King and Kathleen McDermott on the concept of 'humane containment' written in the aftermath of the Strangeways Riot of April 1990 and publication of the Woolf Report in 1991 (King & McDermott, in Downes (Ed.), 1992, pp.96-118).

4 CRIME CONTROL OR CRIME REDUCTION?

THE STRATEGIC ALTERNATIVES

In the course of this chapter my purpose is to suggest that, in the light of all the arguments about deterrence doctrine highlighted so far and recognition of the contra-indications affecting the effectiveness of measures designed to reduce crime and recidivism through increasing severity in sentencing, contemporary thinking about deterrence – in both its specific and general forms – displays serious conceptual flaws. More importantly perhaps, contemporary thinking about deterrence is to an extent 'conditioned' by prevailing attitudes towards criminal punishment at a number of different levels in post-modern societies, and in the conversations (or the absence of such) within a range of institutions with a legitimate interest in shaping criminal justice policies and practices.[1]

After a period of considerable interest during the years pre- and post- World War 2, the rich vein of moral-philosophical writings on the purposes of criminal punishment dwindled significantly. The main reason for this, it must be supposed, was a belief among moral and ethical scholars that what could usefully be written on the subject on the basis of logical reasoning had already been written and that therefore there was little of merit to be added to those (mostly erudite) conversations.

From the late 1970s onwards, interest in criminal punishment widened in a different direction. Sociological, criminological and economic approaches to the subject perceived the need for more empirical explanations, particularly in relation to the deterrence doctrine which had eluded reliable methodological analysis and quantification (see, Gibbs, 1975, *op. cit.* and others). That the methodological problems of deterrence research continued, as Bean (1981, *op. cit.*:29) indicated, to be beset with problems of the control of methodological variables to achieve reliable and refined research outcomes, was, and with hindsight remains, perhaps predictable.

One factor that did emerge with clarity from all the work invested in the deterrence doctrine was the conviction (however unquantifiable) that there was an evident relationship between

1 The term 'levels' as used here relates to strata within the social structure involving government, executive agencies of state, professional groupings, academic institutions, reform groups, the media and the general public. Institutions relate more specifically to organisations directly involved in the criminal justice process and its implementation such as the Police, Prosecution Service, the Judiciary and the Courts, The Prison and Probation Services, and the like.

the certainty and speed of detection of a crime and the bringing of offenders to justice on the one hand, and their evaluation of the risks involved in committing offences on the other hand. This situation was originally perceived and articulated by Beccaria (see *supra*), and has subsequently been retained as a central tenet of deterrence theory.

Coupled with the debate concerning the certainty and celerity of punishment was that of whether the relative severity of punishments had a measurable effect upon the risk: gain calculus consciously or sub-consciously undertaken by criminals in contemplating the commission of illegal acts.[2] Whether or not such is the case or even quantifiable, much would evidently depend upon the extent to which the severity of penalties for various forms of offending was widely known to, or understood by those tempted to commit crime.

A further limitation upon the appropriateness of claims frequently advanced in favour of the deterrence doctrine concerns the extent to which the commission of crimes evades detection and conviction, and whether or not this possibility is perceived by would-be offenders and encourages what has come to be termed 'discounting'. Either way, it must be seen as a limiting factor in deterrence theory since 'enhancing the severity of punishments will have little impact on people who do not believe they will be apprehended for their actions' (Wright, 2010 *op. cit.*:2).

From these somewhat obvious but necessary observations upon the effectiveness and limitations of deterrence theory derives a further assumption that offenders are human beings who are rational free-will actors and who consider the risks and consequences of their actions in a calculated manner before deciding to commit crime. This assumption has been widely challenged in empirical research (Cf. e.g., Mumola, 1999) on the basis that increasing the severity of sanctions alone was less influential than increasing the certainty of detection and apprehension in deterrence of crime and reducing crime rates.[3] In addition, research into public awareness of sentencing practices and the extent of sanctions indicated strongly that such understanding was widely limited (see, in particular, Williams *et al.*:1980; von Hirsch *et al.*:1999).

If the free-will actor hypothesis in relation to crime causation and control through measures of deterrence became fragile, as had previously the positivistic approach originally pioneered

2 Here the reader will recall the question about whether such a calculus is, in fact, widely undertaken, and that even if it is, whether this causes or results in a differentiation between crimes of a pre-meditated nature and those committed spontaneously or under the influence of substances that inhibit such calculation by the impairment of judgement.

3 Here see: Tonry, 2008 *op. cit.*; Williams *et al.*; 1980; von Hirsch *et al.*; 1999; Nagin & Pogarsky, 2001; Farrington *et al.* 1994, all cited in Wright, 2010 *op. cit.*:3-5.

by the classical Italian School following Beccaria, Lomboroso and Ferri,[4] it clearly also refuted the deterministic sociological thesis of crime causation advanced by the first American Chicago School in the pre-World War 2 era as responses to stimuli located within the social structure. Adherents of the second, post-War, Chicago School attempted to adopt a compromise sociological explanation based upon more sophisticated empirical studies of 'urbanisation' and expansion in major cities, and its dysfunctional criminogenic effects upon the social organisation and cohesion of communities which, they maintained, encouraged criminal behaviour.

Whatever the explanations were, however, intuitive confidence in the efficacy of deterrence – both specific and general – remained empirically unsubstantiated and largely unquestioned throughout the later decades of the twentieth century. In spite of this situation, the doctrine continued to feature prominently within discourses on criminal punishment and sentencing policy determination until the late 1990s when the 'justice model' was abandoned in favour of 'law and order' policies of social protection, risk-management and incapacitation. Such policies can neither strictly be termed retributive, having largely abandoned the principles of proportionality and parsimony for severity, nor deterrent since recidivism statistics (at least in England and Wales) indicate conclusively that they fail considerably in that respect.

Crime Control: The Strategy of Despair

In a penetrating analysis of the driving forces within the post-modern societies of Britain and America in the present millennium, David Garland, in the final chapter of his *The Culture of Control* (Garland, 2002), made the following observations:

> The explanation of some of the more puzzling facts of contemporary crime control can be found if we trace their connections to the kinds of social organisation and political culture that dominate in Britain and America today. Why has the prison moved from being a discredited institution destined for abolition, to become an expanded and seemingly indispensable pillar of late modern social life? Not because it was the centrepiece of any penal programme that argued the need for mass imprisonment. There was no such programme. Imprisonment has emerged in its revived, reinvented form because it is able to serve a newly necessary function in the workings of late modern, neo-liberal societies: the need for a 'civilised' and 'constitutional' means of segregating the

4 Based on the belief that criminal and potentially criminal offenders could be identified by scientific study and measurement of their physical features on an anthropological basis.

> problem populations created by today's economic and social arrangements. The prison is located precisely at the junction point of two of the most important social and penal dynamics of our time: risk and retribution. With the absolutist logic of a penal sanction, it punishes and protects, condemns and controls. Imprisonment simultaneously serves as an expressive satisfaction of retributive sentiments and an instrumental mechanism for the management of risk and the confinement of danger. The sectors of the population effectively excluded from the worlds of work, welfare and family – typically young urban minority males – increasingly find themselves in prison or in jail, their social and economic exclusion effectively disguised by their criminal status. Today's reinvented prison is a ready-made penal solution to a new problem of social and economic exclusion.
>
> Why do governments so quickly turn to penal solutions to deal with the behaviour of marginal populations rather than attempt to address the social and economic sources of their marginalisation? Because penal solutions are immediate, easy to implement, and can claim to work as a punitive end in themselves even when they fail in all other respects (*Ibid.*:199-200).

The reader will note that Garland wisely refrained from making any mention of deterrence as an auxiliary purpose of this socio-political agenda, even though the temptation and opportunity to do might be seen to occur in the final sentence. His account is incisive because it precisely encapsulates and accounts for the return to the forms of neo-retributivism, penal instrumentalism and social control during the late 1990s mentioned previously.

Of course, there is no suggestion made here that those incarcerated on the basis Garland described were not convicted of criminal offences: had such not been the case, they would effectively be 'political' prisoners.[5] However, when the extent of their punishment exceeds, for whatever reason, a proportionate response to the gravity and culpability of their crimes, or is extended on the grounds of public protection,[6] the effect is, arguably, much the same:

5 Here I should clarify this contention. If the extent of punishment exceeds the limits of proportionality in relation to the offence (however calculated) but accepted as being generally applicable, then it ceases to be *for* the offence committed and thus transgresses Hart's (1959 and 1968) rules for the justification of punishment. That additional element of the sentence is therefore imposed for other political purposes (e.g. social protection), and not, in consequence, 'of an actual or supposed offender for his offence'. Here see: Hart, H.L.A., *Prolegomenon to the Principles of Punishment*, 60 Proceedings of the Aristotelian Society 1, London, 1960, pp.4-5, and by the same author, *Punishment and Responsibility*, Oxford: Oxford University Press, 1968 *passim*.

6 Sentence extension for the purpose of public protection is based upon a presumption of future criminal dangerousness which has been shown through empirical research to be a fallible concept prone to false-positive predictions. See: Bottoms, 1977:75-77; and Cornwell, 1989 *op. cit.*, *passim*.

their liberty is denied for political purposes, other than punishment, for the duration of the extension period.

The obvious question that arises here is that of the extent to which crime is actually *controllable* within contemporary democratic societies. If this is doubtful, given our former observations concerning the free-will nature of human actions and the risk: gain discounting behaviour of many offenders on either a calculated or spontaneous basis of crime commission, then the potential effectiveness of the crime control agenda is certainly open to question. In terms of socio-economic utility alone, the costs of pursuing reliably effective crime control measures would become so prohibitive, and their intrusive impact upon social freedoms so intolerable, that anarchy might easily result. History reminds us forcefully that even in the most totalitarian of state regimes of the twentieth century, crime remained an endemic feature of social life and even increased in some instances.[7]

Crime control, however apparently desirable, may be an illusory concept that actually runs counter to democratic ideals. Its pursuit in the context of penal policies leads axiomatically towards curtailment of civil liberties, and in extreme instances to the unwarranted use of predictive or preventive incarceration.[8]

The 'culture of control' described by Garland (*supra*) also embraces, and to a significant extent subsumes, attempts made by governments and agencies to manage risk[9] and forestall or prevent predictable system failure. In the criminal justice processes of contemporary England and Wales, and also of the USA in particular, system failure has already occurred and has been evident for at least two decades. This means, in effect, that such measures of control as may or may not have been attempted in the past have failed, and that only a deliberate intervention to reverse the causes of failure can remedy the situation.

The principal cause of system failure in the penal system of England and Wales has been the persistent overloading of its capacity to operate effectively through lack of control over sentencing by the judiciary. However, the culture of control has also, through a significantly

---

7 Particularly in the spread of 'black-market' economies, and of 'gangsterism' and protectionism by the predatory and powerful in pursuit of an illegal monopoly of goods and resources. The outcomes became evident in increased rates of homicide, unexplained deaths, and in crimes of violence.

8 Preventive incarceration involves the use of penal resources including imprisonment or other forms of detention on the basis of predictions of future social risk or dangerousness. Empirical research indicates strongly that the incidence of 'false-positive' predictions (i.e. those predicted to offend who do not eventually do so) can be as high as sixty per cent or even greater (see: Bottoms, 1977:84; Monahan, 1975:20).

9 The term 'manage' is widely used within the literature of contemporary Management Science in relation to risk to imply the processes by which the possibility or the probability of systemic failure can be reduced or limited as far as possible without contingent adverse effects arising as a result of such interventions.

increased volume of legislative provisions since the mid-1990s, widened the net of those liable, many as an outcome of social and economic exclusion, to custodial sentences of increasing severity and duration. As a result, the same culture – however perverse – can only be sustained by expanding prison provision at a cost that has demonstrably become unaffordable in fiscal terms.

But the fiscal costs of such policies are only one element of the social and human costs incurred by their implementation. On frequent occasions during this same period successive governments have been advised in reputable official Reports and authoritative representations of the futility of short-term imprisonment and the adverse effects of sentences that are longer than is strictly necessary.[10] Indeed, the government's own White Paper *Justice for All* (2002) acknowledged that short prison sentences of twelve months or less were not only 'usually ineffective' (*Ibid.*:92), but also 'increase the chances of reoffending' (*Ibid.*:102). However, as early as 1990, government policy-makers in Britain had concluded in a widely quoted White Paper *Crime, Justice and Protecting the Public* that 'imprisonment is an expensive way of making bad people worse' (Home Office, 1990:6).[11] Imprisonment not only carries the risk of further criminalisation, but frequently results in long-term unemployment, family break-up, homelessness, benefit dependency, and ultimately poverty for all involved.

The title of this book was deliberately selected to highlight and reveal the folly of uncritically embracing the crime control thesis with all its dysfunctional socio-economic outcomes. The crime control agenda leads inevitably to a high cost: low yield policy selection, implemented through matching legislative measures permitting and even encouraging the use of disproportionate sentencing practices to create a new form of exclusive 'outlawry' through incapacitation under the guise of social protection. In this manner, the 'outlaws' are segregated and confined within places where, in the words of the psalmist, 'the sun shall not burn thee by day: neither the moon by night'.[12] As the social history of the middle ages in Britain and Europe should remind us, outlaws have a determined instinct for survival and further unlawfulness that can rebound upon the very societies from which they were excluded.

10 These reports include those of the Auld Review Committee (2001), the Halliday Committee (2001), the Coulsfield Inquiry (2003), and the Ministry of Justice (2013). The representations relate in the main to successive Annual Reports by HM Chief Inspectors of Prisons over the same period.

11 The full citation for this assertion is to be found in: Home Office, *Crime, Justice and Protecting the Public*, [White Paper], Cm.965, London: HMSO, 1990, p.6.

12 The Holy Bible, Book of Psalms, 121, v.6.

Crime Reduction: Towards an Inclusive Strategy

If the concept of controlling crime is, as has been suggested, ultimately an exclusive strategy of despair, then a socially more useful and less damaging agenda for reducing the impact of crime calls for consideration. Crime control policies are intrinsically based upon deontological ethical concepts of response to the phenomenon of crime,[13] implying that there is a duty or obligation to punish offences and offenders because punishment is deserved by their actions. If there is a failure to punish, then the wrongful action is condoned or overlooked which is ethically unacceptable.[14] The corollary of this is, of course, the questionable logic that if the punishment fails to deter future offending, then the only recourse is to increase its severity rather than the certainty and swiftness of offence apprehension.

By way of contrast with deontological ethics which focus primarily upon the rightness or wrongness of human actions and a duty to punish the latter, consequentialist ethics are more concerned with the outcomes of actions, seeking to maximise their socially useful consequences and minimise socially dysfunctional ones. There is thus a consonance between consequentialism and utilitarianism which may be helpful in this discussion since it might be proposed that more enlightened penal strategies should focus upon maximising the potential of sanctions to have socially beneficial outcomes, and minimising (through crime reduction and desistence) their socially disadvantageous outcomes of exclusion, recidivism and enhanced criminality as far as possible.

In terms of punishment philosophy, deontology offers only a backward-looking retrospective and retributive approach which has little to say about deterrence other than by implication.[15] The same might also be claimed to be the case in consequentialist utilitarian approaches which, although forward-looking, seek primarily to reduce the 'pain or unpleasantness' of punishment – as expressed in Hart's (1959 *op. cit.*, and 1968) 'Standard

13 Deontological ethics (deontology) is derived from the Greek word 'deon' meaning 'obligation or duty', which is the normative position that judges the morality of an action based on its adherence to a rule or rules. The term was first used by C.D. Broad in *Five Types of Ethical Theory*, New York: Harcourt, Brace and Company, 1930, but was also evident in the writings of Jeremy Bentham in *The Rationale of Reward*, London: John & H.L. Hunt, 1825. This reveals a curious ambiguity in Bentham's work since he was the leading advocate of utilitarianism which is essentially a consequentialist ethical approach often contrasted with deontology as will be evident later.

14 In a more contemporary sense, such an approach is consistent with Frances Kamm's concept of 'Permissible Harm' (Kamm, 2007) identifying the circumstances in which it is permissible for persons to act in a moral way that causes harm to others.

15 Such is to suggest that deterrence might be desirable as an outcome of retributive punishment, but the latter does not depend upon deterrence for its justification in deontological explanations of ethical punishment. Punishment is imposed as a duty based upon desert and the necessity to ensure rule conformity in an evident manner.

Case'[16] – to the minimum, while maximising the prospect of future law-abiding conduct to the general benefit of society.

Crime reduction within societies is a multi-faceted enterprise evidently dependent upon a number of different approaches. One approach lies in the general moral education of the public to perceive crime as an undesirable and disruptive influence in public life and welfare not only because it is intrinsically and morally wrong, but also because it diverts limited national resources away from securing the quality of life and welfare of the population, and towards expenditure on the administration of criminal justice in all its forms.[17]

It can also be approached mechanically and with some success by the installation of surveillance equipment and other devices in buildings and public areas of towns and cities and private properties to detect and record the movements and activities of persons within the zone selected. Such systems are widely used in banks, retail premises and the more expensive and affluent private dwellings as a means of generally deterring offences such as robbery, burglary, and shop theft, and also to detect anti-social behaviour in public places open to leisure activities, sporting fixtures and entertainment.

In a more specific form of approach, crime reduction can be approached on the basis of reducing recidivism by criminal and other offenders by enabling their participation in educational, remedial and vocational[18] programmes to enable them to gain purposeful employment and adopt law-abiding lifestyles. Such programmes can also include counselling and therapeutic interventions to reduce substance abuse and dependency and aggressive behaviour, and also to impart social skills in communication, anger management, and general social tolerance and awareness.[19]

Ultimately, crime reduction can only occur in circumstances in which the risk: gain or gain: pain calculus, whether consciously or subconsciously assessed by individuals, can be re-balanced in favour of desistance, implicitly through operant measures of general

16 See: Hart (1960 *op. cit.*), and also, Husak, D., *A Framework for Punishment: What is the Insight of Hart's Prolegomenon*, Rutgers State University, NJ: Department of Philosophy, 2015. An Occasional Paper available at: <https://s5m.com/5013/papers.cfm?abstract_id=2563290> [accessed on 1 February 2017].

17 Such as policing, prosecution services, courts, prisons and community justice services such as probation and counselling / rehabilitative provision.

18 Such as trade-based or other skills leading to enhanced employability within local communities.

19 If such approaches are to stand a chance of success in the custodial setting of prisons and other forms of detention, they have to be deliberately structured into the daily regime in un-crowded conditions that provide continuity and reliability of delivery by experienced staff specialised in the areas concerned. Ideally, also, such programmes should be directly linked to similar ones available within local communities to provide continuity during the post-release period of supervision and support by probation or equivalent services.

deterrence.[20] This much stated, however, those offences that are committed on a spontaneous or reactive basis might be termed 'calculus elusive', and the perpetrators thereof perceived as altogether unlikely to be cognisant at the time of commission either of deterrence measures or of the extent of risk involved. Such offences, therefore, should not logically be considered to fall within the bounds of specific deterrence theory.

Offence pattern analysis (see Chapter 2 and *Figure* 2:1) of the criminal careers of adult males aged between twenty-one and sixty five years serving sentences of three years or more and with a history of repetitive offending, reveals a number of disturbing aspects of consistency in offence commission over time.[21] In general terms, it became possible to draw the following conclusions:

- the majority of the serious offence patterns[22] were accumulated from the late teenage years and onwards, commencing with less serious offences (e.g. property and motor vehicle theft, lesser assaults, criminal damage, etc.), and subsequently escalating in seriousness;
- the majority of the sample (65%) had accumulated serious offence patterns before the age of thirty years, and had experienced two or more previous custodial sentences;
- frequency of offence convictions for Serious List Offences decreased after the age of thirty years, accompanied by an increase in the time spent at large between convictions;
- offenders with predominant patterns of sexual offending accumulated their serious offence patterns over lengthier periods than violent and property offenders, and generally continued to re-offend until a later age.[23]

The subsequent phase of the research into the relative levels and extent of criminal dangerousness within the sample is not of relevance for the analysis within this work, save to note that its conclusions were consistent with those reached in other earlier studies of a related nature.

---

20 The term 'operant' as used here denotes the psychological process of repeatedly associating the performance of an act or response with positive or negative reinforcement. It is a 'conditioning' process in which the mind is, through repeated experience, induced to respond to a situation or stimulus in an appropriate or desired manner.

21 The sample drawn for the research referred to here (Cornwell, 1989 *op. cit.*) was of 250 male prisoners in a maximum security prison in England between 1985 and 1988, all of whom were serving sentences of between 3 years and life in duration. Though the research methodology was not replicated in detail subsequently, sampling of the offence patterns of similar prisoners in a different maximum security establishment between 1993 and 1995 indicated that there was no discernible change in the manner in which significant and repetitive offence patterns were accumulated over time, and that the range of offences committed was in all respects similar to a significant extent.

22 Offence patterns revealing three or more Serious List Offences committed and sentenced on separate occasions became the baseline criterion for inclusion in the second phase of the research analysis.

23 The general exception to this finding was among those who had been convicted of rape on a single occasion before the age of 30 years, but who had also committed two or more other Serious List Offences.

Re-balancing the Risk: Gain Calculus

One means of achieving this purpose and of reducing crime specifically as a result of recidivism may be approached *via* the process of reparation. The concept of reparation implies that offences cause harm either directly to individual victims or to the wider society, and that as a result a debt is created that should be the responsibility of the offender to repay. Reparation can take a number of forms: of these, financial, practical and psychological recompense being the most frequently considered, either alone or in some combination. The principal feature of reparation is that it should, where possible, be made voluntarily, and at individual 'cost' to the offender whether monetarily in the form of compensation, through work or remedial activity, or emotionally.

The concept of reparation is that of 'repairing' the harm caused which, to a greater or lesser extent, cannot be undone, but which can be mitigated. It is thus not of a retributive perspective, but has a prospective purpose. In terms of our previous analysis it is therefore also of a consequentialist or even a utilitarian nature, seeking 'the good' as an outcome of the 'bad'. Though compensation can be, and in certain circumstances is a component of sentencing protocols, this is normally achieved only with the consent of the offender either alone or in combination with other sanctions.[24, 25]

The purpose of proposing reparation here is to suggest that it has a potential to deter future re-offending or even prospective offending by altering and reducing the 'gain' side of the risk: gain calculus. It might be claimed to do so retrospectively causing the former offender to conclude that the 'net' gain of the offence was marginal if not even negative having made reparation, or by causing the prospective offender to re-evaluate the calculus entirely in the event that reparation would be expected (or even required) to be made if he were to be apprehended and brought to account for the offence under consideration.[26]

Analysis of penal population statistics for England and Wales reveals that sentences of short-term imprisonment have been used, and indeed over-used, since the mid-1990s to

24 Reparation is sometimes described as 'restitution' which implies an 'act of giving back' something of which the owner has been deprived by theft or deception, or of restoring a situation by replacement or reconstruction. This is not strictly what is implied here, since moral or psychological harm or loss frequently cannot be restored to any meaningful extent by subsequent human actions.

25 It should be noted here that in instances of serious offending, reparation might become part of the sentencing outcome, but may be accompanied by additional sanctions – even including imprisonment – as a means of marking the gravity and culpability of the offending action.

26 It will be noted here, however, that the potential for reparation to be prospectively effective would only be applicable to those actual or potential offenders who contemplate the outcomes of their actions, and who might conclude that these would be gain-neutral or gain-negative.

punish[27] many thousands of low-level offenders, the majority of whom were then re-convicted within twelve months of release. This has been the case in spite of the frequent authoritative reminders to successive governments that such sentences are largely counter-productive in reducing recidivism or deterring crime, and which have been discussed previously.[28] A further disadvantage of such punishment is that it makes its outcomes 'invisible' since it operates in the secluded environment of prisons and other places of detention from which the public are specifically excluded.

Setting aside, for this stage of the discussion, the prohibitive cost in financial and human terms of excessive use of imprisonment, it is the victims of crime that receive scant consideration in the penal process as it presently operates in England and Wales. In spite of spasmodic governmental statements from 1996 onwards (Home Office, 1996; 2003; 2005a., b. and c.; and Ministry of Justice, 2012), little of substance other than the specification of procedural arrangements has emerged to improve the situation of victims of crime over the past twenty years. This is the more remarkable bearing in mind the European Union Council Framework Decision of 2001 (European Union, 2001) and the most recent European Commission requirements for victim treatment (European Commission, 2013) from which the United Kingdom negotiated an 'opt-out' derogation effective from December 2014.

Though the response of member states to the Framework Decision of 2001 requiring them to introduce legislative measures for victim support by 2006 was only partial, the Brussels Directive of 2012 was more specific, requiring action to ensure its implementation within national legislations by mid-November 2015.[29] The guidance document issued by the Commission in 2013[30] was a deliberate attempt to ensure that compliance was more universal across the European Union.

There is little doubt that the 'opt-out' derogation negotiated by the United Kingdom in 2012 was prompted mainly by financial considerations, since it would have required considerable investment in substantial victim support provision, and reform within the legal

27 Specifically, sentences of eighteen months or less in duration, of which only half of the sentence period is spent in prison custody. At 30 June 2014, the most recent year for which detailed population statistics are available, a total of 10,901 prisoners (9,942 males and 959 females) were serving such sentences in England and Wales (Ministry of Justice, 2014: Table A1.17).

28 See note 26 *supra*. I have provide a detailed analysis of this situation in recent work (see: Cornwell, 2016, at Chapter 9, pp.93-106 and specifically Tables 9.2 and 9.3) which are not replicated here for reasons of space alone.

29 Council of Europe, *Minimum Standards on the Rights, Support and Protection of Victims of*Crime, [Directive 2012/29/EU], Brussels: Council of Europe, 2012.

30 European Commission, *Rights of the Victim*, [DG Justice, 2013 – Ref: Ares (2013) 3763804-19/12/2013], Brussels: European Commission, 2013.

and penal systems which was politically unwelcome. The Ministry of Justice Consultation Paper of 2012 (Ministry of Justice, 2012a.)[31] set up a consultation period of only three months (January to April), and the Post-consultation Report published in July 2012 by the Ministry of Justice (2012b.)[32] was replete with financial and other 'Impact Assessments' indicating the extent of investment required, the innovative measures including the implementation of Restorative Justice principles, and the legislative provisions necessary to introduce increased reparation to be made by offenders. To date there has been a 'resounding silence' on the part of government in relation to these deliberations.

The reason for mentioning these developments is that had the necessary reforms and initiatives been pursued, much could have been achieved in re-balancing the risk: gain calculus in criminal offending. As matters presently remain largely unchanged, this must be seen as an opportunity for positive reform of the criminal justice process that has either been overlooked or deliberately avoided. Not only could it have resulted in long overdue recognition of the neglected status of victims of crime, but also in the diversion of many less serious offenders from prison custody towards a new generation of community penalties with genuine 'penal bite' and purpose through introduction of a more inclusive crime-reduction agenda for the future.

In relation to the title of this chapter, we may now perceive the true nature of the crime control *versus* crime reduction dilemma within criminal justice. For if crime control is, to any significant extent, achievable without entirely unacceptable social implications within contemporary democracies, crime reduction strategies imply wide ranging reforms of legal and penal processes that involve considerable investment costs. Additionally, both specific and general deterrence are fragile constructs, however appealing to intuitive but uncritical logic, as the foundations for criminal justice policies and practices. It also follows that if we continue to punish on deontological grounds as a matter of duty to impose desert, then the punishment process will remain predominantly retributive and retrospective. If, alternatively, we were to adopt a consequentialist approach based upon a prospective purpose of punishment to change wrongful behaviour, then we must be prepared to accept utilitarian motivations to a greater or lesser extent. The question remains that of to what extent some form of neo-utilitarianism would lead to crime reduction as opposed to crime control.

---

31 Ministry of Justice Consultation Paper, *Getting it Right for Victims and Witnesses*, CP3/2012, London: Ministry of Justice, 2012a. (January).

32 Ministry of Justice, *Post-consultation Report for the Consultation Paper (CP3/2012)*, Cm 8397, London: HMSO, 2012b. (July).

In the chapter that follows we shall examine one particular governmental initiative in England and Wales during the past decade in relation to victims of crime, its curious genesis, its slow implementation, and its debateable outcomes from the perspectives of victims, offenders and the criminal justice process. The initiative became known as the Victim Surcharge from 2003 onwards, and its implications became, and remain, a matter of considerable debate from the viewpoint of criminal deterrence theory.

5 Victims, Villains & Vacillation

The Victim Perspective

In the previous chapter (see *supra*) mention was made of the series of government documents published between 1996 and 2005 and subsequently in relation to the status and support of victims of crime in England and Wales. For a number of reasons this situation requires further examination and clarification, since the terms 'status' and 'support' imply not only procedural provisions for dealing with victims, but also the arrangements necessary to ensure their future material and psychological recovery from the effects of being victimised.

From an historical perspective it is evident that awareness of the needs of crime victims in Britain dates back to the publication of the first Victims' Charter in 1990 (Home Office, 1990).[1] This document was superseded and updated in a subsequent publication *The Victims' Charter – Statement of Standards of Service for Victims of Crime* (Home Office, 1995/6) which became law in 1996. Interestingly, the full title of the 1990 Charter was *Victims' Charter – A Statement of Rights for Victims of Crime*, implying that crime victims had certain rights which were not being met by the criminal justice process, though the nature of these rights remained largely un-clarified and unspecified other than in procedural terms.

In 2003 two quite different events took place in relation to crime victims which need to be noted here. The first was the publication by the Home Office of *A New Deal for Victims and Witnesses: National Strategy to Deliver Improved Services* (Home Office, 2003); the second was the legislative provisions of the Criminal Justice Act 2003. The former document, when reduced to its essential purpose, was a statement of the government's intention to make less threatening the impact of being a victim or witness in the prosecution and conviction of criminal offenders within the justice process in procedural terms.

As to the latter event, deep within the Criminal Justice Act 2003 (at s.161A and s.161B) among a wide range of other legislative provisions with sentencing and punishment

1 This document is not now available as resource material from internet sources other than the National Archive to which access is restricted.

implications,[2] was a statement of intent to introduce a 'victim surcharge' to be imposed on all offenders convicted in the criminal courts of England and Wales from a date to be specified later.[3] This measure was implemented from April 2007[4] onwards through further legislation in the Domestic Violence, Crime and Victims Act 2004 allowing it to become effective on or after 21st March 2007.

The point to note here is that the 'victim surcharge' imposed by the courts becomes revenue of the Victim and Witness General Fund (VWGF) administered by the Ministry of Justice to resource non-governmental organisations and groups offering advice and counselling services to victims of crime and witnesses in criminal cases. It is not a fund set up specifically to compensate crime victims for loss or personal injury resulting from criminal acts. Victims seeking such compensation must pursue claims made either in the Civil Courts, or to the Criminal Injuries Compensation Authority (CICA) in cases of violence, loss or injury in which the criminal courts do not make a Compensation Order.[5]

The legislative provisions governing the Victim Surcharge were revised in 2012 which extended the application of the surcharge to all convictions for criminal offences, but at differing rates for adults (18 years or older), young offenders (aged under 18 years), and offenders not being individual persons (such as companies and similar entities), and again in 2016 (Sentencing Council, 2016)[6] Summarily, the current arrangements are as are as set out in *Table 5:1 below*:

2 For a clear and detailed explanation of the political motivations behind the 2003 Act see generally Michael Tonry (Ed.), Confronting Crime: *Crime Control Policy Under New Labour*, Cullompton, Devon: Willan Publishing, 2003, at Chapter 1, pp.1-25.

3 We shall return to a discussion of this measure, known as the victim surcharge which became effective from April 2007, later in this chapter. The revenue from it was, however, conceived to fund victim services throughout England and Wales through a consolidated Victim and Witness General Fund, later to be administered by the Ministry of Justice which had not, at that stage (2003) been created.

4 In relation to punishment through fines alone until October 2012, and thereafter on conviction for any offence(s) sentenced by the criminal courts of England and Wales.

5 Under the Powers of the Criminal Courts (Sentencing) Act 2003, s.130-133, as amended by the Legal Aid, Sentencing and Punishment of Offenders Act 2012, s.130(2A) in cases of injury, loss or damage.

6 Under the Criminal Justice Act 2003 (Surcharges Order) 2012, and the Criminal Justice Act 2003 (Surcharges) (Amendment) Order 2016.

Table 5.1 Victim Surcharge Rates on Conviction by Type of Court Disposal

OFFENDERS AGED 18 OR OLDER	**One or more offences committed before 8 April 2016**	**All offences committed on or after 8 April 2016**
Conditional Discharge	£15	£20
Fine	10% of fine value with a £20 minimum and £120 maximum*	10% of fine value with a £30 minimum and £170 maximum*
Community Sentence	£60	£85
Suspended Sentence Order	• £80 (six months or less) • £100 (over six months)	• £115 (six months or less) • £140 (over six months)
Immediate Custody	• £80 (six months or less) • £100 (over six months up to and including two years) • £120 (over two years – Crown Court only)	• £115 (six months or less) • £140 (over six months up to and including two years) • £170 (over two years – Crown Court only)
OFFENDERS UNDER 18**		
Conditional Discharge	£10	£15
Fine, Youth Rehabilitation Order, Community Order or Referral Order	£15	£20
Suspended Sentence Order	£20	£30
Immediate Custody	£20	£30
NON-INDIVIDUALS OR ENTITIES		
Conditional Discharge	£15	£20
Fine	10% of fine value with a £20 minimum and £120 maximum*	10% of fine value with a £30 minimum and £170 maximum*

Source: The Sentencing Council, 2016:1-2 [7]. Available at: <www.sentencingcouncil.org.uk/explanatory-material/item/fines-and-financial-orders-made- on-sentencing/wl> [accessed on 9 February 2017].
Note: * denotes rounded up to nearest £. ** denotes at time of offence.

In a Ministry of Justice Press Release published on 8 August 2014[7] it was stated that since 2010 the victim surcharge had raised some £51 million prior to its extension under the 2016 Amendment Order. However, prior to 2014 offenders sentenced in magistrates courts could be exempted from the surcharge if they were financially unable to pay it by having extra days in custody added to their sentence of imprisonment. The practice was abolished in the Anti-Social Behaviour, Crime and Policing Act 2014.

In terms of disbursements from the Victim and Witness General Fund in the three year period 2011-14, the Ministry of Justice made financial awards to groups and organi-

7 Part of: Victims of Crime – <www.gov.uk/government/policies/victims-of-crime>, London: Ministry of Justice, 2014b. (8 August), [accessed on 15 February 2017].

sations throughout England and Wales under eight different headings as shown in *Table* 5:2 below:

Table 5.2 Victim and Witness General Fund Award Allocations 2011-14

Main Organisational Purpose	Award 2011-14 (£ thousand)*
General Range support	£K 989
Burglary victims support	£K 375
Homicide victims support	£K 219
Anti-Social Behaviour victim support	£K 592
Domestic Violence victim support	£K 4,498
Road Traffic victim support	£K 822
Hate Crime victim support	£K 2, 189
Sexual Violence victim support	£K 5, 528
Total Allocations	**£K 15,212**

Source: Ministry of Justice, 2011. Available at: <www.gov.uk/government/uploads/system/uploads/attachment_dat/file/220079/vic-witness-general-fund-awards.pdf> [accessed on 15 February 2017].
Note: * denotes rounded to nearest thousand.

From the data indicated in the previous analysis it will be evident that the revenue generated by the victim surcharge less disbursements from its VWGF between 2011-14 created a net surplus of some £35.78 million based on the Ministry of Justice's own figures. If such is indeed the case, it seems somewhat surprising – allowing for some extent of reasonable departmental costs in administration of the fund – that there has seemed to be no traceable parliamentary curiosity as to if or how the surplus has been used.

Now, since the victim surcharge concept was originally conceived within the 'tough on crime' package of sentencing provisions contained in the New Labour government's Criminal Justice Act 2003, it seems reasonable to suggest that it had some deterrent motivation in relation to crime control in addition to victim and witness support. For such to be to any extent effective it would have to be evident that the existence and extent of prospective surcharges were known to, and considered by actual or 'would-be' offenders, or were discounted in the commission of offences.

Moreover, as Joshua Rosenberg pointed out in 2013, not only has the surcharge had some unintended consequences, but also it is unclear how, and to what extent, the surcharge is actually recovered from offenders sentenced to immediate custody (2013:2).[8] In addition,

8 Here see: Rosenberg, J., 'Victim Surcharge: Unintended Consequences', *The Law Society Gazette*, 2013 (1 July), pp.1-2. Offenders sentenced to immediate custody are normally taken directly from courts to

as Rosenberg suggested, in the cases of many young offenders the surcharge becomes payable by a parent or guardian who may, in some instances, also be the victim of the crime. Where such is the case, it seems entirely perverse that the carer-victim has to pay into a fund designed to provide him/her with support (*Ibid.*).

Between the passing of the CJA 2003 legislation and full implementation of its victim surcharge provisions in 2016, the measure had a long gestation period. Though its revenue is disbursed to fund groups or organisations (many of them charities) engaged in support and advice for crime victims and witnesses, it does not provide actual compensation either for victims or for those immediately dependent upon them. Whatever purposes the surplus revenue mentioned earlier is spent upon, it could otherwise provide some measure of real compensation in cases of genuine need or hardship as victims of criminal acts. From a victim perspective it seems altogether unreasonable that such is evidently not the case.

Courts in England and Wales have limited powers to order offenders to pay financial compensation to crime victims,[9] though such powers are generally applicable only in addition to or in place of a fine, or as ancillary orders providing that the offender has the financial means to make the payment and consents to do so. There is therefore a need for a wider application of the concept of compensation and reparation that is implicit in the principles of restorative justice which has proved slow in acceptance and implementation within the mainstream of criminal justice administration during the past decade (see, Cornwell, 2016 *op. cit. passim*).[10]

The Offender Perspective

Whether or not adoption and implementation of the victim surcharge has had any measurable deterrent effect in causing a re-assessment of the risk: gain calculus by offenders or 'would-be' offenders must remain open to considerable doubt. Reconviction rates within twelve months of release from prison sentences (46% of adults, 48% of women and 68% of under-18 year olds in 2013-14)[11] remain unacceptably high, especially in relation to sentences of twelve months or less in which the rates for adults run at 60% (*Ibid.*). Since it remains unclear how (or if) the victim surcharge is recovered from offenders sentenced

prisons or other forms of custody on conviction and sentencing. This raises the question of whether prison governors have the power or responsibility legally to deduct the surcharge from a prisoner's wages.

9 Under the Powers of the Criminal Courts (Sentencing) Act 2000 s.130-133 as amended by the Legal Aid, Sentencing and Punishment of Offenders Act 2012 s.130(2A).

10 And, in particular, Chapter 9, pp.93-106.

11 See: Ministry of Justice 2016c. *op. cit.*, Tables C1a, C1b, and C2a, and Prison Reform Trust, 2016 *op. cit.*:4.

to short or even longer terms of immediate imprisonment, it becomes difficult to assess any impact that the surcharge may have in practice.[12]

Within the adversarial justice process used in England and Wales and a number of other countries,[13] there is no necessary requirement for accused persons to accept guilt or responsibility for alleged offences unless or until found guilty at trial. Indeed, since adversarial trials are a form of contest between lawyers for the prosecution and the defence with a judge as the 'referee', it is commonplace for accused persons to plead 'not guilty' in the hope that insufficient evidence will be adduced by the prosecution to obtain a conviction, or that they may be acquitted on a legal technicality or by casting doubt on the reliability of the evidence of witnesses called by the prosecution.[14]

As far as the development of the victim surcharge is concerned, and viewed from the perspective of offenders and many lawyers who defend them at trial, the measure adopted in the Criminal Justice Act 2003 and subsequent amendments might reasonably be perceived as being an overt (and possibly somewhat cynical) attempt to increase the 'penal bite' of sentences in pursuit of social control on a retributive and deterrent basis. That this could be proposed and 'coupled-up' to long-promised and unimplemented measures to improve the support and concern for victims of crime became a fortuitous means of giving it also a prospective veneer of 'charitable respectability' within the social consciousness. As Rosenberg (2013 *supra*) observed, 'it was an irresistible opportunity to look tough and raise cash for services that, if really needed, should be state-funded' (*Ibid.*:1).

Recent developments in the spread of reparative and restorative justice initiatives and practices in victim: offender mediation (VOM) worldwide indicate very strongly that many offenders, when confronted with the harm that their offences cause to victims, do express remorse and a willingness to make apology and reparation given an opportunity to do so.

12 An extensive search of internet entries on this matter, and of current Prison Service Orders & Instructions failed to reveal any trace of provisions to recover the surcharge from sentenced prisoners as of 17 February 2017. Prison Service Instruction (PSI) 47/2011, *Prison Discipline Procedures*, [Re-Issue 10 August 2016], 2-127 allows only Stoppage of Earnings (SOE) for proven disciplinary offences against Prison Rules. There appears to be no provision for any other deduction of wages/earnings for any non-disciplinary purpose such as recovery of Victim Surcharges on conviction.

13 Mainly within the British Commonwealth tradition, and as opposed to the Inquisitorial System widely used in Europe and elsewhere to conduct trial processes.

14 Judge Fred McElrea from New Zealand provides an excellent and compellingly readable account of the historical development of adversary trials in his chapter 'Restorative Justice as a Procedural Revolution: Some Lessons from the Adversary System', in D.J. Cornwell, J.R. Blad & M. Wright (Eds.), *Civilising Criminal Justice: An International Restorative Agenda for Penal Reform*, Hook, Hampshire: Waterside Press, 2013, pp.81-114. See also: Louis Blom-Cooper, 'Crime and Justice: A Shift in Perspective', in the same volume at pp.151-170.

Moreover, where mediation between offenders and victims is enabled, many victims express high levels of satisfaction with the outcome (Cf, e.g. Umbreit, 1998; Umbreit & Greenwood, 1999:261 and *passim*; Umbreit *et al.*, 2005:270-285; Shapland *et al.*, 2007).

From an offender perspective also, the negative effects of short custodial sentences have to be taken seriously. Many young adult persons charged with offences involving victims spend some weeks in custody on remand in prisons awaiting trial and sentencing.[15] Time spent in custody on remand is, on conviction, deducted from the effective custodial period of the sentence (50%). Thus, an offender sentenced to twelve months (52 weeks) imprisonment would effectively spend 26 – 9 = 17 weeks in custody in such circumstances. Even if forms of employment or training were available to accommodate every inmate in prisons without waiting lists to access them, allowing for time to assess each prisoner's potential and amenability would result, at best, in providing the equivalent of one normal school term of instruction in the community. Given the crowded situation of many prisons in England and Wales at the present time, even this bleak estimate is widely optimistic.

The reality is that many prisoners serving short sentences spend less than half of every day in custody in purposeful employment to reduce their risk of recidivism on release. This leads to frustration and boredom with the futility of their life in custody, enhanced criminality through enforced association with other more serious and repetitive offenders, and dislocation of their daily lives from families, friends and the wider community outside. All of these effects tend to encourage anti-social attitudes and behaviours which, on release, manifest themselves through reduced employability and frustration to re-offending. In such circumstances, it must be unlikely that measures such as the victim surcharge will significantly affect any future cost: gain analysis that ex-offenders may consider in relation to deterrence from further offending.

The Causes and Effects of Delay in Penal Reform

It will be recalled from Chapter 3 (*Figure* 3:1) that between 1995 and 2017 the average daily prison population of England and Wales rose from around 52,000 to slightly over 85,500 at an average annual growth rate of +3.4%. This increase also occurred during a period in which crime rates recorded by the police throughout Western Europe were

15 In England and Wales during the twelve months to March 2014, more than 49,300 people were remanded in custody in local prisons or Remand Centres to await trial or sentence, 33,585 of them convicted but awaiting sentence. Of these, 10,832 (11%) were subsequently acquitted, and a further 16,024 (21.9%) eventually received a non-custodial sentence. The average time spent in custody on remand was nine weeks (Prison Reform Trust, 2015:25).

generally declining (Aebi & Delgrande, 2014) with the exception of crimes of violence against the person and theft in some countries including Britain. This year on year reduction was maintained steadily, and the chances of an average citizen becoming a victim of serious crime reduced by almost half from 43% to around 24% (European Commission, 2016 *passim*).[16]

As we have already noted earlier also, by mid-May 2016, 74 of the 118 prisons in England and Wales were overcrowded,[17] and of these prisons the number whose performance rating was 'of concern' or 'of serious concern' had risen from 13% (one in eight) in 2012-13 to 24% (one in four) in 2014-15.[18]

All the indicators of concern mentioned within this chapter, when considered together, lead to only one plausible conclusion on the enduring nature of the 'prison crisis' of England and Wales since this millennium began. It is that successive governments not only ignored or overlooked the warning signs of impending crisis, but actually accelerated its scope and intensity by adopting legislative measures of a retributive and deterrent nature which were bound to exacerbate the situation. Options were available throughout this period, and even in the final years of the 1990s, to stabilise the situation which, by 1995, had already become of serious concern when the average daily prison population stood at around 52,000 – an all time post-War high.

From 1995 onwards, crime rates throughout Western Europe began to decline, and continued to do so steadily year on year into the new millennium. Yet over these same years the penal population of England and Wales was driven upwards by another 30,000, and was allowed to massively overspill the capacity of the prisons to accommodate it in conditions of security, control and decency. Now, as this book is nearing completion, there are once again signs of simmering instability in a number of prisons in which security and control are threatened by the widespread availability of psycho-active drugs such as 'spice' – a synthetic cannabinoid substance which evades routine drug-testing and detection procedures. Use of these drugs leads to violence among inmates and upon prison staff, severe addiction, and even mental illness and death.

---

16 Available at: <http://ec.europe.eu/eurostat/statistics_explained/index.php/Crime_and_criminal_justice_statistics> [accessed on 19 February 2017].

17 Ministry of Justice, Monthly Population Bulletin May 2016, London: Ministry of Justice, 2016d.

18 Ministry of Justice, Prison Annual Performance Ratings 2014-15, London: Ministry of Justice, 2015, and see also: Prison Performance Digest 2012-13, London: Ministry of Justice, 2014b, and Prison Reform Trust, 2016 op. cit.:5.

Even so, the previous Justice Secretary Elizabeth Truss has indicated in parliament[19] that she had no intention of seeking 'an arbitrary reduction in the number of prisoners in our prisons' when introducing the government White Paper *Prison Safety and Reform* (Ministry of Justice, 2016d.) on 3 November 2016. To the contrary, the White Paper revealed the government's intention to build six new adult male prisons, five new community prisons for women, and a 'further wave of new prisons' starting in 2017.[20]

Reaction to the White Paper from MPs was decidedly robust, typified to a significant extent by the following extract from the statement made by Richard Burgon, an opposition member for Leeds East (Labour):

> This morning the Secretary of State said that it was in July that she had realised that there was a problem in our prisons. The rest of the country was aware of that reality well before then. There is a crisis in our prisons, although the Secretary of State refuses to admit it openly. The story of our prison system since 2010 is a story of spiralling violence and drug use. The root cause of the prison crisis is the political decision to cut our prison service back to the bone, and today's announcement feel a lot like "too little too late". The Secretary of State wants the headline to be "2,500 extra prison staff", but 400 of those jobs have already been announced, and, in fact, it is 2,500 "extra" after a reduction of more than 6,000 on the front line.
> .. We have a prison capacity of 76,000 and a population of 85,000 which has remained at about the same level since 2010. We had 24,000 prison officers to deal with 85,000 prisoners: now we have 18,000 to deal with the same number. What has that meant? It has meant a record number of prison deaths, including a record number of suicides. The rate is nearing one death every day. There have been 324 deaths this year, including 107 suicides. There are now 65 assaults each day, and this year there have been nearly 24,000: there has been a huge surge in both prisoner-on-prisoner assaults and assaults on our hard-working prison staff. The statistics show that there have been more than 100,000 assaults in prisons since 2010 (House of Commons, 2016:5-6).

During the same debate, a former Justice Secretary Kenneth Clarke asked his successor but two whether 'she agreed that her overriding aim of protecting the public by reducing reoffending and preventing prisoners from committing crimes in the future is almost impossible to achieve so long as prisons are overcrowded slums, and was she prepared to

19 House of Commons, Prison Safety and Reform, Hansard Online, 03 November 2016, Volume 616:7, 2016.
20 See: <www.gov.uk/government/publications/prison-safety-and-reform> [accessed on 20 February 2017].

make the courageous decision to start addressing some of the sentencing policies of the 1990s and 2000s, which accidently doubled the prison population in those overcrowded slums? Would she ensure that our prisons are reserved for serious criminals who need to be punished, and find better ways of dealing with problems of mental health and drug abuse, and with irritating trivial offenders?' (*Ibid.*:6). The Justice Secretary's reply was: 'I am not in favour of an arbitrary reduction in the number of prisoners in our prisons' (*Ibid.*:7).

From what has been noted above, it is clear that at least for the foreseeable future the policy of the incumbent government is to do 'more of the same', accompanied by a potential expansion of the prison population with increased capacity at a short term cost of £1.3 billion in capital terms, and a relatively modest increase in staffing levels. There is to be no initiative to curb the sentencing behaviour of the judiciary in the use of short term imprisonment, and neither is there any expressed intention of reducing the incidence of cell-sharing leading to overcrowding. Altogether, it would appear to present a prospect aptly summed up in the words of Jean-Baptiste Karr in his journal *Les Guêpes*, 'Plus ça change, plus c'est la même chose' (Karr, 1849).[21]

The most alarming feature of this situation is the fact that it takes a crisis to bring it about, and that even when the crisis is recognised, only palliative action is taken to deal with its root causes. The 'separation of powers' doctrine enshrined in British constitutional law makes the status of the judiciary independent of the executive and legislative arms of government, and thus – other than through legislation – largely immune from governmental pressure to act in any particular manner. Though the judiciary are bound to comply with the statute law, they have some latitude in its interpretation in the administration of justice through sentencing in particular, even though reasons must be stated for decisions made which fall outside sentencing guidelines. The appellate process provides the mechanism through which judicial decisions can be challenged on an *ultra vires* basis as being unreasonable in particular circumstances.[22]

The judiciary of England and Wales have traditionally proved to be extremely protective of their independence, and resist strongly any executive interference in sentencing matters as a matter of principle. The only way in which the use of short prison sentences could be eliminated or severely restricted would have to be approached through changes to statute

21 Translated into English from the French original quotation: The more things change, the more they are the same' (Karr 1849).

22 From the Latin, meaning 'beyond the legal power or authority of a person, official, agent or other body.' The principle is enshrined within the rules of Natural Justice largely in relation to the duty to act fairly (without bias) in the making of decisions.

law sentencing powers enacted by parliament. If this were imposed, there would be a danger of an alarming escalation in sentencing severity for less serious offences presently attracting short sentences to levels on or above the new threshold for immediate custody. Consequently, the last case would be worse than the first unless the judiciary could be persuaded to accept the necessity for such a moratorium, and had alternative non-custodial measures made available to them, perceived as having an equivalent 'punitive bite'.

The further problem in pursuing such a policy would arise from what might be anticipated to be a media-inspired furore about 'public safety', and accusations that the government had 'gone soft on crime' which, for entirely electoral reasons, politicians would perceive as potentially threatening to their prospects for re-election by their constituents. Though this is not, in fact, an insurmountable difficulty as the Finnish experience of the 1960s and 1970s bears witness (Lappi-Seppälä, 2013:501-524), it requires a wide public and parliamentary consensus that such reform is necessary, and the essential ministerial determination to make it happen.

Another means of achieving much the same purpose lies in executive action to 'cap' occupancy levels in prisons by imposing strict and legally enforceable limits on occupancy of accommodation – that level formerly prescribed as 'certified normal accommodation' or CNA.[23] The corollary of such an approach would require courts proposing to sentence offenders to immediate custody to ascertain, prior to commitment, where the offender was to be confined and that a vacancy was immediately available. Such a procedure would also impose upon prison governors the duty and authority, in the event of full occupancy of their prison, to make a place available by releasing on licence the prisoner nearest to his/her scheduled release date.[24]

As I have noted in earlier work, however, (Cornwell, 2016 *op. cit.*:69-80), building a consensus for reform is the first stage in a protracted process to make reform possible. There are no 'short cuts' or 'quick fixes' that can be adopted in approaching this task, and it must include all the main stakeholders in the criminal justice arena – politicians, policy makers, courts and judiciary, police, prosecution, prisons and probation professionals, academic advisers, reform groups, and most importantly the media. Without a consensus that significant change is necessary, the process will be undermined and wasteful of time and resources.

23 Such is to imply that level of occupancy which the prison was originally designed to accommodate, normally in single cells, and in conditions of decency and security. This would eliminate the practice of 'doubling-up' prisoners two to a cell in accommodation designed for single occupation.

24 Providing that the prisoner to be so released had less residual days of sentence remaining to be served than the effective custodial period of the sentence to be passed upon the incoming offender.

The history and experience of the past two decades indicates unequivocally that reform of criminal justice processes cannot be achieved through measures of net-widening and incapacitation which draw into prisons increasing numbers of already disadvantaged people and send them back into society unchanged and further marginalised. Prisons, as presently used in Britain and elsewhere do not change people for the better: such places merely 'warehouse' them and 'make bad people worse'. Whether prisons can rehabilitate to any meaningful extent remains an open question, but one thing is certain: prisons in which overcrowded conditions are prevalent breed violent, resentful and predatory people dependent upon drugs and other stimulants to survive the experience.

Working in prisons and with offenders is, even in the most stable of circumstances within such places, a stressful and potentially dangerous profession. It requires staff with the dedication, self-discipline and motivation to work together in an enclosed and altogether unnatural and sometimes uncongenial environment with patience, tolerance and determination. Many prisoners lack basic social skills or the ability to communicate orally in a reasoned manner. Some are manipulative, devious, mistrustful and exploitive by nature, or due to their personal environments and relationships with others. Others have personalities damaged by substance or other abuse, mental impairment, neurosis, homelessness, or an inability to form or sustain relationships. Many need help but perceive seeking it as a sign of weakness and vulnerability. Almost all of them resent the necessarily rule-driven circumstances of prison life, and have little respect for the authority that has removed their liberty and limited their personal autonomy. Such are the inhabitants of prisons amongst whom prison staff live out their daily professional lives.

One further question remains to be answered honestly by politicians and opinion formers concerned about criminal 'justice'. To use contemporary jargon it is simply this: is the present situation in prisons and the social purpose for which such places are used ultimately 'sustainable' and 'fit for purpose' both morally and economically? This is the question which must concern us in the remaining part of this work because if deterrence means anything, the uses to which it is presently put amount to an exceedingly blunt instrument for changing lives.

In Chapter 6 and onwards, the focus of attention in this work changes towards consideration of ways in which the dysfunctional situation described in the foregoing chapters might be reversed to provide better criminal justice in the future for all of the stakeholders in that process. Continued failure by politicians to heed the warning signs that the penal system of England and Wales is in danger of degenerating into a chaotic and rudderless state can no longer be ignored with impunity since the lives of those in prisons are now seriously at risk. Exploration of the potential of reparative justice provides the key to a long overdue reform process, abandonment of dependence upon the deterrence doctrine that has largely precipitated the present crisis, and opens up a vision of a more enlightened means of delivering effective correctional services in the years to come.

Part II
Looking to the Future

6 DETERRENCE AND REPARATIVE JUSTICE

IS THERE NO BETTER WAY?

In view of all that has been said in the previous chapters of this book, we might conclude that we have almost reached a point of no return in criminal justice at which difficult choices and decisions have to be made. For if the present 'unacceptably violent and dangerous' situation in the prisons of England and Wales as reported by HM Chief Inspector of Prisons in July 2016[1] and noted in the Justice Secretary's Statement to the House of Commons on 3 November 2016 (House of Commons, 2016 *op. cit.*) is indeed widespread due to increased violence and the availability of psycho-active drugs, then urgent remedial action is necessary to safeguard the lives of both prisoners and prison staff.

Part of the causes of unrest and lack of safety in many prisons lies in the extent of overcrowding within the prisons estate and the reductions in front-line prison officer numbers since 2010 which the Justice Secretary has pledged to remedy to some extent as a priority (*Ibid.*:1). As we have also seen previously, however, the cause of overcrowding is too many offenders being sentenced to imprisonment above and beyond the capacity of the prisons to accommodate and deal with them in conditions of safety, security and control. The remedy for this situation lies either in fewer prisoners or more prisons. It seems evident that the present government proposes to adopt the latter option, and attempt to 'build its way out of trouble' as have others in the past two decades, and without much success.

Post-release reconviction statistics clearly indicate that however bad conditions in prisons may be, imprisonment does not deter re-offending – especially following short prison sentences. Many prisoners have extensive records of previous convictions and periods spent in prison or other forms of custody and still do not desist from re-offending whenever they are released. To make matters worse, a considerable number of those released are recalled to prison for short periods in breach of their licence conditions,[2] either for committing further offences or for failing to comply with their licence requirements.

Desistence requires a change of direction within the offender away from the commission of crime and towards lawful behaviour. Securing desistence is, however, not that simple.

1 HM Chief Inspector of Prisons for England and Wales *Annual Report 2015-2016*, Session: June-July 2016, HC 471, London: House of Commons, (2016), pp.18-19 and *passim*.

2 In the twelve months to March 2014, 17,515 people were recalled to prison custody, and on 30 June 2014 there were 5,300 recalled prisoners in prisons in England and Wales (Ministry of Justice, 2014b. and c.).

Many offenders are genuinely socially disadvantaged, and rebuilding their lives requires not only an effort from them, but also considerable support and encouragement from other sources to empower them to do so. It is here that prisons in their present state cannot achieve such a purpose, even supposing that they were ever able to do so to any significant extent in years gone by. The reason for this is that the closed and secluded nature of the prison environment is not conducive to 'directional change' other than in a small minority of cases.

If the notion of deterrence is so deeply embedded within the folk-wisdoms of traditional penology as to be irreducible as presently seems to be the case, is it possible to conceive a means of harnessing it to other concepts of 'better justice' than that predominantly of retribution? In this chapter I shall attempt to outline how this might be approached with a view to securing desistence from crime rather than, necessarily, deterrence as it has been understood hitherto in a crime control context.

The reader will recall here the discussion concerning crime control in Chapter 4 *supra*, and the essential differences between the deontological and consequentialist approaches towards it outlined at that stage. These differences, despite the apparent consonance noted earlier, will become central to an understanding of the discussion in the subsequent parts of this chapter.

Distancing Deterrence and Desistence

One of the many problems with the deterrence doctrine is that, somewhat like a coin, it might be said to present two distinctly different faces. One of these faces is directed at pre-emptive crime control through the threat of penalties for offending; the other is focused on the use of punishment to secure future compliance as a result of the unpleasant consequences of sanctions imposed upon those who have offended. In liberal democracies the state has a duty to preserve public safety and order by limiting crime and the opportunities to commit it as far as possible, and it does so from a deontological motivation through law enforcement.

As to the second face of deterrence, instances occur in which the extent of the punishment imposed is greater than that strictly necessary to mark the gravity of offences and the culpability of offenders, and the principle of parsimony is set aside by the addition of a 'deterrence premium' supposedly to secure either individual or general future compliance. Such evidently was the intention of the legislation within the Criminal Justice Act 2003 in England and Wales providing for the use of the indeterminate IPP and ESPP sentences (see: Gibson, 2009 *op. cit.*:87) which have subsequently been abandoned. Though these sentences were ostensibly designed for public protection on an indefinite (indeterminate) basis,[3] detention beyond the tariff period set for punishment and retribution was entirely at the discretion of the Parole Board.

These retrospective and deontological considerations apart, the morality of the use of excessive punishment has always been questionable to the extent that a number of the more enlightened liberal democracies of Western Europe have abandoned such practices almost entirely.[4] It is also of interest to note that they have done so without any significant increase in public risk of victimisation (van Dijk *et al.*, 2007:45-47).[5] Though victimisation rates per hundred thousand of population do differ across the main countries of Western Europe, with those in the United Kingdom among the highest (22%), rates in the Netherlands (19%), Sweden (17%), Norway (15%), Germany (14%), Finland (13%) and France (12%) are all clustered around the mean rate of 15.7% (*Ibid.*:47).

The statistics cited briefly above also suggest a strong correlation between those countries using imprisonment the least (per hundred thousand of population) and those that display the lowest rates of public victimisation. The deterrent effect of imprisonment in pursuit of crime prevention thus becomes further questionable. Indeed, when or if imprisonment is used unnecessarily, then high rates of post-sentence recidivism may actually be encouraged by the overall effects of the custodial experience.[6] For many ex-offenders who may leave prison anxious not to return, the will to desist from crime can quickly be eroded by the lack of skills enabling them to gain purposeful employment.

---

3 Of serious sexual or violent offenders. The ISPP sentence was imposed for offences carrying a maximum penalty of ten years imprisonment or more, and the ESPP sentence was given to similar offenders for offences carrying a maximum sentence of at least two but less than ten years imprisonment. For a critique of these sentences see: Gibson, B., *Criminal Justice Act 2003: A Guide to the New Procedure and Sentencing*, Waterside Press, 2004.

4 Amongst these democracies are most notably the Scandinavian countries of Norway, Sweden, Finland, and to a lesser extent Denmark also.

5 Such is to suggest without any marked increase to the most prevalent forms of crimes of inter-personal violence such as robbery, rape, serious assaults occasioning actual bodily harm and aggravated burglary. Other forms of prevalent crime such as consumer fraud, deception, motoring offences and motor vehicle theft were also included in the EU International Crime Statistics Survey 2005, and the Council Of Europe Statistical Survey of 2007. See: van Dijk, J.J.M., Manchin, R., van Kesteren, J.N. & Hideg, G., *The Burden of Crime in the EU: A Comparative Analysis of the European Survey of Crime and Safety (2005 EU ICS)*, Council of Europe, Brussels: Gallup Europe, 2007, pp.45-47.

6 Insofar as the fact of having served a period of imprisonment affects employment prospects and the break-up of family relationships, frequently leading to homelessness, social welfare dependency, and the temptation to return to criminal activity as a means of subsistence.

Facilitation of desistence from crime in offenders and ex-offenders can only be viewed as a prospective enterprise of a consequentialist nature. It requires an investment of time and resources to equip such people with the necessary skills and abilities to seek legitimate employment and compete in the labour market on equal terms with non-offenders, and the confidence to do so. This investment has financial and structural costs that have to be balanced against those of re-offending by ex-prisoners and those who breach the conditions of non-custodial sentences. Recent statistics compiled by the National Audit Office (NAO) in England and Wales estimate the cost of re-offending to the economy to be between £9.5 and £13 billion GBP annually, some £7 to £10 billion GBP of which is attributed to former short-sentenced prisoners (NAO, 2010; Prison Reform Trust, 2016 *op. cit.*:4).

Many offenders have histories of low educational achievement on leaving school, of persistent truancy and exclusion for anti-social behaviour while at school, and a need for remedial education to enable them to assimilate skills training in preparation for the world of work. This calls for deliberate programmes of vocational training that combine literacy and numeracy with the acquisition of craft skills over a period of at least two years of full-time study and practical experience. During this period, basic minimum wage payments would also have to be made to enable these students to subsist in order to desist from further offending.

In many respects, embarking on such a programme of skills training requires a deliberate investment in people who have hitherto been regarded as undeserving due to their criminality, and have become the outcasts of modern democratic societies. Though some would object that this amounts to 'positive discrimination' in favour of those who least deserve it, it can also be seen as an investment in necessary social reform that has, for too long, been almost totally ignored. Though the costs involved are considerable in times of economic uncertainty, these have to be weighed against the potential savings that could accrue in the reduction of recidivism and lesser resort to, or even eventual abandonment of, the use of short term imprisonment.[7]

7 For the sake of clarity here, the costs of recidivism include not only the material costs of re-offending, but also those of the police, prosecution and courts in dealing with re-offenders and re-sentencing them. The costs also include those of re-imprisonment or community sanctions for those re-convicted, and of maintaining high levels of prison occupancy for short term prisoners for whom little or no capacity is available to provide adequate employment and training to reduce re-offending.

REPARATIVE JUSTICE

Even if the costs of such reform are high in fiscal and economic terms, the social benefits that might flow from such investment are considerable. It is the central thesis of this work that these benefits could be realised not by increasing resort to deterrent measures and incapacitation, but through what is now widely recognised as 'reparative justice' which is the potential key to desistence from crime. Though reparative justice is grounded in the principles of restorative justice, it is a development of the latter with a specific emphasis on making offenders responsible for their wrongful actions, and on enabling them to make amends for these through reparation both to victims of crime and to the wider society against which crimes are committed.

Reparative justice is ultimately about what Lode Walgrave (2008) has so aptly described as 'responsible citizenship' in a criminological context. Responsible citizens refrain or desist from crime out of respect for laws that reinforce social norms of behaviour which in turn govern the safety and security of fellow citizens and the societies in which they live their daily lives. Responsible citizenship is, to use an analogy, the cement that secures the foundations and the structure of social life in democracies, enabling populations to live together in peace and common respect for each other's humanity and well-being. It protects individual and collective rights and freedoms from abuse and disregard, while at the same time placing responsibility upon individuals to conform to generally agreed standards of behaviour and probity.

Reparative justice could also be termed 'repairative' justice since it seeks to put wrongs right through positive action taken by offenders to make good, as best as possible, the harm caused by their offending behaviour, by offering apology for it, and by making reparation either directly or indirectly to crime victims. It embraces the ancient notion of 'expiation'[8] which has its origin in many religious and secular movements across the world. In medieval England, and in particular during the reign of the Plantagenet King Henry II (1133-1189), the first centralised system of justice administration was brought into being. Central to its operation, through the creation of local magistrates and travelling justices of assize, was the enforcement of compensation of victims through the payment of '*wer*' or '*bot*' (otherwise known as *wergeld*) by the offender in cases of theft, violence and property disputes.[9] This form of financial compensation (*wer*) could also be discharged by way of work done (*bot*)

8 The term derives from the sixteenth century Latin verb *expiare* – to atone or make amends for wrongdoing or sin as found in many of the religions worldwide. Through making expiation the offender was to an extent forgiven for the harm done, and allowed to regain his/her place within society having done so.

9 For an excellent and scholarly account of this development see: Briggs, J. *et al.*, *Crime and Punishment in England: An Introductory History*, London: UCL Press, 1996, pp.1-11 and *passim*.

for the victim(s) of crime on an agricultural basis, or in the form of repairs to damaged property, in cases in which the victim had become disabled or even killed in commission of the offence.[10]

At the core of this medieval justice process was the preservation of community relationships and cohesion which became disturbed by criminal acts. It also made possible the pursuit and apprehension of fugitive offenders from county to county, and their enforced return to the place in which the crime was committed to stand trial. Interestingly, during this period the crime of theft was regarded as the most heinous of all offences, punishable almost more rigorously than that of manslaughter or homicide as an outcome of interpersonal disputes being settled. Due to the poverty of most citizens and low rates of wages, a *wergeld* fine equivalent to £10 GBP or €12 would, if discharged in *bot*, bind an offender to the service of crime victims for almost half a lifetime.[11]

From the foregoing account it will be noted that the process of victim compensation is of ancient origin in Britain as in a number of other Western European countries. There is some evidence that the process lapsed considerably during the later Middle Ages when punishment of serious offenders became widely imposed by execution or banishment, and the use of trials by county Courts of Assize and judges became formally established.[12] The role of magistrates' courts also became more centralised, many of the powers of which are traceable to the system of justice administration which has survived to the present millennium.

Reparative justice in a contemporary context is based upon this ancient concept to a considerable extent as advocated in this work. It seeks to re-focus criminal justice away from its traditional pre-occupation with retrospective and retributive punishment and deterrence towards a prospective and inclusive paradigm of correctional logic. Bad people can change their behaviour, but only if they have a positive incentive to do so. The change process requires support and guidance and the will to change, but it cannot be imposed by threats. Deterrence, as Franklin Zimring and Gordon Hawkins (1973, *op. cit.*) reminded us almost

10 *Wer* in the form of financial compensation for loss of life became payable to the family of the deceased person, payable by the offender according to his means and income assessed by local justices. If necessary, the offender would have his property and livestock confiscated or sold to provide such payment, or transferred to the ownership of the victim in lieu of financial compensation.

11 *Wergeld* fines accrued to the King's Treasury through taxes upon local feudal lords and holders of manorial rights. It later became the responsibility of travelling justices and county magistrates to impose and enforce fine payments payable to the Treasury.

12 For a clear and concise account of the development of the adversarial trial process in England from the Middle Ages and onwards, see: McElrea, F.W.M. (J), 'Restorative Justice as a Procedural Revolution: Some Lessons from the Adversary System', in D.J. Cornwell, J.R. Blad & M. Wright (Eds.), *Civilising Criminal Justice*, Hook, Hampshire: Waterside Press, 2013 *op. cit.*, pp.81-114.

half a century ago, is the legal threat in crime control: it has taken too long for the correctional world to understand that threatening people is not the way to change them.

Reparative justice does what traditional justice significantly fails to do. It makes offenders take responsibility for their past actions, understand the harmfulness of what they have done, and make amends for the harm through the positive process of making apology and offering to make reparation. Reparation can be made either directly to the victims of a particular crime, or indirectly to victims of crime in a more universal sense. The fact that it is offered and made is more important than whether it is made directly or indirectly.

The direct reparation process itself requires professional facilitation. It will only be appropriate in cases in which there is a genuine willingness on the part of the offender to accept his/her guilt, and also on the part of the victim(s) to enter into the process voluntarily. Decisions also have to be made concerning the classes and seriousness of offences that should be considered potentially amenable to direct reparation, having due regard for the welfare of victims and the risk of their becoming further traumatised.

Indirect reparation, either to identified victims or to victims of crime generally, presents an entirely different aspect. It could be made available to all offenders whether dealt with by means of a custodial or a non-custodial sentence. In the majority of cases it could be made from the earnings of offenders in custody or in the community, payable to a Crime Victim Welfare and Compensation Fund (CVW&CF) centrally or regionally managed by Justice Ministry officials and independently audited. It might be proposed that some 'sentencing discount' would be appropriate where offenders accept guilt and agree to make reparation as part of the pre-trial process, thus saving considerable court time by avoidance of speculative 'not guilty' pleas.[13]

In cases in which direct reparation is offered and accepted, the extent, nature and duration of the reparative activity should be recorded in a court-enforceable Reparation Order with a default penalty included. In cases in which the court might consider a further sanction to be necessary, due regard must be paid to the Reparation Order conditions to ensure that the offender is capable of full compliance with its requirements.[14] Once made, Reparation Order compliance must be supervised by a Responsible Officer, being a Probation

13 The term 'speculative' as used here involves cases in which, particularly in systems of adversarial justice, defendants are encouraged to enter 'not guilty' pleas at trial on the basis that the prosecution case may fail, or that the accused may be acquitted on some legal technicality. Prior agreement to make reparation is not part of any 'plea-bargaining' process, and should not be seen as such.

14 For example, if having agreed the terms of a Reparation Order the court might consider it necessary to impose a secondary sanction in the form of a curfew or treatment condition in the form of a Community Punishment Order, the two must not be mutually exclusive.

Officer or Social Services official responsible for the case management of the offender whether in custody or in the community.

Reparation Orders made in conjunction with custodial sentences should specify that the sentence be served in a prison or similar establishment in which the facilities provide for a full working week regime with vocational training, employment and an earnings structure that enable compliance with the Order. Deductions from a prisoner's earnings for reparation should not exceed one-third of the weekly wage earned, and be remitted at source either to a nominated victim specified in the Order or to the CVW&CF administered by the Justice Ministry. Since this requirement has resource and structural implications for prisons as presently operated in many countries including the United Kingdom, we shall return to a further discussion of its potential in the chapter which follows.

The strength of the concept of reparative justice lies in its potential to encourage desistence from recidivist crime in a positive manner, while at the same time giving long-overdue acknowledgement to the situation of victims of crime. The concept has a positive social purpose which could, if followed, revolutionise the entire rationale of criminal punishment as it is presently conceived. In many countries correctional services have a negative social image as significant consumers of national revenue with a poor record of crime prevention. Recidivism statistics provide ample evidence of the extent to which this failure is an endemic feature of criminal justice administration in the contemporary world.

In many individual instances young men and women drift into crime for a wide variety of reasons. A significant proportion of these people are not intrinsically wicked at the start of this process of decline, but display deep-seated symptoms of social disadvantage and an inability to compete adequately within contemporary societies. Many are the product of poor parenting, environmental poverty, substance abuse and addiction, and lacking in social skills, literacy and numeracy, or any sense of purpose in their lives. Others have untreated medical symptoms, poor dietary and hygiene habits, or have suffered abuse or neglect. These are more the casualties of modern societies who, like wandering and uncared-for animals, become predatory, aggressive, withdrawn and anti-social. All too frequently, prisons become a refuge for such people, but have a strictly limited ability to remedy their condition other than to house them, feed them, treat their basic health needs, and ultimately release them.

A much smaller proportion of the people sentenced to imprisonment are bad and dangerous individuals from whom society has to be protected, and prisons are the only places that can provide this protection – in some few cases for the remaining duration of their lives. Unfortunate as this may be, it is the reality which has to be faced in understanding what prisons are capable of achieving. Overcrowding prisons and mixing together these two quite different populations serves neither purpose and is ultimately entirely counter-productive. The concept of reparative custody is strictly limited in its applicability: it is to empower those who offend but who genuinely wish to change the direction of their lives by making amends for what they have done and reparation for the harm caused. Such an agenda for reform would provide some un-crowded and properly resourced prisons with a positive purpose to reduce recidivism, uncontaminated by the more extensively criminal population previously discussed.

As to the first of these populations, a sizeable proportion are serving short sentences of two years or less with a custodial period of twelve months or less. Many are relatively minor offenders who do not present a vivid threat to society in terms of their dangerousness, and who could be dealt with otherwise than by imprisonment which may only make them worse in terms of their life chances. The second population consists predominantly in those serving long sentences of five years or more in duration, and whose regime conditions and levels of security require entirely different considerations. We shall return to discussion of each of these quite different populations and the non-custodial sector of corrections in subsequent chapters of this book.

WHERE DOES THIS LEAVE DETERRENCE THEORY?

However much, or to what extent, observers of criminal justice processes in action might be tempted to accept deterrence theory on an intuitive level,[15] it remains a controversial and unquantifiable concept to adopt as a purpose of criminal punishment. It is controversial because it has morally questionable implications for sentencing practices, and it is unquantifiable because it has always defied the accepted standards and requirements of rigorous methodological and statistical evaluation. This much stated, deterrence theory still maintains a strong appeal for proponents of 'tough on crime' policies as a means of increasing the severity and duration of sanctions, and in particular as a means of incapacitating and excluding those believed or predicted to be criminally dangerous in pursuit of public protection. Such policies have their risks, for as David Garland (2002:204) has

15 Such is to suggest holding a belief that deterrence through criminal punishment must be effective for the majority of offenders in the majority of instances. The difficulty is that deterrence remains elusively resistant to empirical evaluation, and the reliable statistical evidence from recidivism statistics indicates that the majority of offenders are not deterred from re-offending as a result of experiencing current sentencing practices, and periods of imprisonment in particular. On the contrary, the evidence suggests that increasing the severity of sentences to achieve deterrence has, at best, only a marginal, if any, effect upon rates of reconviction within twelve months of release from prison custody.

reminded us: 'A government that routinely sustains social order by means of mass exclusion begins to look like an apartheid state'.

The wider question that deterrence theory raises and leaves largely unanswered is why it has for so long remained unquestioned. In correspondence relating to my former published work, a much respected friend and colleague[16] said that he had noted with some interest in my most recent work (Cornwell, 2016 *op. cit. passim*) that I drew a distinction between the *criminal* law and *penal* law, and he wondered why I did so. My reply was to the effect that I perceive the criminal law as being that body of statute law that defines what actions or neglects constitute criminal offences that are punishable by state-approved sanctions, while the penal law stipulates how punishments are to be administered by the authorities legally constituted to impose them, their extent or duration, and the powers, responsibilities and accountability of the authorities for doing so.

To some this might seem to be an over-fine distinction to draw, but it seems to me to have some importance – particularly in relation to deterrence theory. In modern democracies governments have the power to define criminal acts in statute laws with the approval of parliaments. On the one hand, governments with significant majorities (or alliances) within parliaments can pass good laws or bad laws in legislation, but these are still laws that must be obeyed and have sanctions specified for non-compliance. Penal authorities, on the other hand, have no discretion over the implementation of sanctions, have no powers to waive or moderate them, and are bound by their accountability to parliaments to ensure compliance with the punitive decisions of the courts in enforcing laws.

Rather too frequently within contemporary democracies, laws enacted by governments are, to a considerable extent, based upon expediency reflective of the dominant political ideology within parliaments. Political expediency may be driven by pressures exerted by the mass media, by the perceived need to retain or restore electoral credibility, or by reaction to events without due consultation, deliberation or consideration of the outcomes. Such was almost certainly the case in the passage of the Criminal Justice Act 2003 in England and Wales providing for the IPP and ESPP (q.v.) measures which legislated for the indeterminate incapacitation of violent and/or sexual offenders for prevention and public protection, and had, subsequently, to be abandoned.

As we have seen all too clearly within this work, criminal laws grounded in retribution and deterrence cannot be other than speculative in their provisions since there is no reliable

16 Professor John R. Blad, until recently of Erasmus University, Rotterdam, the Netherlands, in e-mail correspondence with the author during March 2017.

means of measuring either the extent or the effectiveness of their outcomes. Despite this undeniable fact, however, the politicisation of criminal justice and its associated policy development has become a matter of profound complexity and concern within many contemporary jurisdictions.[17] It bears heavily upon the nature of electoral systems, of party leadership, of the status of advisory groupings and civil servants in policy development, and of the relative extent of decision-making independence vested in ministers within justice ministries and cabinets. Nicola Lacey summed this up as follows:

> [In] liberal market economies with majoritarian electoral systems, particularly under conditions of relatively low trust in politicians, relatively low deference to the expertise of criminal justice professionals, and a weakening of the ideological divide between political parties .. the unmediated responsiveness of politics to public opinion in the adversarial context of the two-party system makes it harder for governments to resist a ratcheting up of penal severity. As Newburn[18] has shown in relation to the British case, these dynamics become particularly strong where both parties take up a law and order agenda: they probably also become more acute under circumstances of weak party discipline and leader-dominated politics (Lacey, 2008:76).[19]

The situation described in this quotation precisely describes the developments in British penal policies during the period 1995 – 2016 in which successive governments, both Conservative and New Labour, adopted increasingly punitive penal policies without any significant regard to the moderating advice of senior civil servants and criminal justice professionals as to the outcomes of doing so. The result has been evident in the increased average daily prison population of England and Wales from around 52,000 in 1995 to over 83,000 in 2016 (Ministry of Justice, 2016b. *op. cit.*:3).

Unquestioning faith in the deterrence doctrine in tandem with retributive punishment has fuelled the expansion of the penal estate to above capacity on a continuous basis and continues to do so. Even as this book is nearing completion, the previous Justice Secretary for England and Wales had, in late-March 2017, stated in defence of the programme for

---

17 Here see, for example, the excellent account of this situation provided by Nicola Lacey in *The Prisoners' Dilemma: Political Economy and Punishment in Contemporary Democracies*, Cambridge: Cambridge University Press, 2008, pp.55-112, and especially, pp.70-77.

18 See: Tim Newburn, '"Tough on Crime": Penal Policy in England and Wales', in M. Tonry (Ed.), *Crime and Justice: A Review of Research*, Chicago, ILL: University of Chicago Press, 2007, pp.425-470.

19 And see also M. Cavadino and J. Dignan, *Penal Systems: A Comparative Approach*, London: Sage Publications, 2007, for a similar analysis in relation to a number of Western European and other countries: Germany, pp.102, 105; the Netherlands, pp.114-123; France, p.132; Finland and Sweden, pp.35-6, 151-2, 164; and Japan, pp.180-3; all quoted in Lacey, 2008 *op. cit.*:75 at fn.22.

further expansion of prison capacity that it would be 'an economic lifeline for the local communities – creating hundreds of jobs for local people'. This extraordinary claim was immediately challenged by Richard Garside, Director of the Centre for Crime and Justice Studies, asking her to prove her contentious claim, starting with the publication of a secret government report on the economic impact of new prisons.[20]

Now, while it is self-evidently true that building new prisons will, at least in the short term, create some local jobs within the construction industry, such employment will be of relatively short duration – possibly lasting at most five years and thereafter disappearing altogether. New prison staff are centrally rather than locally recruited and trained for employment in public sector prisons, or provided by re-location or re-deployment of existing Prison Service staff from prisons that are being closed due to age or becoming uneconomic, and not necessarily from within the immediate area of the communities in which the new prisons are built. Therefore, the Justice Secretary's claim is contentious, and particularly so since it was made in the immediate wake of the formal notification of the British government's decision to leave the European Union on 29 March 2017,[21] and the period of economic uncertainty that must inevitably follow during negotiation of the terms of its exit.[22]

This strange coincidence notwithstanding, the intention of the government to continue to expand the capacity of prisons in England and Wales signals very clearly the absence of any intention to depart from existing penal policies based on retribution, deterrence and incapacitation, or to take any substantive action to reduce its excessive penal population. In the chapter that follows we shall explore how, and to what extent, that population might be reduced by adoption of a reparative justice paradigm for the future that would significantly reduce the dysfunctional nature of such policies in a pragmatic manner.

In Chapters 7 and 8 which follow, we shall examine possible means of reducing prison populations while at the same time increasing the sector and impact of community corrections through the implementation of policies of mediation and reparation. In so doing, a new paradigm of criminal justice will emerge as a means of lessening dependence upon

---

20 E-mail 'Will new prisons bring a jobs bonanza?' from the Centre for Crime and Justice Studies to subscribers on Thursday 30 March 2017 timed at 05.43am GMT enclosing March Monthly Bulletin.

21 Triggering Article 50 of the European Union Constitution to leave the EU in a process widely known as 'Brexit'.

22 To the cynically-minded, it would seem suspiciously propitious that the Justice Secretary's announcement was timed to coincide almost precisely with the formal notification to the EU of British departure from the Union under Article 50, and thus, at least, in part a palliative gesture to reduce economic doubts among the 'Remain' lobby and population opposed to 'Brexit' and its uncertainties for the future economic situation of the United Kingdom.

deterrence-based sentencing practices, reducing the present high rates of post-sentence recidivism, and of restoring prisons to their primary purpose of changing rather than further damaging the lives of serious criminal offenders.

7 Reducing Dependence on Prisons

The Dismal Face of Custodial Justice

Anyone who has been inside even the most modern of prisons within many contemporary democracies would recognise them for what such places represent: unnatural structures of last resort. The imposing and enclosing atmosphere of gates and surveillance devices, the purely functional nature of the architecture, the regimentation of the residents known only by surnames and numbers, the almost clinically impersonal design of cell-block accommodation and the clock-driven routines of daily life stifle individuality to its barest essentials. Such places are, ultimately, human warehouses specifically designed to contain the outcasts of every national society out of sight and out of mind.

Many prisons in the United Kingdom and elsewhere do not meet more than the minimum requirements of decency, hygiene and cleanliness on a day to day basis. Prisoners lodged two to a cell designed for single occupancy to meet overcrowded conditions are required to eat, sleep, and carry out their personal ablutions in the same space without any but the most basic privacy. I have visited prisons in South Africa in which inmates were accommodated in locked dormitories housing up to forty persons together with access to a single shower and only two toilets, and with less bunk spaces than two-thirds of the number confined in them. In Poland also, both the Remand and Convicted prisons I visited were severely overcrowded and the sanitary and hygiene provisions were inadequate and squalid.

To make matters even worse, overcrowded prisons become incapable of delivering a full day of regime activities and purposeful employment, with the result that inmates spend many hours each week locked in their cells watching television or otherwise in idleness. Many prisons have difficulty in attracting other than the most menial of work contracts to occupy inmates, or providing vocational training to assist other than a few of them in gaining employment on release. In addition, educational facilities – even of a basic remedial nature – become inadequate to meet the demand for them, healthcare provision becomes overburdened, and those with symptoms of mental impairment or substance addiction remain largely untreated other than with basic suppressive medication.

Between 1995 and 2016 the average daily prison population of England and Wales increased by more than 35,500 people, a rise of 62.5%. Convicted admissions during 2015-16 exceeded 77,000 of whom more than 37,000 were sentenced to less than or equal to six months, of which only half (three months or less) would be spent in custody.[1] Many of these people would receive little or no substantive help to avoid re-offending on release, and recent recidivism statistics indicate that more than 60% of persons serving such sentences were reconvicted within twelve months in 2013-14 (Ministry of Justice, 2016c. *op. cit.*; Prison Reform Trust, 2016a. *op. cit.*:2).[2]

The concerning fact about these and other dismal statistics previously included in this work is that they are not new, and reveal an extent of political rather than operational failure that has persisted for two decades past. Prisons have become increasingly dangerous places for both prisoners and prison staff, particularly since 2010 due to budgetary reductions and decreased staffing levels. Levels of self-harm, assaults, homicides and self-inflicted deaths have reached unprecedented levels, combined with escalating rates of stress-related illness and sickness absence affecting prison staff. In addition, the recent scourge of psycho-active drugs[3] entering prisons undetected or un-intercepted has become a matter of serious national concern, particularly because of their capacity to provoke erratic and irrationally violent behaviour among inmates and towards prison staff.

All of this leads to a much deeper and more profound question of why, in this twenty-first century, governments like the one in the United Kingdom persist in legislating to preserve the *status quo* in a bankrupt criminal justice non-system that is so evidently unfit for purpose and does more harm than good. It surely cannot escape the understanding and recognition of ministers and senior Justice Ministry officials that the *status quo* is fragile to the point of having become untenable, that its fiscal and social costs are unsustainable, and that the penal system itself is on the brink of disintegration in both moral and operational terms. Perpetuation of, and blind adherence to, the notions of the deterrence doctrine are but one part of this overall political myopia which is ultimately promoted and reinforced by a mendacious mass media and a deep-seated fear among politicians of losing electoral credibility.

1 Ministry of Justice, *Offender Management Statistics*, Table 1.9 and Annual Table A2.6, London: Ministry of Justice, 2016, and see also Prison Reform Trust, *Bromley Briefings Prison Factfile Autumn 2016*, London: Prison Reform Trust, 2016b., pp.8-9.

2 In fact, the same statistics apply for sentences of up to and including twelve months, of which only up to or less than six months would be spent in prison custody.

3 Such as the substance known as 'spice' which is a synthetically made substance combining herbs or tobacco 'spiked' with cannabinoids of the family known as cannabicyclohexanol (or CBC) which is a psycho-active or psychotropic drug inducing irrational or hallucinating behaviour, and can be fatal. Due to its synthetic nature it is difficult to detect using standard drug detection scanners, and is effectively a 'designer' drug widely available for 'recreational' use. See: <https://en.wikipedia.org/wiki/synthetic_cannabinoids> for an excellent description of its origins, method of production and effects [accessed on 4 April 2016].

Fear is a powerful driving force within the criminal justice arena. Prisoners in unsafe conditions live out their daily lives in fear of assault and intimidation by their peers.[4] Prison staff report for duty on a daily basis recognising that the possibility of being assaulted by prisoners is an ever-present aspect of their profession. Prison governors manage their establishments mindful that incidents can arise entirely unpredictably, leading to concerted disorder, casualties, damage, the need for forcible intervention, and the loss of accommodation. Even the most senior Prison Service officials can be removed from their posts in the event that they incur the displeasure of ministers when serious incidents occur beyond their personal control.[5] And, ultimately, even Justice Ministers can find themselves 're-shuffled' if the policies they adopt meet with the disapproval of their cabinet colleagues, the Prime Minister and his/her senior civil service advisers.[6] It all seems to be as William Shakespeare is often quoted: 'Uneasy lies the head that wears a crown' (Henry IV, Pt2, III, i, 231).

Thinking about Reducing Prison Numbers

Once excessive prison populations have become established as 'business as usual', the options for reducing their overall size become strictly limited. People end up in prisons because they are sent there by the courts either on remand awaiting trial or conviction, or having been sentenced to custody. This relatively simple, and to some extent self-evident statement is all too frequently overlooked or ignored by both politicians and those responsible for sentencing offenders. The axiom that imprisonment should be used as a last resort has, in many jurisdictions, been supplanted by the notion that 'public safety' will be placed at risk if lesser use were to be made of prison custody, or finite limits were to be imposed on the capacity of prisons to accommodate inmates in conditions of decency and socially purposeful use.

4 Safety within adult male prisons in England and Wales was assessed as below required standards or 'not good enough' in almost half of the prisons inspected by HM Inspectorate of Prisons (HMCIP) in 2015-2016. HMCIP *Annual Report 2016*, London: The Stationery Office; Prison Reform Trust, 2016:10. 42% of adult males and 49% of women stated that they felt unsafe at some time while in custody. Serious assaults (prisoner on prisoner) have almost doubled in the last three years. In the year to June 2016 there were 2,462 such assaults, the highest annual level ever recorded.

5 As became the fate of Derek Lewis the Director General of the Prison Service in 1995 when he was dismissed by the (then) Home Secretary Michael Howard following the escape of notorious prisoners from Whitemoor and Parkhurst maximum security prisons (see Chapter 3 *supra*).

6 As seems to have been the case when Kenneth Clarke, Justice Secretary from 2010-2012, announced his 'Rehabilitation Revolution' which became contrary to the more punitive criminal justice policies preferred by the Prime Minister David Cameron and his cabinet colleagues (see further below).

A much maligned former Justice Secretary for England and Wales during the present decade Kenneth Clarke[7] perceived very clearly the uselessness of sending offenders to prisons that were incapable, often due to overcrowding, of changing their criminal behaviour into law-abiding lives. He announced the need for a 'rehabilitation revolution' to give prisons a revived sense of purpose, and prisoners some substantive assistance towards avoiding re-offending on release.[8] For whatever reasons, his message that matters could not be allowed to remain as they were found him isolated within the Cabinet of the day, and led to his early replacement by a successor whose preferred and more punitive approach had greater resonance for the 'law and order' lobby within the conservative-dominated coalition government, the wider political constituency, and the mass media.

Whatever the problems that might have arisen from the Green Paper published in December 2010, it focused precisely on the needs of the criminal justice system to reduce the prison population, make prisons more effective in reducing recidivism, placing necessary limitations on the use of short prison sentences, and the expansion of more demanding community sentences. It met with opposition from an influential group of conservative MPs anxious not to lose electoral credibility, the National Association of Probation Officers (NAPO) claiming that it would lead to further 'privatisation' of their role, and some sections of the media asserting an increase in public risk and critical of the government becoming 'soft on crime'.[9] The new Justice Secretary Chris Grayling was quick to announce withdrawal of the Green Paper which did not survive its planned consultation period.

The saddening aspect of this development was that Kenneth Clarke, a former barrister and QC and thus an experienced legal practitioner in addition to being a long serving and distinguished MP, was uniquely well-placed to propose such a purposeful reform agenda. He had also been a former Home Secretary in the government led by John Major as Prime Minister between 1992-3, and was a political moderate with an extensive understanding of the workings and the shortcomings of the criminal justice process. This was an opportunity missed as a matter of political expediency by a government with a slender majority

7 Kenneth Clarke who was Justice Secretary from 2010-2012 during the early years of the administration headed by David Cameron as Prime Minister. He was replaced by Chris Grayling whose public stance on criminal justice issues was considerably more disposed towards maintenance of the *status quo* insofar as imprisonment was concerned.

8 The proposals for reform were set out in a Green Paper: Ministry of Justice, *Breaking the Cycle: Effective Punishment, Rehabilitation and Sentencing of Offenders*, Cm 7972, London: The Stationery Office, 2010 (December) which was subsequently withdrawn.

9 However, media criticism was by no means universal and some of the more responsible national newspapers gave the Green Paper balanced coverage. See, for example, A. Travis & H. Mulholland, 'Prison System Failing to Tackle Re-Offending Says Ken Clarke', *The Guardian*, Tuesday 7 December 2010.

in parliament, and which could not rely on the loyal support of its own members in matters of urgently needed criminal justice reform.

Selection of the term 'rehabilitation revolution' as the catchphrase for the proposed reforms was, in a number of ways, an unfortunate, even though well-intentioned, choice. Indeed, 'sentencing revolution' would have been more appropriate in the circumstances since it was prevailing sentencing practices more than anything else that had persistently lead to the over-burdening of the penal system. Moreover, it remains a debatable question whether prisons can effectively rehabilitate offenders in the closed and secluded environment in which such places have to operate, whether overcrowded or not.[10] We shall return to a further discussion of this important debate in Chapter Eight which follows. Implicit within the concept of the abandoned Green Paper of 2010 was a deliberate intention to reduce the use of short custodial sentences, and therefore the prison population. Such a proposition had considerable implications for the perpetuation of the deterrence doctrine within penal philosophy, and for contemporary sentencing practices based, at least in part, upon its supposed efficacy in crime control and reduction. It would be encouraging to believe that this amounted to a carefully considered re-evaluation of the public safety: public risk dimension within criminal justice administration, combined with at least a realisation and acknowledgement that the actual effectiveness of the doctrine was open to serious questioning.

THE ROUTE TO ACTUAL PRISON REDUCTION

The economic circumstances prevailing in different countries and their penal populations vary considerably, and particularly so within Western Europe. The extent of these differences is indicated very clearly in *Figure* 7:1 which displays a sample of sixteen nations with their rates of imprisonment *per* one hundred thousand of the population and their daily *per capita* expenditure on maintaining individual prisoners in custody (Council of Europe, 2017). Here, it is of interest to note that the five nations making the greatest use of prison custody are amongst the lowest in terms of daily *per capita* expenditure, and that the five

10 Because there is an established school of thought among many modern criminologists that rehabilitation has at its core a motive and context of social re-adaptation which has to be implemented and tested under conditions of supervision and guidance within the community which is offended by crime. Importantly, this concept implies a relationship between offenders, victims of crime and communities inclusive of restitution and reparation which has subsequently been developed within the concept of reparative and restorative justice. Here see: A. Keith Bottomley, *Criminology in Focus*, Oxford: Martin Robertson, 1979 at Chapter 4, pp.153-157, and R.E. Barnett, 'Restitution: A New Paradigm of Criminal Justice', *Journal of Ethics*, Vol.87, pp.279-301 as early instances of this development.

countries with the lowest rates of imprisonment spend the highest amounts on maintaining prisoners in custody.[11]

Figure 7.1 Comparison Charts Rates of Imprisonment & per Diem Expenditure per Capita in Western European Countries

Imprisonment Rate per 100,000 of Population in 2017*

COUNTRY	RATE PER 100 K
England & Wales	146
Scotland	145
Spain	140
Portugal	136
Belgium	108
Austria	102
France	101
Northern Ireland	93
Republic of Ireland	92
Italy	90
Germany	78
Norway	72
Netherlands	71
Denmark	64
Sweden	59
Finland	58

Expenditure in Penal Institutions Per Capita Daily in 2017 (€ and £GB)**

COUNTRY	PER DIEM €	PER DIEM £GB
Sweden	354.00	439.35
Norway	348.00	431.90
Netherlands	273.00	338.82
Denmark	191.00	237.05
Republic of Ireland	189.00	234.05
Finland	175.00	217.19
Italy	141.76	179.94
Belgium	137.28	170.38
Germany	129.35	160.54
Scotland	125.00	155.10
England & Wales	115.76	143.67
Austria	112.97	140.21
Northern Ireland	112.20	139.25
France	102.67	127.42
Spain	59.72	74.12
Portugal	41.22	51.16

* Source: Council of Europe, *Annual Penal Statistics SPACE1, Prison Population Survey 2015 Final Report*, Table 17, Strasburg: Council of Europe, 2017 (14 March).

** Source: *Ibid.* Table 19. Based Exchange Rate £1 = E1.241 as at Bank of England Rate at 3 January 2017

What does remain a matter of concern within this work is the question of why the five nations with the highest rates of imprisonment within Western Europe find it necessary to use custodial sentences at more than twice the rates of the lowest five. Though it must remain a matter of conjecture because it is cannot be proved with certainty, it seems altogether likely that persistence with excessively punitive sentencing practices based upon

11 This much stated however, the Council of Europe statistics do not specify precisely which costs are and which are not included in the compilation of the daily rates of expenditure in penal institutions. For instance, in England and Wales annual average costs *per* prisoner place are quoted exclusive of the costs of Healthcare and Educational provision which are considerable. The reason for this is that such costs are met by other Departments of State than the Ministry of Justice.

retributive and deterrent justifications has played at least a significant part in bringing this situation into existence.

At the other end of the scale, the quality of prison regimes in terms of the emphasis placed upon reducing re-offending and changing lives towards crime-free future social behaviour cannot be envisaged in overcrowded prisons operated at relatively low cost and with a lack of resources for purposeful employment and training on a full-time daily basis. Such requires an investment in people rather than in prison places which some countries – particularly those in Scandinavia – have recognised for decades past and have implemented with considerable social benefit in terms of reducing recidivism.

The conclusions to be drawn from this analysis are self-evidently clear: high use of imprisonment leads inevitably to high rates of re-offending; and high rates of re-offending lead to further use of imprisonment and high rates of prison occupancy. This is the cycle of despair which currently affects England, Wales and Scotland in particular, and quite simply has to be reversed. It requires a determined investment in better quality criminal justice, a long overdue overhaul of sentencing practices to reduce the prison population, and a significant expansion of community sanctions and resources with the potential to change lives through enhancing skills and employability which will, in turn, reduce re-offending or the perceived need for it.

Better quality criminal justice requires political determination and consensus beyond the narrower confines of justice ministries and individual party agendas with traditional preferences within government. It also requires a unified acceptance that penal reform is now unavoidable in the national interest, and must involve all the stakeholders in the justice process.[12] Such an agenda and consensus for reform is not without precedent, such as that established in Finland (see, for instance, Lappi-Seppälä, 2013 *op. cit.*:501-524; Cornwell, 2016 *op. cit.*:69-119; Blom-Cooper, 2013 *op. cit.*:151-170), but it has to be deliberately promoted by an administration determined to pursue it to a definitive conclusion and implementation within a specified time frame.

12 These stakeholders include parliament, the judiciary, the Justice Ministry, Home Office, police, prison and probation services, the media, penal reform groups, and academic advisers drawn from universities with established faculties of expertise in criminology, sociology and law. Ideally, it would be conducted as a Royal Commission on the Penal System of the United Kingdom, required to report to parliament within a specified period not exceeding two years.

Figure 7.2 Prison population – England & Wales 2017

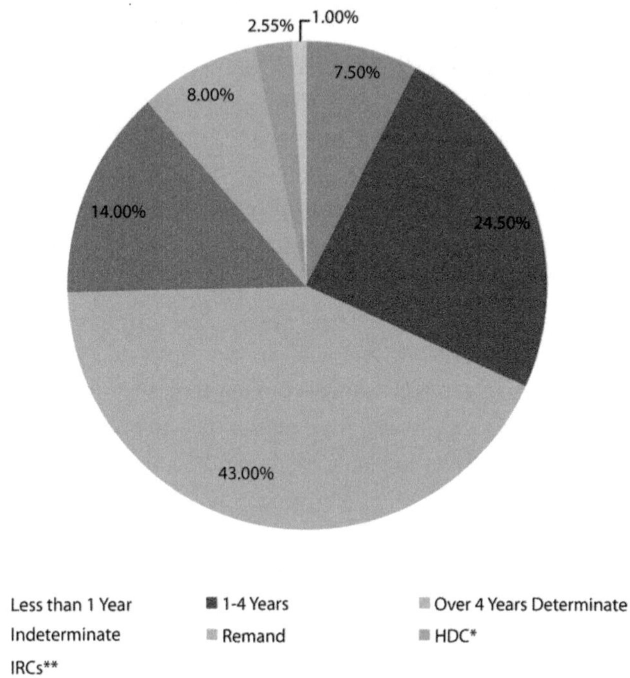

Source: Extracted and adjusted from: House of Commons Library, UK Prison Population Statistics [Briefing Paper SN//SG/04334], G. Allen & C. Watson (Compilers), London: House of Commons, 2017 (April), available at: <http://researchbriefings.parliament.uk/documents/SN04334.pdf> [accessed on 24 April 2017].

Key to Population Sentence Values

Less than 1 Year	7.50% = 6,350
1 – 4 Years	24.50% = 20,750
Over 4 Years Determinate	43.00% = 36,760
Indeterminate	14.00% = 11,970
Remand Prisoners	8.00% = 6,850
Home Detention Curfew (HDC)	2.55% = 2,180
Immigration Removal Centres (IRCs)	1.00% = 860
Total Prison Population	**100.00% = 85,720**

NB. Values rounded up/down to nearest ten.
* = HDC Prisoners liable to recall for non-compliance.
**= IRC detainees awaiting deportation not sentenced.

In the specific instance of the penal situation in England and Wales at the present time, the causes and symptoms of which have already been clearly explained, the options for reform are strictly limited to a process of reversing the causal factors of the crisis. The chart at *Figure* 7:2 provides a snapshot breakdown of the prison population as at the end of April 2017, and the proportion of prisoners in each of the main sentence bands. The reader will recall that under existing sentencing conditions in England and Wales, the length of time spent in prison custody for those serving determinate (fixed) sentences is actually one-half of the total sentence period (i.e. two years for a four year sentence, etc.), but in the case of indeterminate sentences, release is at the discretion of the Parole Board once the minimum custodial period imposed by the sentencing court has been served.[13]

One of the concerning features of sentencing practices in England and Wales is that since 1994, the average length of sentences of imprisonment has steadily increased in all sentencing bands, and so too has the time spent in custody by those thus sentenced (Ministry of Justice, 2016b, *op. cit.*:4 and *passim*). This single factor, though not alone, has contributed significantly to the increasing size of the prison population, and also to the extent of overcrowding throughout the prison system.[14, 15] In considering the potential for reducing prison numbers, therefore, it is logical to focus attention on that sector of the population which spends the least time in custody, but which also adds the most pressure on the prison system and prevents it from performing effectively in reducing re-offending following release.

Two further aspects of the existing situation also have to be considered in looking for a potential reduction in prison numbers. The first is the extent of the use made by prisons of the temporary release of prisoners to serve part of their sentences in the community prior to release; the second is the escalating rate of recall of such people to serve short periods in custody for breaching the conditions of their temporary release licences, and also the re-sentencing of offenders serving non-custodial (community) sentences or suspended sentences for breaches of the conditions imposed by the courts upon them. This particular element of the prison population does not feature separately in the chart at

13 For a further explanation of this procedure see: Gibson, B., *Criminal Justice Act 2003: A Guide to the New Procedures and Sentencing*, Hook, Hampshire: Waterside Press, 2004, at pp.87 and 99.

14 It is, however, not the only contributory factor in the expansion of the prison population of England and Wales since 1994. There is considerable (though unquantifiable) evidence that in the lower (magistrates') courts in particular, sentencing officials have widely opted to impose short prison sentences in cases in which a non-custodial sentence could have been ordered, due to a general decline of confidence in the effectiveness of community penalties in reducing re-offending.

15 At the end of May 2016, 74 of the 118 prisons of England and Wales were officially overcrowded, with almost 22,000 (more than one-quarter) of the population held in overcrowded accommodation. Here see: Ministry of Justice, 2016d. *op. cit.*, and Prison Reform Trust, 2016b. *op. cit.*:14-15.

Figure 7:2 since the majority of such prisoners are subsumed within the numbers serving sentences of less than one year. However, in the year to June 2016, over 7,500 such persons were recalled to prison serving sentences of less than twelve months.[16]

The use of release on temporary licence (ROTL) enabling low and medium risk prisoners to serve pre-release periods working in the community has seen a significant (37%) decrease in recent years despite the fact that until 2012 the rate of successful completion of such placements without further offending was as high as 99.93%.[17] Part of the reason for this situation is the risk-averse attitude of prison managers seeking to avoid adverse media publicity, and also new restrictions imposed upon the use of such release by Justice Ministry politicians for similar reasons following the replacement of Kenneth Clarke as Justice Secretary in 2012 mentioned earlier. However, in 2014-15 only 1,273 prisoners were granted such release, an average of 368 each month out of a population of some 27,000 serving effective sentence lengths of two years or less in custody (Ministry of Justice, 2015b.: Table 20; Prison Reform Trust, 2016a. *op. cit.*:4, at fn.55).

Given the factors outlined in the preceding analysis, and the fact that short prison sentences are considerably less effective than community sanctions of equivalent duration in reducing re-offending[18], it becomes logical to consider seriously why such sentences are imposed in the first instance. It is difficult to escape the fact that short prison sentences are predominantly punitive in nature, and particularly so since the overcrowded conditions in which these are served are evidently unsatisfactory and also ineffective in reducing recidivism or deterring future criminal activity.

A bold strategy to overcome this situation would be to impose a sentencing threshold for imprisonment set at over two years in custodial duration which, under present circumstances in England and Wales, would enable all sentences of four years imprisonment or less to be replaced by community sanctions. Such an initiative would immediately reduce the prison population by some 27,000 places, while at the same time eliminating prison overcrowding. It would also have the significant advantages of resolving the recall to custody situation which is widely over-used, and of enabling prisons to provide regimes properly equipped to address offending behaviour, and also educational and skills training to enhance the employability of prisoners on their eventual release.

16 Ministry of Justice, 2014d. *op. cit.*: Table 5.2.

17 Ministry of Justice, *Offender Management Statistics – Prison Releases 2015*, London: Ministry of Justice, 2016e., Table A3.7.

18 According to Ministry of Justice statistics, people serving prison sentences of twelve months or less had a re-offending rate within one year of release seven percentage points higher than similar offenders serving an equivalent community sentence (Ministry of Justice, *2013 Compendium of Re-Offending Statistics and Analysis*, London: Ministry of Justice, 2013, and Prison Reform Trust, 2016a. *op. cit.*:4).

A further determined penal reform measure of a significant and overdue nature would address the present conditions in which remand imprisonment is used in England and Wales, involving more than 10,000 people who are untried, un-convicted or convicted but un-sentenced on an average daily basis. In 2015, almost 40,500 people were imprisoned before trial, spending an average of over ten weeks in custody while on remand. Of this population, three-fifths (60%) were accused of non-violent offences, one in ten (almost 11,000) were subsequently acquitted, and a further 15,500 (15%) received a non-custodial sentence (Prison Reform Trust, 2016a. *op. cit.*:3).

There are compelling reasons for such reform, not least because the use of prisons for un-convicted or un-sentenced persons is morally questionable, but also because their presence in prisons exacerbates the overcrowding situation, resulting in them being held in entirely inappropriate conditions. In circumstances in which their detention can be justified as a matter of public safety, a strong case can be made for this to be implemented in secure accommodation operated by an entirely separate custodial entity under the jurisdiction of the Courts & Tribunals Service and the Police Services rather than in prisons. It would also enable persons in custody awaiting trial to be held in locations near to the court in which they will be tried, and save considerable expense in secure escort transportation.[19]

The moral issue involved here is that confinement of un-convicted and even convicted but un-sentenced persons in prisons inevitably infringes the principle that they should suffer no more extensive deprivation of their rights and liberties as citizens than is strictly necessary to ensure public safety and the administration of justice. The extent and nature of the deprivations imposed by imprisonment regimes is considerably greater than that justifiable on such grounds, and in many instances places logistical constraints or limitations on their access to dependents and legal advisers due to distance and the pressure of excessive prison numbers on the visitation capacity of prison establishments. In a strict sense, these persons remain 'civil prisoners' until they are both convicted and sentenced, and as has already been mentioned, almost one-quarter of them are eventually either acquitted or given non-custodial sentences when their trials are concluded.

Up to this stage in the discussion of the potential for necessary penal reform, the focus has been upon those serving short and ineffective prison sentences, and those subjected to remand custody. In combination, these populations (totalling some 33,900) account for more than one-third of the total average daily prison population of England and Wales

19 Such, for instance, is the case in the Crown Court adjacent to the present HMP Belmarsh in London in which the two facilities are connected by an underground tunnel enabling pedestrian movement between the two.

which currently stands at just over 85,000. As to the remaining prisoners serving longer (over four year) sentences, an altogether different problem arises. For as we have noted in Chapter 6 (*supra*), such persons are less likely to be suitable for reparative custodial regimes due to the relative seriousness of their offences, at least until they reach the period leading up to their eventual release. This particular population comprises some 36,200 individuals serving a mix of longer determinate sentences, mandatory and other life sentences, and the residue of the former IPP and ESPP sentences, and for whom the existing traditional form and security levels of prison custody must remain entirely appropriate.

TOWARDS COMMUNITY INVOLVEMENT IN PRISONS

It is possible to envisage a situation in which a number of prisons with dedicated reparative regimes might be established to accommodate selected inmates in the final two years of their sentences who are willing to comply fully with the requirement to work to make reparation to victims of crime while at the same time acquiring training and skills to enhance their employability on release. These prisons would work within the framework of Community Justice Forums (CJFs) in close liaison with local police, the judiciary, probation and local government agencies, voluntary sector organisations,[20] employers, and educational authorities. I have described in outline a blueprint for community involvement of this nature in former work (Cornwell, 2016 *op. cit.*:119-127), based upon those in Canada and Scotland already in existence (see: Mirsky, 2005; Scottish Government, 2013; Criminal Justice Voluntary Sector Forum, 2014). It was further suggested in the proposed blueprint that CJFs should be chaired by Police and Crime Commissioners (PCCs) assisted by a small secretariat to coordinate their work.[21]

The emphasis here is to make reparative prisons an integral feature of the communities in which they are located, and provide low and medium risk offenders with the opportunity to re-integrate in local communities on a supervised basis as deliberate preparation for release without re-offending. It is also, however, a two-way strategy to involve communities with prisons in a manner that encourages building public confidence in the purpose of reparative imprisonment, and confidence within prisons in the routine release of prisoners on temporary release to gain work experience within communities. For this reason,

20 Including representatives of the Mediation and Reparation Service (M&RS), Victim Support Groups, and local media. Further description of the role of the M&RS may also be found in the same work (Cornwell, 2016 *op. cit.*:93-106), to which we shall return subsequently.

21 The proposal made here lies beyond the present role description of Police and Crime Commissioners (PCCs) as set out in 2012 (Home Office, 2012), which would require consultation and amendment. The document is available at: <www.gov.uk/government/uploads/system/uploads/attachment_dara/file/117463/role-as-pcc.pdf> [accessed on 13 March 2015].

reparative prisons should have integral hostel-type accommodation designed into them to enable prisoners on temporary release to return each evening to a semi-secure environment under the supervision of prison staff.[22]

It would also be essential that reparative prisons operate regimes with a full eight hour working day of vocational training or employment with realistic pay and incentive structures from which deductions could be made at source for the VW&CF. External work placements should be of similar daily duration and remuneration on a five day working week basis. The purpose of these routines is to encourage the development of a regular work ethic in offenders, enabling them to be released into their communities able to compete effectively with non-offenders within the employment market and thereby reduce the risk of their re-offending and returning to a criminal lifestyle and re-imprisonment.

The initiative for reparative prisons outlined briefly in the previous paragraphs of this section represent a deliberate prescription for reducing dependence on imprisonment as a means of deterring crime. Reparative prisons could contribute significantly to overall crime reduction and also, importantly, to a reduction in offender recidivism and its costs – both financial and social – to national economies.[23] There is, however, one further means of reducing prison populations, extending reparative justice, giving victims of crime greater consideration, and at the same time increasing the likelihood that offenders will desist from further crime. This lies in the lessened use of deterrence as a threat, and in the implementation of mediation within the criminal justice process as an alternative strategy for crime reduction. In the chapter that follows this paradigm is examined with its implications and potential to deliver better justice for future generations.

22 It is important to note here that prisoners undertaking daily work placements outside the prison should be accommodated separately from those who have not yet qualified for temporary release. This reduces the risk of the importation of contraband items into prisons, and also the risk of those offenders working outside prisons being placed under pressure to act illegally by doing so.

23 In England and Wales a Report compiled by the National Audit Office in 2010 estimated that re-offending by all recently released offenders costs the economy between £9,5 and £13 billion annually. As much as three-quarters of this cost can be attributed to former short-sentenced prisoners: some £7 – £10 billion annually (National Audit Office, *Managing Offenders on Short Custodial Sentences*, London: HMSO, 2010 *op. cit.*; Prison Reform Trust, 2016a. *op. cit.*:4).

8 Mediation and Reparative Justice

A Justice Paradigm for the Future

The previous chapter concluded with a glimpse of how reparative justice might reduce dependence on imprisonment of those offenders convicted of less serious offences, involve communities more closely as stakeholders in the criminal justice process, and give victims of crime greater consideration. In this penultimate chapter we shall explore the way in which mediation might be incorporated within the criminal justice process, enabling lesser reliance upon deterrence as a central purpose of criminal punishment and opening the way to a new and more inclusive justice paradigm for the future.

If reparative justice represents a door to this new conception of justice, then mediation provides the key to opening it. At the present time there are encouraging signs that a number of democratic countries worldwide are actively considering the inclusion and implementation of mediation practices within their justice processes. In a number of instances these practices are closely allied to the principles of reparative and restorative justice as an alternative strategy to the widely espoused and traditionally punitive retributive mode of criminal and civil offence resolution.

It is, of course, self-evidently obvious that serious offences deserve a serious response, and that the response should bear some evident relationship to the extent of the harm that each offence causes to both the victim(s) and the social order. Moreover, offences differ in the extent of the harm occasioned, and thus the relative seriousness with which each must be viewed and the response that is justly appropriate. Hence, issues of proportionality in sentencing arise.

By way of contrast, experience in the field of mediation practice indicates that the harm and trauma endured by victims of crime can be reduced to a significant extent through the process of dialogue, between themselves and the perpetrators of crime, that professionally conducted mediation can achieve. It is a regrettable fact that within many criminal justice processes in particular, victims become the marginalised parties since there is no necessary expectation that those who commit crime should take responsibility for their actions and make amends for the harm that they cause.

Failure to make the potential benefits of mediation an integral part of justice processes results in relegation of its social and psychological importance to a peripheral activity within many Western-style democracies that focus predominantly on punitive responses to crime and its control rather than upon crime reduction. Such a focus is ultimately detrimental to the lives and well-being of all of the stakeholders in the delivery of fair and effective justice – victims, offenders and communities alike.

It is argued by some criminal justice practitioners, policy-makers and academic criminologists that inclusion of mediation within justice processes extends the time taken to bring offenders to justice, and thus detracts from the principle of certainty and celerity in its administration and the demonstrable punishment of offenders. This contention has to be weighed against the potential benefits that mediation can offer to the future lives of those most centrally affected – both victims and offenders – to crime reduction, and to the social cohesiveness of communities.

This analysis acknowledges that certain risk factors are inherent in mediation processes, identifies these, and some of the ways in which they can be avoided or reduced. It will also propose a number of principles upon which mediation in a justice context should be based, and the implications of these principles for the delivery of better justice in the future.

Within many contemporary jurisdictions there is no evident requirement that offenders should accept or take responsibility for their wrongful behaviour or its harmful effects upon those offended against. Indeed, in many respects the adversarial processes of justice administration and trial encourage denial of guilt and evasion of responsibility until conviction becomes inevitable. This situation effectively sidelines both victims of crime and the communities in which crime is committed. Yet both crime victims and communities are principal stakeholders in the maintenance of social order and cohesion, and it is their security that is violated by criminal acts.

At the present time, the absence of any requirement within the adversarial justice process in England and Wales for offenders to take responsibility for offences and 'put wrongs right' points to the similar absence of any formally established mediation process. If such a process were to be established, then logically it should provide for mediation to be considered at the stage at which decisions are made as to prosecution in cases in which the conflict caused by offences might be resolved (or mitigated) by the offender accepting guilt and responsibility, and indicating a willingness to apologise and make reparation to the victim(s) of his/her wrongful behaviour. This raises the issue of which forms of offending and its relative seriousness might be considered as being potentially amenable to resolution by mediation (alone or in part) if both parties were willing to participate in the mediation process.

Establishment and formalisation of mediation processes within either adversarial or inquisitorial justice systems requires a structure that includes the designation of officials appointed specifically to examine and decide, at the prosecution stage of offence consideration, which cases might be suitable for resolution by mediation, either entirely or partially, in conjunction with a subsequent trial process. It also requires the recruitment and training of professional mediators to exacting standards of accreditation as members of a National Mediation and Reparation Service (NM&RS) as an agency within the Ministry of Justice. In earlier work (Cornwell, 2016 *op. cit.*) I have described the outline and purposes of such a structure to which the attention of interested readers is directed, rather than for it to be repeated in its entirety here.[1] This much stated, however, *Figure* 8:1 provides a step-by-step description of a process for decision-making and the disposal of offences within a reparative model of correctional justice.

At this stage it seems appropriate to indicate that within the field of restorative justice studies and literature, there is an evident divergence of view on mediation within criminal justice processes. On the one hand, and at the philosophical level, there are those (*f.i.* Walgrave 2008:20-24 and *passim*; 2013:347-73 *passim*) who propose that mediation processes should, in principle, be available to all offenders who are willing participants, and particularly those who commit serious offences, who perhaps need it most. On the other hand there are those, possibly of a more pragmatic disposition, who perceive establishing the principle of mediation in criminal justice as necessarily limited, initially at least, to less serious offences and offenders. The latter is the approach which I have adopted here, in the belief that if it proves to be successful its potential can be extended, though in a somewhat different and holistic approach, to the rehabilitation of more serious offenders for whom longer terms of imprisonment are presently perceived as unavoidable within a predominantly retributive mode of punishment and incapacitation.

1 Here, see: D.J. Cornwell, *Desert in a Reparative Frame: Re-Defining Contemporary Criminal Justice*, The Hague, The Netherlands: Eleven International Publishing, (2016), Chapters 9-11.

Figure 8.1 Disposal of Offences in Mediated Reparative Justice

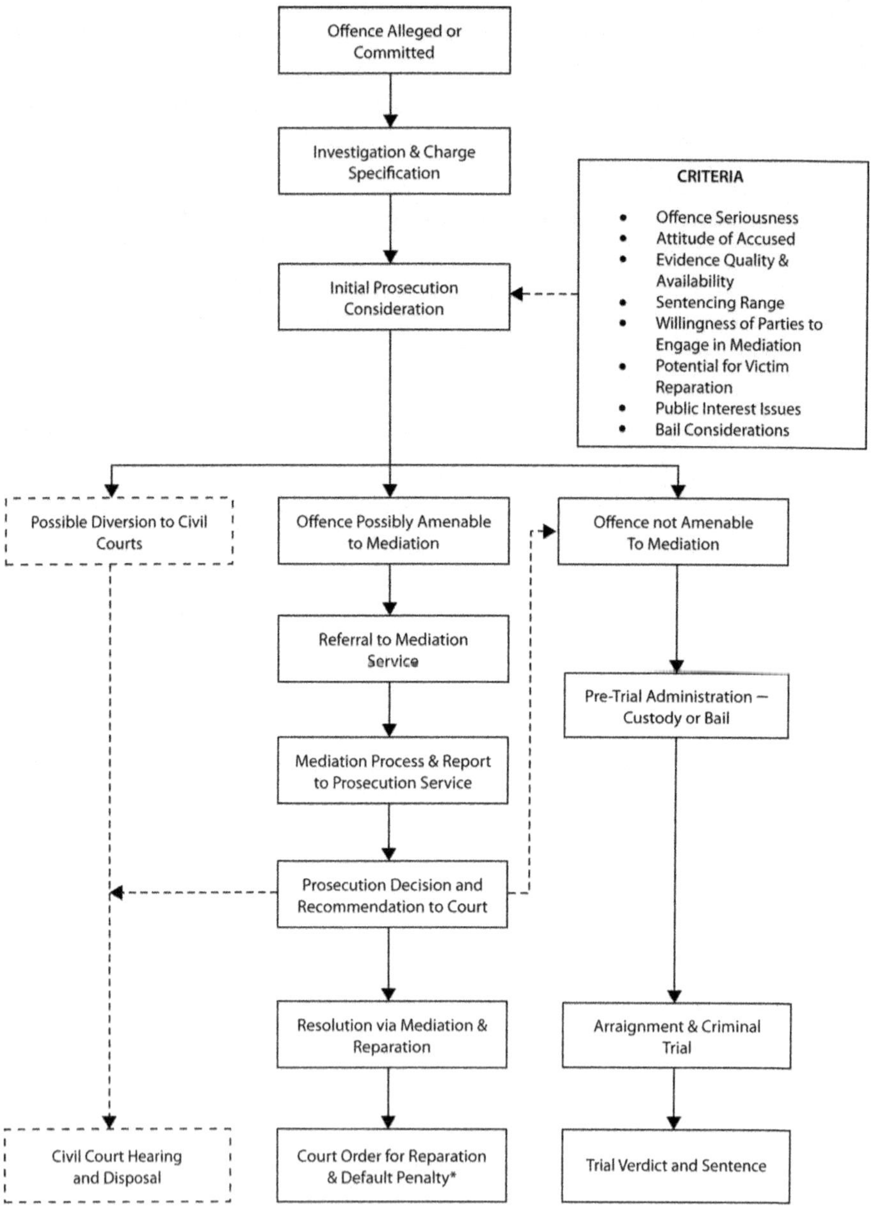

* Note: may include additional orders or penalties decided by court in addition to reparation.

But mediation within criminal justice is equally about giving victims of crime proper attention and support, and, moreover, a substantive and hitherto largely neglected status as genuine stakeholders in the justice process.[2] The needs of victims as involuntary sufferers of personal violation and even traumatisation extend beyond that of mere reparation and compensation, important as the latter may be in instances of financial loss or material hardship. Mediation between victims and offenders who willingly agree to participate in the process can produce win: win outcomes: victims can reach some measure of vindication and closure, while offenders can reach some understanding of the harm they have caused and resolve to apologise and make reparative amends to those whom they have violated.

There are risks inherent in any negotiation process that cannot be discounted. Some victims of criminal acts, especially those involving personal violence, can be heavily traumatised and need care and support to recover either physically or psychologically. Having to re-live their experiences can lead to further traumatisation, particularly in face to face contact with their aggressors. Others may harbour deep-seated feelings of anger towards those who have wronged them, and either refuse the offer of apology and mediation or insist on trial outcomes as a means of 'getting their own back' on offenders. Some offenders may attempt to manipulate the justice process by opting for mediation as a means of avoiding the extent of punishment deserved by their offences. Mediators have to be conscious of these and other situations on the part of either party to the mediation process, and seek to eliminate or minimise their effects. However, Family Group Conferences (FGC) and Healing Circles can often assist in mitigating these risks providing that there is a genuine willingness on the part of the parties to resolve their differences in a positive and generous manner.

Above all else, perhaps, the inclusion of mediation processes and procedures opens up valuable and much-needed options for dealing with criminal offences in a more rational manner than that which essentially retributive justice provides. Many less serious offences could, with mediated resolution, be diverted to civil courts for hearing and disposal without the delays and expenses of criminal trials and the legal manoeuvrings of the adversarial mode of justice. Even with mediation having arrived at a successful outcome in more serious cases of offending, entry of a 'guilty' plea and willingness to make reparation could obviate the need for a jury trial and speed up the disposal of offences, giving the accused some credit for saving the court time and expense. In instances of heinous crime, however, an early decision by prosecution officials that the alleged offence is not amenable to

2 Such is to suggest beyond that of potential witnesses in the prosecution process, but not to the extent of allocution within trial proceedings beyond the existing procedure for them to submit Victim Impact Statements (VISs) or Victim Personal Statements (VPSs) for mandatory consideration by the courts prior to sentencing decisions being made.

mediation would assist in bringing the case to trial without undue delay due to court lists being overloaded with unnecessarily contested hearings of lesser offences.

Such is not to exclude really serious offenders from mediation processes completely, since some express genuine remorse for their victims and crimes, particularly when the latter cause death or lifelong trauma to those offended against. In cases in which victims or their relatives are eventually prepared to extend forgiveness, it may be possible for some form of dialogue to be created between the parties to the benefit of both. Many serious offenders do, however, have a need for therapeutic counselling to help them to come to terms with the seriousness of their criminal conduct, understand its effects upon others, and regain a measure of self-esteem and confidence in the future. This is quite different from mediation.

Mediation processes have to be structured into criminal (and civil) justice systems as an integral part of the reparative and rehabilitative paradigm rather than as a means of diversion from the due process of law enforcement. Thus viewed, mediation services have to be perceived as having a significant potential to reduce re-offending and enhance rehabilitation while also being a means towards the after-care and vindication of victims. Mediation thus becomes a professional vocation working to rigorous accreditation criteria and ethical standards of conduct. In many respects it mirrors the skills, competencies and personal characteristics required in hostage negotiation practice.[3]

Disposal of Offences in Mediated Reparative Justice

As *Figure* 8:1 indicates, the process required for mediation of offences involves the police, prosecution authorities, mediation service and the courts in a sequence of activities designed to determine the outcome of offences from the time that these are first alleged through to final disposal in the courts. Key decisions have to be made at stages within this process, including:

- by the police as to the offence(s) to be charged;
- by the Prosecution Service according to the criteria for considering prosecution;

3 A detailed analysis of the skills and personal characteristics required by mediators would occupy more space than this account can include. It is, however, essential that mediators approach their role in a demonstrably impartial and empathetic manner that creates a safe environment for the parties involved to seek resolution of feelings of hurt, guilt, anger, frustration and the like out of respect for each other's humanity and dignity. The reader may find the explanations set out in Elizabeth Bader's article 'The Psychology of Mediation, Part 1, The Mediator's Issues Of Self And Identity', *10 Pepperdine Dispute Resolution Law Journal*, 183 (2010) helpful as background reading. For an abridged version see: <www.mediate.com/articles/baderE2.cfm> [accessed on 16 June 2016].

- by the Mediation Service as to amenability to mediation procedures, referral and report compilation (with recommendations including any agreed reparation);
- by the Prosecution Service in recommending disposal to the courts;
- by the courts in deciding upon diversion, mediation or criminal trial, and sanctions upon conviction (including reparation orders, default and additional penalties).

The critical stages in the process are those at which the Prosecution Service completes its initial consideration as to whether cases are or are not potentially amenable to mediation or diversion (to the civil courts), and, following receipt of the Mediation Service report as to the likelihood of a mediated outcome in possibly amenable cases, its final recommendation(s) to the courts on disposal.

Insofar as the Mediation Service is concerned, once a case has been referred to it as possibly amenable to a mediated outcome, the agreement of the parties to participate must be sought and an initial conference held to establish the potential for a mediated outcome.[4] The outcome of this stage should determine the recommendation(s) made by the Prosecution Service to the courts as to final disposal of the case.

In instances in which resolution could be reached *via* mediation, it would fall to the court to decide upon the extent of any Reparation Order made, default penalty to be imposed, and any additional conditions or restrictions with which the offender must comply.[5] The key consideration would be the ability of the offender through employment to make the required reparation from earned income on a reliable basis.

In more serious cases in which a sentence to immediate imprisonment might otherwise be justified, it would be for the court to decide whether part, or all, of the sentence should be served in a reparative prison and make an order accordingly to ensure that the agreed reparation is made. This should, however, be avoided if a suspended sentence would serve the same purpose and the offender was in full-time employment at the time of consideration.[6]

---

4 This conference need not necessarily involve face to face contact between offender(s) and victim(s) initially, however desirable (or otherwise) this might become in due course. Its purpose would be to establish willingness to participate in mediation, and whether, a mediated outcome including reparation would be acceptable as a means of resolving the differences between the parties. The Report to the Prosecution Service would hinge on this issue primarily.

5 For instance, seeking and undertaking treatment for addiction or behavioural issues, or skills training for employment to ensure that reparation is made. In cases in which an immediate custodial sentence might otherwise have been imposed, this might be suspended for a similar period as a default penalty.

6 Such is to suggest where a sentence of more than two and less than four years might be considered, in accordance with the recommendations made earlier in Chapter 7 *supra*.

Learning from the Scandinavian Experience

Some Western European nations, most notably Norway and others within the Scandinavian group of countries, already have mediation processes, such as that suggested here, incorporated within their criminal justice processes. These were not, however, implemented without some structural modification during the early stages of their development. The reasons for this require some explanation at this stage of the discussion.

The traditional preference within the countries comprising the Scandinavian bloc within North-Western Europe, and in Norway in particular, was originally the principle of devolving the administration of criminal justice to a marked extent away from central government control and towards regions and municipalities. The philosophical basis for this form of decentralisation was to encourage a communitarian participation in the justice process at local level, and this was reflected strongly in the establishment of the national Mediation Service within that country in the Municipal Mediation Service Act 1991. One of the main architects of this philosophy was the widely respected criminologist Nils Christie whose writing, dating back to the late-1970s, significantly influenced such a development (Christie, 1977 and later 2004 in particular).

In fact, as Per Andersen has indicated (2013:484-5), the devolved initiative largely failed because the municipalities perceived criminal justice administration as a state task, and were also ambivalent about the concept of restorative practices as expressed in the Mediation Act as an alternative strategy for crime control or reduction, over which they might have established ownership. If this was unfortunate, it was also due, in part, to the fact that structural changes in the nature of local communities during the last two decades of the twentieth century had resulted in the migration of many of the younger working age population to the cities in pursuit of more affluent and contemporary lifestyles.

As has also been evident in many Western European nations of the post-modern era, the concept of 'community' has changed considerably over recent decades with the expansion of urbanisation in and around cities as centres of housing, employment, education and recreation. Many occupants of suburban areas and housing estates have no particular sense of civic affinity with neighbours or neighbourhoods, but retain and rely upon more distanced ties with close family and relations widely dispersed from their places of origin.

The result of these developments in Norway proved to be the centralisation of responsibility for, and control of the Mediation Service as a national entity under the *aegis* of the Ministry of Justice. Christie's original prescription for a significant extent of local autonomy over the resolution of both criminal and civil disputes and offences became, effectively, an almost romantic pipe-dream of a bygone age. The wider question for this work remains that of whether this situation was either inevitable or ultimately desirable.

With the benefit of hindsight it might be contended that the drafting of the 1991 Act in Norway was conceptually flawed because it confused the relationship between the Mediation Service as a devolved organisational entity and the Ministry of Justice as the centralised state controller of the criminal justice system. In such a situation, as Andersen has suggested, it was unrealistic for the municipalities to be expected to assume responsibility for delivery of a service over which they did not exercise ultimate control.

On the one hand, whether or not the concept of 'communities' within post-modern democracies is illusory or outdated remains a moot matter open to considerable discussion. The recent upsurge in international terrorism within Western Europe and its member nations, and the aftermath of these incidents, suggests strongly that in times of crisis the immediately affected communities still spontaneously unite in grief, concern for those harmed, and support for bereaved families and for each other. Communal expressions of solidarity and cohesion require a unifying purpose to generate and energise responses and awareness of need, but where no consciousness of necessity for cohesiveness is widely felt or considered necessary, social solidarity becomes weakened and fragmented.

On the other hand, in many contemporary societies and their criminal justice systems there exists a public perception that where processes are centralised and state-controlled in a bureaucratic manner these become remote from, and beyond the ownership of the population. The protective behaviours of civil servants shield these policies from external participation, and make revision or reform difficult to accomplish. However, if a considerable extent of public involvement is necessary for effective functioning of the processes, then their operational control has to be devolved to entities closer to the *locus* of delivery. This inevitably involves a risk that the policies or procedures become 'customised' or 'localised' to some or another extent, and uniformity of the practices becomes degraded.

Balancing these alternatives is a matter of public interest if community justice is to become a reality. Effective community justice absolutely implies a considerable extent of lay participation and voluntarism that still has to be financially backed by central revenue distribution. This in turn suggests that, to use a traditional Scottish analogy, 'he who pays the piper calls the tune'. However, to extend the musical analogy, if the party is to be a success the payee has to be satisfied only that the piper is paid and allow those participating in the dance to decide which tune is played.

Delivery of community justice requires the state to make a reasoned investment in the delivery process at an administrative level below that of centralised control. Now, while it is entirely reasonable that the state should require and ensure that the piper is musically competent to a verifiable extent[7] and that the nature of the music to be played is in every respect appropriate, it must then permit the dance to continue without further overt interference. It is for all of these reasons that the prescription for community justice in England and Wales proposed in this work has been set at the area level of public administration in the form of Community Justice Forums (CJFs) under the chairmanship of Area Police and Crime Commissioners (PCCs) as suggested in Chapter 7 (see *supra*).

The Pipers and the Dancers

Since the central purpose of community justice is to reduce crime rather than to deter it, CJFs should be designed to bring together those organisations and entities whose primary interest as stakeholders is in crime reduction within their areas of operation. *Figure* 8:2 provides an indication of the span of these organisations within geographic areas that might actively contribute to this purpose. Selection of PCCs as independently elected public officials as chair persons would ensure that CJFs remained non-partisan, while at the same time adding a measure of accountability for their performance to central government (see Figure 8:2 and below).

Though at first sight the span of potential interests in community justice appears to be wide, the core work of CJFs could be handled by Standing Committees and a small secretariat meeting at regular intervals and more frequently than the full membership. CJFs could also delegate various aspects of their work to sub-committees with appropriately co-opted participation drawn from the full forum membership.

7 Such is to suggest accreditation at a national level of professional competence having completed training to assured standards of qualification.

Figure 8.2 Suggested Membership for a Community Justice Forum (CJF)

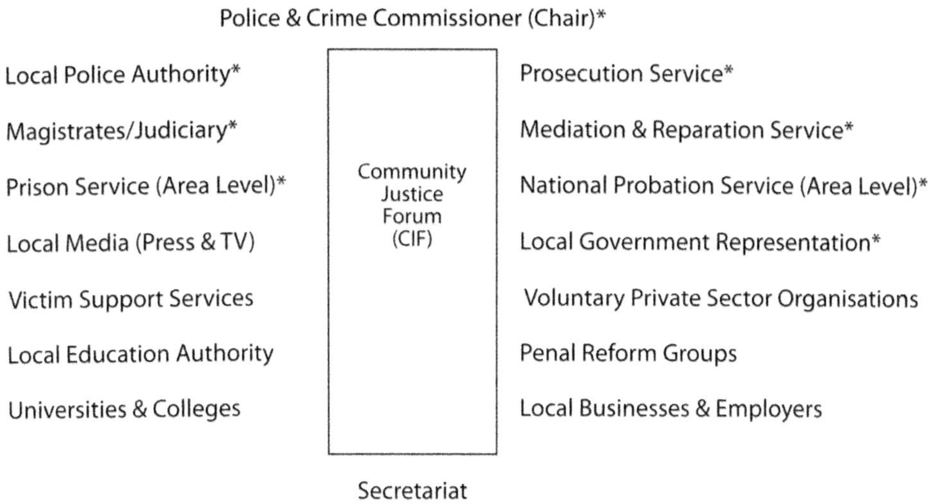

* Indicates Standing Committee Membership

One practical difficulty that would have to be overcome in this prescription is the fact that as matters presently stand in England and Wales, PCCs are accountable to the Home Secretary rather than the Minister of Justice for the conduct of their official duties.[8] As the footnote indicates, however, this situation may not be as insurmountable as might at first sight be imagined. Indeed, since both ministers are members of the Cabinet Committee on Crime and the Criminal Justice System (CCCCJS), a measure of joint accountability for PCCs might even be desirable and advantageous at the highest level of state administration.

If such an arrangement were to prevail, these ministers would become the pipers in our musical analogy, and the CJFs the dancers, with the Mediation and Prosecution Services cast somewhat in the role of joint masters of ceremonies. A structure of this nature might overcome some of the difficulties of municipal *versus* national ownership of CJFs as experienced in the Norwegian experience cited by Andersen and described previously.

---

8 The Home Secretary is the Minister of State responsible, *inter alia*, for policing in England and Wales in addition to Homeland Security, borders and immigration policies. For a more detailed analysis of the relationship between the Home Secretary and the Justice Secretary see Gibson, 2009 *op. cit.*:81-2. The Home Secretary is, however, a member of the Cabinet Committee on Crime and the Criminal Justice System (CCCCJS) as is the Justice Secretary, so a measure of joint accountability to both in relation to the role of PCCs might be manageable within that committee.

The overall structure for criminal justice administration in England and Wales in this new millennium is an extremely complex affair, having its roots in both antiquity and modernity. To the outside observer it defies description as a 'system' due to the involvement of so many different departments of state in its operational practices, and thus differing lines of accountability to parliament for the day to day delivery of its services. This somewhat confusing situation need not detain the reader of this work since a detailed account of its working practices would occupy a complete volume of explanation which would serve to confuse rather than clarify the issues described here. Formation of the Ministry of Justice in 2007 resulted in some clarification of the roles of the principal participants in the criminal justice process, but the relationships between the various ministries involved in the delivery of justice remain intricate and even confusing to the lay person.[9]

TOWARDS UNIFIED CORRECTIONAL SERVICES

In previous work (Cornwell, 2006; 2007; 2009 and most recently 2016 all *passim*) the case has been made for the urgent need in England and Wales to re-structure the existing custodial and non-custodial penal complex into a unified correctional service. The need has arisen because both the present Prison and Probation Services have existed for at least two decades in a state of perpetual crisis, their resource capacities overloaded, and their morale in danger of disintegration. Neither of these services can be described as 'fit for purpose' in reducing crime and recidivism as matters currently stand, and both have been subjected to severe financial retrenchment which has threatened their required operational effectiveness to an unacceptable extent.

This situation has arisen for a number of reasons, foremost among which has been political ambivalence and prevarication in penal policy-making due, in considerable measure, to persistence with ideological preferences for increasingly punitive crime control measures grounded in incapacitation and deterrence for electoral expediency.[10] It is also due to failure in successive administrations since 1995 to place limitations on the extent of the prison population, the use by the judiciary of short prison sentences, and an escalation in length of sentences in all determinate sentence bands.

9 Such as those between the Home Secretary, Justice Secretary, Attorney General, Lord Chief Justice, Director of Public Prosecutions and a number of others. For some clarification of these roles see Gibson, 2009 *op. cit.: passim*.

10 Evident in provisions such as those for extended sentences (ESPP) and increasing use of indeterminate imprisonment, combined with decreased use of Release on Temporary Licence (ROTL) for low and medium risk prisoners as previously noted.

It is, however, a matter of note that during the period in which this work has neared completion (in March 2017), the National Offender Management Service (NOMS) of the Ministry of Justice has been re-named HM Prison and Probation Service. A Prisons and Courts Bill 2017 was introduced in parliament in February 2017 seeking, *inter alia*, changes in prison management, court practices and the treatment of witnesses in cases of domestic violence. The bill has since been abandoned by the government in the run-up to the June general election. It would be encouraging to believe that the re-naming of NOMS signalled a genuine desire on the part of government to integrate the two services into a single correctional entity, thus visibly closing the considerable gap that presently exists between custodial and community justice. Realistically, however, this might be just one further instance of '*plus ça change*' in the history of the penal process in England and Wales.[11]

Unification of correctional services will depend to a considerable extent upon making prisons more open to community involvement, and making communities (and the media) more amenable to the involvement of prisons and their occupants in reparative community work participation as a means of their restoration to full and law-abiding citizenship. This requires development of an effective and mutually acceptable partnership between the two services to work together to deliver better justice rather than from different professional motivations. It is also in the interests of communities to participate in this process since it is within them that most imprisoned people must return on release from custody. Whether or not prisons can effectively rehabilitate prisoners within their boundaries, it remains a fact that more than 90% of all prisoners will eventually return to communities, and the better prepared they are for their release the better their chances of avoiding re-offending.

It is also an established fact that the longer people spend in prisons, the more likely they are to fail on release.[12] Insistence upon imposing increasingly lengthy prison sentences beyond that which is strictly necessary, and for the purposes of deterrence and retribution,

11 If only because historically there has existed a deeply entrenched difference in ethos between the two services, their *raisons d'être*, and their *modi operandi*. The Prison Service, dating back to the mid-eighteenth century, has always maintained a *quasi*-militaristic disciplinary structure of conduct, many of its members being traditionally recruited from the Armed Forces. The Probation Service was formally established in the Probation of Offenders Act 1907, though its history prior to that formation dates back to the practice of courts 'binding over' offenders with sureties to be of good behaviour, first used in Boston, USA and in England during the 1880s (see: Jordan, 1983:184). In the 1907 Act, probation officers were charged with 'advising, assisting and befriending' offenders placed under their supervision by the courts, frequently as an alternative to imprisonment. The Probation Service thus has a social work ethos relying much more upon persuasion than coercion.

12 Predominantly because the closed environment of prisons 'institutionalises' their occupants by reducing their self-reliance and autonomy, and relieves them of all responsibility other than to conform to regimes that provide for all their daily needs. Many offenders serving longer sentences leave prison unable to deal adequately and independently with their survival needs on a daily basis, or compete effectively in the employment market and earn a sufficient income without public welfare support.

effectively enhances the chances of failure and the likelihood of recidivism. It is for this reason in particular that abandonment of short prison sentences should now be seriously considered if crime reduction is the over-arching purpose of the criminal justice process.

The concept of CJFs is designed to actively encourage community involvement in partnership with the justice process, rather than to expect that process to function effectively in isolation from the real life of the every-day world. This should be done in a structured manner that increases public confidence while at the same time reducing the public risk caused by re-offending with its very considerable costs against national expenditure. Public confidence in the delivery of justice could be significantly enhanced by the visible inclusion of mediation and reparation procedures as a means of resolving lower level crime issues within community boundaries. Victims of crime would be seen to be dealt with in a more considerate manner than at present, and offenders seen to be making amends for the harm caused to them in an evident and constructive manner.

In the final chapter of this book an attempt will be made to draw together all the strands of this work, and return to the true nature of Philip Bean's assertion about the deterrence doctrine and its impact upon criminal justice in the contemporary world of correctional theory and practice. That it has proved to be a malign influence is, it could be claimed, evident in what has been recorded in the foregoing chapters. What remains to be done is to suggest how this influence, which is almost universally accepted as an irrefragable aspect of criminal justice, might be mitigated to an acceptable extent.

9 Better Justice or Future Uncertainty?

Learning from the Lessons of the Past

Within the chapters of this book we have traced the development of the deterrence doctrine from its early sixteenth century formulation to the present day. Having done so, it seems reasonable to assert that the early writers on the subject perceived deterrence within the criminal justice punishment process primarily as a means of social control within their disorderly societies in which the poor, the feckless and the ill-educated under-classes represented a significant threat to social stability. That these societies were largely un-policed – particularly in England and Wales – until the nineteenth century placed justice very much in the hands of local officials (such as magistrates) and travelling justices of assize.

From the early seventeenth century onwards, policing in Britain was carried out by parish constables elected by parishioners, and appointed by magistrates. It was not until the nineteenth century that formal police forces were established in England, initially in London and subsequently within the counties throughout the country.[1] During this period also, apart from the frequent use of hanging as the prevailing form of capital punishment, the practice of transportation as a form of expulsion became widely used between Britain and its overseas colonies – principally North America, Australasia and the Caribbean (Forsythe, 1983:223-5).[2] The point of note here is that in its heyday transportation was widely regarded as the principal deterrent punishment available to the courts as a means of dealing with, and expelling, those found guilty of serious crime, persistent vagrancy and certain forms

1 The term 'constable' is of ancient origin throughout Western Europe, but the roles of these unpaid officials differed considerably from jurisdiction to jurisdiction. Constables were originally to be found in English towns that had a duty to make horses and armaments available to the crown, and thus these constables were primarily 'ostlers' or stable workers who maintained horses ready for military service, and the armour of those who rode them in battle. Constables as police officers in Britain remained 'keepers of the local peace' on a largely unpaid basis until the nineteenth century when formal policing became established in the Metropolitan Police Act 1829 and the County Police Act 1839. Thereafter, constables of varying ranks were full-time officials, sworn to their duty, and paid annual salaries. They had powers of arrest and detention of criminals to be tried in the courts, and were charged with patrolling duties within towns to maintain order and protect the public.

2 Transportation was used as a punishment for felonies (serious crimes), persistent vagrancy, subversive sedition, and for those cases in which the death penalty was reprieved in favour of lengthy imprisonment. Those transported were conveyed in ships to their destinations where they were used as forced labour until the expiry of their Transportation Orders – normally issued for seven years, fourteen years or life. Many survived this ordeal and became settlers in their new countries rather than return to Britain if they could afford the fare. The practice of transportation was eventually abandoned in 1867 with the increasing reluctance of the colonial administrations to accept further transported criminals on the basis of the cost of doing so. Here see also generally: A.G.L. Shaw, *Convicts and the Colonies*, London: Faber & Faber, 1966.

of seditious behaviour. To an extent this policy backfired on Britain insofar as those thus banished might otherwise have become a much needed source of manual labour within the home economy.[3] The deterrent effect of transportation was also significantly reduced by the fact that many of those transported actually welcomed the opportunity that it made available to escape from poverty and start a new life in more convivial surroundings.

Returning to Phillip Bean's assessment of the deterrence doctrine (page 1 *supra* and *passim*), it becomes clear that on an historical basis at least, the concept of deterrence was originally conceived as a sociological theory based on social control. Unruly and largely impoverished populations of uneducated and menial people and vagrants under feudal systems of social subjugation had to be frightened into compliance with the wishes of the dominant ruling classes who needed their labour for their own survival. Intermittent rebellions such as the Peasants Revolt of 1381 in Southern England were ruthlessly crushed by the forces of the crown, and their leaders publicly executed as a deterrent example to others who might be tempted to behave in a similar manner.

Similar instances are recorded in Germany and France during the same period,[4] and also somewhat later within the turbulent life histories of Hugo Grotius and Samuel von Pufendorf briefly recorded in Chapter 1. With barbaric forms of retribution high on the agendas of monarchs and rulers of the period, deterrence, if it was even conceived as a grand theory and component of criminal punishment, was at best a subsidiary issue within the pursuit of social control. The works of Locke, Beccaria, Bentham and Mill outlined in the same chapter tend to reinforce this assertion, though as the nineteenth century dawned increasing emphasis upon the need for prison reform and centralisation reflected the impact of the Enlightenment era upon national social structures and institutions.

At which stage in the development of penology in Europe the concept of deterrence achieved the status of a psychological theory remains unclear. Evidently, it started out in the belief that deterrent policies and practices would prove to be amenable to measurable and quantifiable outcomes using statistical research techniques. However, as became apparent in Chapter 2, there was an extent of wishful thinking in such an approach and the outcomes of the research that was attempted were, to say the least, equivocal as Gibbs (1975 *op. cit.*)

3 It has been estimated that by the time transportation ended in 1867 with the introduction of penal servitude in the Penal Servitude Acts of 1853 and 1857, the ships used to transport convicts had carried more than 108,000 people to the Australian continent alone since 1800.

4 Here, see: J.M. Bennett & C.W. Hollister, *Medieval Europe: A Short History*, New York: McGraw-Hall, 2006, *passim*. In the various states of Germany between 1336 and 1525 there were some sixty incidents of peasant unrest, focused mainly upon the conditions of the labouring underclass and their remuneration (Bickle, 1988 *passim*). Similar incidents occurred in Flanders 1323-28 and Northern France 1356-58.

indicated so clearly. There is, to this time, no substantial evidence that this situation has changed.

This much stated, however, there was in the earlier writings of Sutherland (1924 *op. cit.*), Ewing (1929 *op. cit.*), Andenaes (1952 *op. cit.*), and Becker (1968 *op. cit.*) among others, an evident acceptance that deterrence had a rightful place within the philosophy of criminal punishment. Unquantifiable as it might be in operational effect, much space was afforded within the philosophical literature of the post-World War 2 period to the inclusion of deterrence within its extensive debates.[5]

The question that arose to trouble and even to haunt the philosophical explanations and justifications of criminal punishment was that of where, precisely, the deterrence doctrine as articulated differently by many of the leading scholars fitted within the punishment debate. Some perceived it as axiomatically tied to the retributive function of sanctions; others as an altogether more forward-looking concept designed to negate the necessity for extensive and excessive punishment. It was in this particular respect that the general and specific components of the deterrence doctrine almost collided.

The twentieth century was to prove a turbulent era within criminological history. Immediately pre- and post-World War 2, the combined literature of established sociology, philosophy and the emergent science of criminology became replete with explanations of crime causation, the impact of increasing urbanisation, and social dislocation. The debate about the purposes of criminal punishment among the leading scholars of the period reflected the changing attitudes within the national institutions in response to rising crime rates as post-war societies became more affluent and the differences of wealth distribution and amenity between the various social classes became more marked.[6]

During the first three decades of the post-war period (1945-1975) criminal justice processes almost worldwide underwent a period of transition during which emphasis on predominantly retributive punishment gave way to the welfare focused and *quasi*-medical model of the 'treatment and training' concept. With its belief that crime could be 'cured' and criminal lives transformed by therapeutic intervention and remedial education combined with instruction in basic industrial trades, the model encouraged the use of indeterminate sentences, release from which became a matter of executive discretion exercised by civil servants on the recommendation of prison professionals. During this phase, deterrence

5 See: Acton, 1969 *op. cit., passim.*
6 For a fascinating and comprehensive account of British national life during that particular period see: David Kynaston, *Tales of New Jerusalem 1945-1979*, [Four volumes], London: Bloomsbury Press, 2007.

had a relatively low profile within the hierarchy of criminal punishment purposes, predicated largely on the tacit assumption that 'changed' lives would desist from further crime as a consequence of corrective treatment and industrial training.

As we have seen in Chapter 3, however, by the early 1970s faith in the 'rehabilitative ethic' of the treatment and training model was declining rapidly in America and subsequently in Europe. This was due largely to the AFSC Report 1972 (see *supra*) and the pessimistic analysis of treatment programmes recorded by Martinson (1975 *op. cit.*) and Lipton *et al.* (1975 *op. cit.*). In 1976 the influential Committee for the Study of Incarceration Report *Doing Justice: The Choice of Punishments* (von Hirsch, 1976 *op. cit.*) strongly condemned the rehabilitative model for its cruelty and injustice, and urged its replacement by a 'justice model' of corrections based upon a return to retributive sentencing with a renewed emphasis on general deterrence, denunciation and incapacitation. Now, once again, deterrence was to be re-instated as a primary purpose of criminal punishment.

Though, as was also noted in the same chapter, the justice model was welcomed by the 'law and order' lobbies in Europe and America, it signalled a return to punitive sentencing and increasing use of imprisonment for longer periods of time and also severe restrictions on parole and temporary release from prisons. This in turn led to escalating prison populations in overcrowded accommodation, and subsequently to widespread incidents of rioting and unrest in British and American prisons in the mid-1970s and onwards as a response to conditions and considerably reduced regimes. By the end of the 1980s the 'prison crisis' in England and Wales had become 'business as usual', culminating in the Strangeways siege at Manchester in April 1990.[7]

As Chapter 3 further recorded, from 1993 onwards in England and Wales there occurred what Cavadino and Dignan (1997:5 *op. cit.*) described as the 'law and order counter-revolution' with its emphasis on retributive incapacitation and deterrence which restored these purposes of criminal punishment to pride of place in the political agenda for the decade to follow. The result was seen in an escalation in sentence lengths which drove up the daily penal population from just below 50,000 in 1993 to over 76,000 a decade later (see *Figure* 3.1 *supra*). To make matters even worse, the aftermath of two notorious prison escapes in late 1994 and early 1995 plunged the Prison Service into turmoil, leading to the dismissal of its much respected Director General Derek Lewis in the following October.

7 Here see the account in Adams, 1992 *op. cit.*, *passim* for a comprehensive description of the onset of rioting in British and American prisons during the late 1970s and onwards.

Crime Control versus Crime Reduction

The situation described above left few options for penal policy reform as the new millennium began. Ultimately the choice had to be made about whether crime control or crime reduction was to become the dominant purpose of criminal justice in England and Wales. In Chapter 4 it became evident that this particular issue dominated the penal agenda, and the discussion focused on the implications of that situation. Crime control, whether achievable or not, implied measures to increase the use and duration of prison sentences with a corresponding decrease of emphasis on non-custodial sanctions. It also required an expansion of prison capacity at considerable financial cost at a time of increasing pressure to reduce national borrowing through fiscal retrenchment in the provision of public services such as health, education and infrastructural development. If public and media confidence in the justice process was to be maintained, then a larger number of offenders had to be taken out of circulation without any significant concern for changing their lives through rehabilitative assistance and preparation unless overcrowding of prisons could be significantly reduced.

On the other hand, crime reduction ultimately had to focus on reducing post-sentence recidivism in particular, and its cost to the national economy. This would demand a multi-faceted approach requiring a seamless 'bridge' between custodial and community corrections, a unification of custodial and non-custodial correctional services, and genuine community involvement in the process. It would also require substantial resource investment in community justice rather than in prison expansion. Fundamentally, therefore, whatever measures were to be taken, the risk: gain calculus of criminal offending had to be re-balanced in favour of law-abiding rather than criminal behaviour.

Victims of Criminal Justice

Mixed in with this dilemma were the promises made by successive governments from 1996 onwards that, in the new millennium, victims of crime would receive greater consideration within the justice process, not only as potential prosecution witnesses but also as those most harmed by criminal behaviour. In the closing section of Chapter 4 it became evident that delivery of these pledges and compliance with the Europe-wide initiative to ensure its inclusion within statute law became a matter of vacillation and eventual derogation as the United Kingdom opted out of its responsibility to implement by November 2012.[8]

8 Here see in particular the discussion included in the concluding part of Chapter 4 and the beginning of Chapter 5.

The most striking development in relation to victims of crime that occurred during the first decade of the new century was a legislative measure within the Criminal Justice Act 2003 to introduce the 'victim surcharge' described in some detail in Chapter 5 and Table 5:1 *supra*. It is interesting to speculate whether this measure was, when implemented progressively from 2007 onwards, a genuine attempt to support victims of crime, or rather a means of revenue earning to offset the increasing costs of expanding the custodial penal system in England and Wales, combined with a deliberate attempt to increase the deterrent component of penal sanctions.

Of the £51 million that the surcharge was claimed, by the Ministry of Justice, to have raised between 2010 and 2014, disbursements of some £15.2 million were made to fund new non-governmental organisations to provide 'support services' for crime victims between 2011 and 2014, but it is evident that little or none of the net surplus of £35.7 million was paid directly in compensation to the victims themselves. It also remains entirely unclear how the surcharge is recovered from offenders sentenced to immediate imprisonment during their time spent in prison.

Offenders have also become victims of criminal justice to a considerable extent during the past two decades in England and Wales. Overcrowded prisons result in reductions to regimes that address offending behaviour, most particularly for those sentenced to short (two years or less) custodial sentences. Restrictions on the use of, and risk-aversion in relation to temporary release make it almost impossible to bridge the 'custody and community' gap that, if made seamless, could actively assist in reducing recidivism. Continued use of such sentences now urgently requires serious re-consideration with a view to reducing or even abandoning the use of short term imprisonment altogether on the basis that it is evidently more harmful than useful in human terms, and counter-productive in its costs to the economy. This much became evidently clear within the discussion in Chapter 5. To make matters even worse, it emerges with considerable certainty from the analysis of that chapter and those preceding it that the deterrence doctrine as presently conceived, both in theory and in operation, fails significantly to achieve either crime control or crime reduction.

Looking to the Future

The remaining chapters of this work have been devoted to the search for a new justice paradigm which could overcome and even reverse the present *malaise* in criminal justice in the future. Though there is much to be learned from the mistakes of the past, these cannot be undone and the future concept of criminal justice has to be advantageous to all its main stakeholders – victims, offenders and communities as well as the state. Deterrence theory also has to be recognised for what it is in reality: at best a speculative and largely unquantifiable notion that may have an emotional appeal, but is no basis upon which criminal punishment policies should be conceived.

In Chapter 6 the need to distance or separate deterrence from desistance was explained with the reasons for its necessity. Doing so would enable a consequentialist rather than a deontological approach to be taken in dealing with offenders and crime victims, with an emphasis on making their futures more secure, rather than focusing on past actions that cannot be undone other than in a remedial manner. It was proposed in this chapter that reparative justice provides a preferable paradigm for achieving future desistence and also for alleviating victim trauma that the present, essentially punitive, mode of justice simply cannot deliver.

Desistence from future offending requires offenders to be convinced that a law-abiding lifestyle is preferable to one of repetitive re-offending and increasingly punitive sanctions. Many offenders require guidance, access to education and skills acquisition, and actual employability to make this transition in their lives. Where and when possible, this is more likely to be successfully achieved in the real world of the community than in the isolation and criminalising environment of prison.

Encouraging desistence is an integral part of the process of rebalancing the risk: gain calculus in the perception of offenders who may never have considered it seriously in the course of previous offending, or who discounted it altogether. Though desistence might be perceived as being linked to the notion of deterrence, in a prospective consequentialist sense of inhibition, the desire for change has to come from within the offender as a preferred life pattern rather than as a result of being threatened with excessively punitive sanctions. Access to the process of reparative justice as described in Chapter 6 encourages change towards what Lode Walgrave (2008 *op. cit.*) has termed 'responsible citizenship' in offenders willing to take responsibility for the harm they have caused and make amends for it to crime victims and their communities.

In countries like the United Kingdom where parsimony in the use of criminal punishment is widely disregarded as a political strategy in pursuit of social control, excessive prison populations accumulate over time, and as a result penal reform can only be achieved by deliberate policies of reduction and the curbing of sentencing discretion. Chapter 7 was devoted to a discussion of how these trends can be reversed given the political will to create a consensus to do so. Drawing on the experience of the Scandinavian traditions of justice administration and the Finnish example of down-sizing its custodial penal population in particular, it became possible to envisage a bold strategy for reduction without significantly increased public risk.

This strategy was based upon two main components and the implementation of policies to make them effective in operation. The first was the virtual elimination of short sentences of imprisonment with effective custodial periods of two years or less by imposition of a 'custody threshold' in the courts; the second involved an alternative strategy for dealing with the remand prison population in secure accommodation adjacent to the Crown Courts, but not within prisons for convicted and sentenced offenders.

Delivery of Unified Correctional Services

These components envisaged two further strategic policies to deliver the new justice paradigm. The first of these was the establishment of reparative prisons for offenders willing to work to make reparation to victims and address their offending behaviour with a view to desistence in the future. The second was the creation of a truly unified Correctional Services[9] structure bridging the gap between prisons, probation services, and their local communities with the support of Community Justice Forums (CJFs) described in greater detail in Chapter 8.

The discussion at this stage required further elaboration of the concept of reparative justice and its implementation in prisons and communities. It also envisaged the creation of the new entities that would be necessary to make the new justice paradigm effective in operational practice. Chapter 8 then outlined the structural and procedural considerations that would enable the reformed justice process to become both systematic and capable of delivering crime reduction. Foremost among these recommendations was the creation of a National Mediation Service as part of the Ministry of Justice, transfer of un-convicted remand detainees to facilities operated by the Courts and Tribunals Service,[10] the organisation of CJFs, and the establishment of a network of reparative prisons. However, for more serious and long sentenced offenders, the present provision of traditional prisons would remain appropriate until at least the final stage of their sentence with its resettlement needs, providing that such prisons were free of overcrowding.

---

9 Principally comprising the existing Prison and Probation Services operating within areas with coterminous geographic boundaries and in partnership with Community Justice Forums (CJFs). Here see *Figure* 9:1.

10 Such facilities might be secure accommodation contracted out to the private sector, but ideally should be located close to the courts before which remand detainees would be brought for trial, where they would be held until convicted and sentenced.

Mediation in its criminal justice context requires the close collaboration of the prosecution authorities, the courts, and the Mediation Service in deciding which cases might be appropriately resolved through mediation, where both offenders and their victims are amenable to the process either directly or indirectly.[11] Considerable care has to be taken to ensure that victims are not subjected to further traumatisation during the mediation process, and that offenders do not perceive it as a means of evading the deserved extent of sanctions for the harm caused by their offences. Financial sums recovered in reparation by offenders should be remitted to the Victims of Crime General Fund administered by the Mediation Service as an agency of the Ministry of Justice, and thus accountable to parliament.[12]

The concept of unified correctional services implies a structural re-organisation of the various agencies that participate in the criminal justice process into a coherent and integrated system with the common purpose of administering justice through the combined rather than independent working of its constituent elements.[13] This structure is illustrated at *Figure* 9:1 below with the sole observation that in March 2017 the Prison and Probation Services were combined into a single entity as HM Prisons and Probation Service.

To what extent the recent 'marriage' of these two services will resolve their differences of professional ethos and operational structure remains to be seen. It also remains a matter of considerable doubt whether the outsourcing of responsibility for the post-sentence supervision of low and medium risk offenders from the Probation Service to private sector contracting entities will succeed in reducing subsequent recidivism and its prohibitive financial costs to any measurable extent.

---

11 Some cases can be resolved satisfactorily in face to face mediation where the parties are willing participants. Other cases may have to rely upon indirect mediation in which the mediator conducts the process as an independent and impartial go-between in contact with both parties in the negotiation of a settlement between them. It would then fall to prosecution officials to inform the court of the outcome, and make a recommendation as to whether the settlement should be accepted as part or all of the court's sentencing decision.

12 In some instances decisions made at the prosecution stage might make a recommendation to the criminal court that the case be diverted to the civil courts for hearing and disposal of a mediated outcome. Both criminal and civil courts would have the power to make Reparation Orders and impose additional sanctions on offenders with default penalties as appropriate.

13 For a more extensive explanation of such a structure see: Cornwell, 2016 *op. cit.*:94 and Chapter 9 – A Reparative Justice Model in particular.

Figure 9.1 A Strategic Model for Reparative Justice

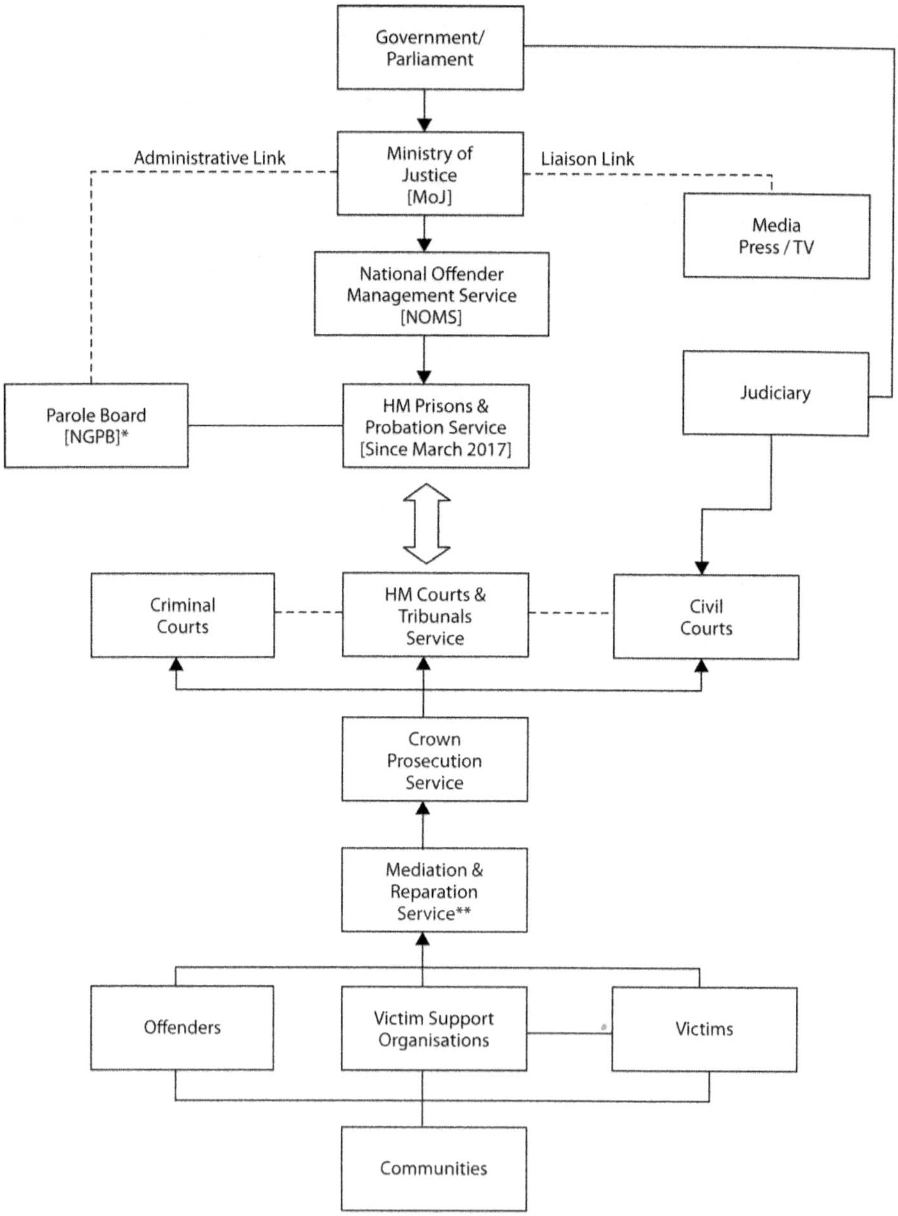

Note: * The Parole Board is a Non-Governmental Public Body [NGPB]
** Proposed Mediation & Reparation Service as an Agency of NOMS

Concluding Observations

Though, as has become evident throughout this book, perceptions of deterrence and its place within criminal justice have changed since the sixteenth century, its taken-for-granted status as a principal component of criminal punishment has rarely been robustly challenged. That deterrence theory has consistently defied rigorous empirical evaluation of its effectiveness is, however, beyond dispute. The reasons for this situation have emerged with clarity in this work.

Until the end of the seventeenth century criminal punishment remained a barbaric and largely public spectacle imposed by feudal rulers and their adherents and some ecclesiastical authorities on a predominantly retributive basis. If some would-be offenders were deterred as a result of witnessing such spectacles, such was not a primary purpose but rather a desirable outcome of the punitive process.

During the Enlightenment period of the eighteenth century described by Thomas Paine (1737-1809) and others subsequently as the Age of Reason,[14] the attention of social reformers began to focus on the human wastefulness of arbitrary and barbaric punishment practices. Alternative means of dealing with criminal offenders without killing or mutilating them began to gain acceptance, including in Britain the use of transportation to reduce the rising costs of imprisonment and maintain social order.

The nineteenth century witnessed the development of a new penology based, in Western Europe and America, largely upon religiously inspired reformative ethics and increasingly centralised state control of penal processes. During this period, the notion of deterrence became an almost dormant consideration within the administration of criminal punishment, overtaken by zealous ideas of human redemption and reformation.

Developments during the twentieth century and into this millennium have been traced as the central thesis of this work, and require only limited rehearsal here save to note the resurgence of interest in deterrence (in both its specific and general forms) during the pre- and post-World War 2 period onwards, and its entirely inconclusive outcomes in both empirical and operational terms. However, from such evidence-based research as is available, it becomes clear that increasing sanction severity and the use of short term imprisonment for deterrent purposes significantly fails to reduce recidivism, and probably encourages it.

---

14 See: Paine, T., *The Age of Reason*, Paris: Barrois & London: D.I. Eaton, 1794.

Criminal justice policies and practices are ultimately a matter of politics at governmental level. Politicians and their policy advisers are notoriously risk-averse and highly sensitive to media criticism – particularly in the field of criminal justice administration. Being considered to be 'soft on crime' heralds the imminent departure of many a justice minister from that office as the recent political history of England and Wales bears witness. Justice ministry officials repeatedly proclaim the need for policies to be based upon evidence-led research, but consistently fail to seek the advice and expertise of the academic faculties that could make such research available to them. This might be due in large part to the likelihood of being offered evidential advice that ministers might not wish to hear or consider.

The 'bottom line' as Michael Tonry (2003:6 *op. cit.*) so aptly pointed out is that 'current policies, political rhetoric and patterns are as they are because politicians, however motivated, wished it so. Looking on the bright side, that conclusion means that directions can change if politicians wish it so'. On the dark side, however, it seems that the British government is once again trying to build its way out of penal crisis rather than address its causes. Such a policy seems completely perverse in an era of financial retrenchment and reduction in public sector services and their delivery.

Continued pursuit of deterrence-based criminal justice policies and incapacitation drives up the costs of criminal justice and will continue to do so unnecessarily when other less damaging and socially more beneficial options are available. Reparative justice provides a more positive prescription for reducing dependence on imprisonment in particular, and of restoring the social purpose of prisons capable of fulfilling their stated mission of serving the public and changing the lives of offenders into those of law-abiding and responsible citizens.

What, then, is the future for deterrence theory? Surely, from all that has become evident within this book, it must be concluded that at best it remains just a theory with an intuitive appeal to punitive instincts, but nonetheless a theory based on an unsubstantial and mythical belief that it must be beneficial in controlling human behaviour. The substantial evidence of recidivism statistics strongly indicates the contrary. But can deterrence theory be justified on a moral philosophical basis, constructed as it is, as Ted Honderich (1976 *op. cit.*:51-65) so eloquently argued, on a set of suppositions which are tenable only on a somewhat tenuous circumstantial basis? Once again, the conclusion must be that it cannot be thus justified because it leaves more questions unanswered than it actually answers.

Of course it remains true that some offenders and would-be offenders will be deterred by the threat of punishment, but the statistical evidence points to the contrary especially when that punishment is short-term imprisonment. How many of these people are deterred and why remains shrouded in the mythical beliefs that sustain continuing political adherence to criminal deterrence as a basis for policies of crime control. Crime reduction might be more achievable if these myths were to be consigned to the status of historical irrelevance.

Finally, we should return to Philip Bean's assertion noted at the beginning of this book. Whether deterrence doctrine is a psychological theory based on threats, or a sociological theory based on social control actually appears to matter very little, if at all. That its effects are both malign and unquantifiable does matter considerably since it has given rise to increasingly counter-productive and punitive penal policies wasteful of human lives and resources. If nothing else, that has been demonstrated in this work and every thinking politician should read and consider it.

The title of this book was deliberately chosen to reveal its purpose. The historical survey indicated how the concept of criminal deterrence came into being. The post-World War 2 analysis of penal policies and punishment practices and their dysfunctional outcomes has exposed the myths and assumptions about deterrence upon which those policies were predicated. The reality of criminal deterrence is that, in combination with retributive and incapacitative approaches to justice administration, it fails to deliver either crime control or crime reduction. Until other more preferable means of dealing with criminal offenders are seriously explored, the existing penal crisis will continue to be 'business as usual', and at a cost that is both unaffordable and unnecessary. Reparative justice offers one potential means of alleviating this situation to the benefit of all the stakeholders in criminal justice – offenders, victims and communities.

One means of resolving the existing chaotic situation within the penal processes of England and Wales and building a consensus for radical reform remains unexplored at this time. It lies in the setting up of a truly independent Royal Commission on the Penal System to examine and identify the causes and effects of the existing crisis, its costs in social, human and economic terms, and propose a blueprint for reform having carefully considered the potential of alternative strategies for delivering better justice including that of reparative and restorative justice proposed and discussed in this work.[15] In this way the history, myths and realities of perpetuating reliance upon deterrence theory could be fully exposed to

15 Here it is suggested with a Chairperson of eminent reputation without parliamentary or judicial status, but with a thorough understanding of the history and practical working of the courts and the entire criminal justice system of England and Wales. The membership of the Commission to be drawn from the principal stakeholders in criminal justice delivery including, but not limited to, representatives of the Judiciary, Ministry of Justice, HM Prison and Probation Service, The Parole Board, Police, Academic Centres of Criminology, Psychology and Psychiatry, Penal Reform Groups, Victim Support Organisations, Inter-Faith Groups and the Media.

serious debate, and the way opened up for a more humane, effective and less wasteful justice system to be adopted in the future.

All that has been recorded in this work indicates the necessity of lifting the debate over penal reform to a national level above that of partisan parliamentary politics and media sensationalism of crime which have so evidently contributed to the existing crisis rather than resolving it for several decades past. As my friend and colleague Dr. John Blad from the Netherlands once described the situation:

> 'Criminal justice seems to me to have come to resemble an old hospital that should be demolished because it has collected so many viruses that it is, in fact, pathogenic. Some of the viruses that infect criminal *procedure* .. have become present because the focus or aim of criminal procedure is deliberately to cause pain. The root cause is not the desire to do justice, but our misconceptions about, and misuse of punishment' (Blad, 2006:135).

His wise words provide a fitting epitaph for this work.

Postscript

In concluding this work and reflecting upon those that have preceded it dealing with criminal punishment from different perspectives, there seems to be little more that I can usefully add to this particular and complex debate. Without doubt it remains a contentious issue morally, philosophically, sociologically and politically in our post-modern world in which expediency has become a dominating influence, possibly above all else, in many aspects of national governance almost everywhere. This is a saddening aspect of contemporary 'civilisation' that exercises a marginalising effect on considerations of what is the 'good' which lies at the heart of all rigorous philosophical enquiry.

Undeniably, crime has an almost universal impact upon the fiscal economies of nation states and the quality of life of their citizens. The science of criminology is, or at least should be, devoted to the serious study of crime as a social phenomenon, its causal aetiology, and its prevention or reduction. In this particular respect it represents a potentially valuable adjunct to effective government and social equilibrium. But crime is also a reflection of social dissonance which has causes deeply embedded in the social structure, and in its relative distributions of status, equality, opportunity and affluence between citizens. Poverty in its various forms[1] arises from mal-distributions of these life-enhancing qualities of citizenship.

Lesser eligibility remains a significant issue in many contemporary societies. Circumstances of birth, nurture (or the lack of it) and subsequent development have a major influence upon access to opportunities and success in adulthood. Children raised in deprived environmental conditions, without effective parental and moral guidance and encouragement, become prone to failure even though, individually, they may have innate abilities which are not recognised or fostered. Sadly, too many of these disadvantaged youngsters become attracted to dishonesty and crime as a means of 'equalising' their perceptions of social marginalisation. As the British sociologist Joe Sim once cogently described their situation: 'When You Ain't Got Nothing, You Got Nothing To Lose'.[2] As importantly, once a person has a criminal record the downward spiral of disadvantage and exclusion all too frequently develops into a lifestyle of increasing criminality.

---

1 Such is to suggest poverty expressed and experienced predominantly in parental, financial, environmental, emotional, educational, dietary and general health terms.

2 Title of a paper presented by Joe Sim at the British Criminology Conference held at the University of York in 1992 and reprinted in K. Bottomley, T. Fowles & R. Reiner (Eds.), *Criminal Justice: Theory and Practice*, London: British Society of Criminology, 1992, pp.273-300.

This work has focused on the failure and futility of criminal justice policies grounded in retribution and deterrence as a means of reversing the situation described above, most particularly in relation to 'lower level' criminality. Imprisoning young and relatively less serious offenders with increasing severity in the supposed interests of either general or individual deterrence results in 'making bad people worse', at very considerable expense and with adverse social consequences. The concept and principles of reparative and restorative justice and mediation outlined in this work provide a blueprint for 'doing justice better' and for repairing the damaged lives of offenders, victims and communities who are most affected by crime. It is a message that politicians and judiciaries alike have proved remarkably reluctant to accept for fear of being perceived as 'soft on crime' and suffering consequent loss of credibility. It is, however, a message with considerable resonance for the well-being of civilised democratic societies and which, if it continues to be resisted, will ultimately rebound upon and discredit those who continue to ignore its potential.

Guide to British Prime Ministers & Home Secretaries/Justice Ministers 1945-2017

DATES	PRIME MINISTERS	HOME SECRETARIES
1945-51	Clement Attlee (Lab)	Donald Somervell 1945 James Ede 1945-51
1951-55	Winston Churchill (Con)	David Maxwell Fyfe 1951-54 Gwylym Lloyd George 1954-57
1955-57	Anthony Eden (Con)	
1957-63	Harold Macmillan (Con)	R.A. Butler 1957-62
1963-64	Alec Douglas-Home (Con)	Henry Brooke 1962-64
1964-70	Harold Wilson (Lab)	Roy Jenkins 1964-67 James Callaghan 1967-70
1970-74	Edward Heath (Con)	Reginald Maudling 1970-72 Robert Carr 1972-74
1974-76	Harold Wilson (Lab)	Roy Jenkins 1974-76
1976-79	James Callaghan (Lab)	Merlyn Rees 1976-79
1979-90	Margaret Thatcher (Con)	William Whitelaw 1979-83 Leon Brittan 1983-85 Douglas Hurd 1985-89 David Waddington 1989-90
1990-97	John Major (Con)	Kenneth Baker 1990-92 Kenneth Clarke 1992-93 Michael Howard 1993-97
1997-07	Tony Blair (Lab)	Jack Straw 1997-2001 David Blunkett 2001-04 Charles Clarke 2004-06 John Reid 2006-07
2007-10	Gordon Brown (Lab)	Jacqui Smith (2007)
		JUSTICE SECRETARIES Charles Falconer 2007 Jack Straw 2007-10
2010-16	David Cameron (Con)	Kenneth Clarke 2010-12 Chris Grayling 2012-15 Michael Gove 2015-16
2016-	Theresa May (Con)	Elizabeth Truss 2016-2017 David Lidington 2017 -

Bibliography

Acton, H.B. (Ed.), *The Philosophy of Punishment: A Collection of Papers*, London: Macmillan, 1969.

Adams, R., *Prison Riots in Britain and the USA*, Macmillan Press, 1992.

Advisory Council on the Penal System (ACPS), *Non-Custodial and Semi-Custodial Penalties*, London: HMSO, 1970.

Advisory Council on the Penal System (ACPS), *The Length of Prison Sentences*, London: HMSO, 1977.

Aebi, M. & Delgrande, N., *Council of Europe Annual Penal Survey 2012*, Strasbourg: Council of Europe, 2014.

American Friends Service Committee (AFSC), *Struggle for Justice*, New York: Hill & Wang, 1972.

Andenaes, J., 'General Prevention – Illusion or Reality?' in *Journal of Criminal Law, Criminology and Police Science*, 43, July-August, 1952, pp.176-198.

Andersen, P., 'Development of Restorative Justice Practices in Norway', in D.J. Cornwell, J.R.Blad & M. Wright (Eds.), *Civilising Criminal Justice: An International Restorative Agenda for Penal Reform*, Hook, Hampshire: Waterside Press, 2013, pp.479-499.

Armstrong, K.G. 'The Retributivist Hits Back', in H.B. Acton (Ed.), *The Philosophy of Punishment*, London: Macmillan, 1969, pp.130-137.

Ashcraft, R., *Locke's Two Treatises of Government*, London: Unwin Hymen Ltd, 1987.

Auld, Sir R. (LJ), *Review of the Criminal Courts of England and Wales – Report*, London: The Stationery Office, 2001.

Bader, E., 'The Psychology of Mediation, Part 1, The Mediator's Issues of Self and Identity', *10 Pepperdine Dispute Resolution Law Journal*, 183, 2010.

Barnett, R.E., 'Restitution: A New Paradigm in Criminal Justice', in *Journal of Ethics*, Vol.87, 1999, pp.279-301.

Bean, P., *Punishment: A Philosophical and Criminological Inquiry*, Oxford: Martin Robertson, 1981.

Beccaria, C., *Dei Delitte e delle Pene – On Crimes and Punishment*, 1764, [Tr. H. Paolucci], Indianapolis: Bobbs Merrill, 1963.

Becker, G.S., 'Crime and Punishment: An Economic Approach', in *Journal of Political Economy*, Vol.76, No.2, 1968 (Mar-Apr), pp.169-217.

Becker, H.S., *Outsiders: Studies in the Sociology of Deviance*, New York: Free press of Glencoe, 1963.

Becker, H.S. (Ed.), *The Other Side*, New York: Free Press Macmillan. 1964.

Bennett, J.M. & Hollister, C.W., *Medieval Europe: A Short History*, New York: McGraw-Hall, 2006.

Bentham, J., *The Rationale of Reward*, London: John and H.L. Hunt, 1825.

Bentham, J., *Rationale of Judicial Evidence*, J.S. Mill (Ed.), [Five Volumes], London: Hunt & Clarke, Covent Garden, 1827.

Bickle, P., *Unruhen in der Ständischen Gesellschaft 1300-1800*, Munich: Oldenburg, 1988.

Blad, J.R., 'The Seductiveness of Punishment and the Case for Restorative Justice: The Netherlands', in D.J. Cornwell, *Criminal Punishment and Restorative Justice: Past, Present and Future Perspectives*, Winchester, Hampshire: Waterside Press, 2006, pp.135-148.

Blom-Cooper, L., 'Crime and Justice: A Shift in Perspective', in D.J. Cornwell, J.R.Blad & M. Wright (Eds.), *Civilising Criminal Justice: An International Restorative Agenda for Penal Reform*, Hook, Hampshire: Waterside Press, 2013, pp.151-170.

Bottomley, A.K., *Criminology in Focus*, Oxford: Martin Robertson, 1979.

Bottoms, A.E., 'Reflections on the Renaissance of Dangerousness', *Howard Journal*, Vol.xvi, No.2, 1977, pp.70-95.

Bottoms, A.E., 'The Suspended Sentence in England and Wales 1967-1978', in *British Journal of Criminology*, 21(1), 1981, pp.1-26.

Box, S., *Recession, Crime and Punishment*, Basingstoke, Hampshire: Macmillan Education Limited, 1987.

Briggs, J., Harrison, C., McInnes, A. & Vincent, D., *Crime and Punishment in England: An Introductory History*, London: UCL Press, 1996.

Broad, C.D., *Five Types of Ethical Theory*, New York: Harcourt, Brace & Company, 1930.

California Assembly Committee on Criminal Procedure, *Deterrent Effects of Criminal Sanctions*, Sacramento, CA: Assembly of the State of California, 1968.

Carr, C.L. (Ed.), *The Political Writings of Samuel Pufendorf*, [Tr. M.J. Seidler], New York: Oxford University Press, 1994.

Cavadino, M. & Dignan, J., *The Penal System: An Introduction*, [second Edition], London: SAGE Publications, 1997.

Cavadino, M. & Dignan, J., *Penal Systems: A Comparative Approach*, London: Sage Publications, 2007.

Cavender, G, & Musheno, M.C., 'The Adoption and Implementation of Determinate-based Sentencing Policies: A Critical Perspective', unpublished paper presented to the American Society of Criminology, 1981.

Christie, N., 'Conflicts as Property', in *British Journal of Criminology*, 17(1), 1977, pp.1-15.

Christie, N., *A Suitable Amount of Crime*, London: Routledge, 2004.

Church of England Board for Social Responsibility, *Prisons and Prisoners in England Today*, London: CIO, 1977.

Claessen, J., 'Straffen en Herstellen in Bijbels Perspectief: De Geestelijke Erfenis van Hermann Bianchi', in *Tijdschrift voor Filosofie*, 78(4), 2017.

Clear, T. & Frost, N., *The Punishment Imperative: The Rise and Failure of Mass Incarceration in America*, New York: University Press, 2015.

Cornwell, D.J., *Criminal Dangerousness and Its Punishment: Beyond the Phenomenological Illusion*, D. Phil. Thesis, York: University of York, 1989.

Cornwell, D.J., *Criminal Punishment and Restorative Justice: Past, Present and Future Perspectives*, Winchester: Waterside Press, 2006.

Cornwell, D.J., *The Penal Crisis and the Clapham Omnibus*, Hook, Hampshire: Waterside Press, 2009.

Cornwell, D.J., *Desert in a Reparative Frame: Re-Defining Contemporary Criminal Justice*, Den Haag: Eleven International Publishing, 2016.

Cornwell, D.J. & Boag, D., 'The Multi-Perpetrator Dimension in Prison Siege Negotiation: Psycho-Strategic Considerations', in *Proceedings of the Prison Service Psychology Conference 1991*, London: HM Prison Service, 1991, pp.104-124.

Cornwell, D.J., Blad, J.R. & Wright, M. (Eds.), *Civilising Criminal Justice: An International Restorative Agenda for Penal Reform*, Hook, Hampshire: Waterside Press, 2013.

Council of Europe, *Minimum Standards on the Rights, Support and Protection of Victims of Crime*, [Directive 2012/29/EU], Brussels: Council of Europe, 2012.

Council of Europe, *Annual Penal Statistics Survey 2014*, [M. Aebi *et. al.*(Eds)], Strasburg: Council of Europe, 2016, Table 7.

Council of Europe, *Annual Penal Statistics SPACE1, Prison Population Survey 2015 Final Report*, Table 17, Strasburg: Council of Europe, 2017 (14 March).

Criminal Justice Voluntary Sector Forum, *Redesigning the Community Justice System: A Policy Briefing for CJSVF Members*, Edinburgh: CJVSF, 2014.

Dean, C.W., Brame, R. & Piquero, A.R., 'Criminal Propensities, Discrete Groups of Offenders, and Persistence in Crime', *American Society of Criminology*, Vol.34, No.4, (November), 1996, pp.547-574.

Durkheim, E., *The Rules of Sociological Method*, [Tr. S.A. Solovay & J.H. Mueller], New York: Free Press of Glencoe, 1958.

Durkheim, E., *The Rules of Sociological Method and Selected Texts on Sociology and Its Method*, [Tr. W.D. Halls, S. Lukes (Ed.)], New York: Free Press, 1982.

Erlich, I., 'The Deterrent Effect in Law Enforcement', in *Journal of Legal Studies*, Vol.1, No.2, 1972 (June), pp.259-276.

Erickson, K.T. 'Notes on the Sociology of Deviance', in H.S. Becker (Ed.), *The Other Side*, New York: Free Press Macmillan, 1964, pp.9-22.

Esmée Fairbairn Foundation, *Crime, Courts and Confidence: Report of an Independent Inquiry Into Alternatives to Prison*, [The Coulsfield Report], London: The Stationery Office, 2004.

European Union. *Council Framework Decision of 15 March 2001 on the Standing of Victims in Criminal Proceedings*, [2001/220/JHA], Official Journal L 82, 22.3.2001, Brussels: European Union, 2001.

European Commission, *Rights of the Victim*, [DG Justice Ref: Ares (2013) 3763804-19/12/2013], Brussels: European Commission, 2013.

European Commission, *Crime and Criminal Justice Statistics*, Brussels: European Commission, 2016, at: <http://ec.europe.eu/eurostat/statistics_explained_/index.php/Crime_and_criminal_justice_statistics> [accessed on 19 February 2017].

Ewing, A.C., *The Morality of Punishment*, London: Kegan Paul, Trench & Trubner, 1929.

Farrington, D., Langan, P. & Wikstrom, P-O., 'Changes in Crime and Punishments in America, England and Sweden Between the 1980s and 1990s', *Studies in Crime Prevention*, 3, 1994, pp.104-131.

Fitzgerald, M. and Sim, J., *British Prisons*, [Second Edition], Oxford: Basil Blackwell, 1982.

Flew, A., 'The Justification of Punishment', in H.B. Acton (Ed.), *The Philosophy of Punishment*, London: Macmillan, 1969, pp.83-104.

Forsythe, W.J., 'Transportation', in D. Walsh & A. Poole (Eds.), *A Dictionary of Criminology*, London: Routledge & Kegan Paul, 1983. pp.223-5.

Garland, D., *The Culture of Control: Crime and Social Order in Contemporary Society*, Oxford: Oxford University Press, 2002.

Gibbs, J.P., *Crime, Punishment and Deterrence*. New York: Elsevier Publishing Company, 1975.

Gibbs, J.P, 'Crime, Punishment and Deterrence', in *Social Science Quarterly*, Vol.1, No.4. 1968, pp.515-530.

Gibson, B., *Criminal Justice Act 2003: A Guide to the New Procedure and Sentencing*, Hook, Hampshire: Waterside Press, 2004.

Gibson, B., *The Pocket A-Z of Criminal Justice*, Hook, Hampshire: Waterside Press, 2009.

Gillin, J.L., 'Social Factors Affecting the Volume of Crime', in *Physical Basis of Crime: A Symposium*, Easton, Pennsylvania: American Academy of Medicine, 1914, pp.53-67.

Glueck, S., 'Crime Causation', in *National Probation Association Yearbook*, 1941, pp. 86-108.

Gov.UK, *Press Release: Offenders to Pay More Towards Victim Support Services*, London: Ministry of Justice, 2014 (8 August), Part of: Victims of Crime (<www.gov.uk./government/policies/victims- of-crime>) [accessed on 15 February 2017].

Greene, J.E. (Ed.), *100 Great Thinkers*, New York: Simon & Schuster, Vol.2, 1967.

Grotius, H., *De Jure Belli et Pacis*, Paris: Buon Publishers, 1625, re-published by LibertyFund, Indianapolis, [Three volumes], 2005.

Haley, H.J., 'Retribution and the Definition of a Just Measure of Pain', in D.J. Mueller, D.E. Blackman & A.J. Chapman (Eds.), *Psychology and Law*, London and New York: John Wiley & Sons Limited, 1984, p.393 and *passim*.

Hart, H.L.A., *Prolegomenon to the Principles of Punishment*, 60 Proceedings of the Aristotelian Society 1, London, 1960, pp.4-5.

Hart, H.L.A., *Punishment and Responsibility*, Oxford: Oxford University Press, 1968.

HM Chief Inspector of Prisons for England and Wales, *Annual Report for 2015-2016*, Session: June- July 2016, HC 471, London: House of Commons, 2016.

HM Prison Service, *Prison Discipline Procedures*, [Prison Service Instruction (PSI) 47/2011], London: HM Prison Service, 2016 (Re-Issue).

Hennessey, J., *Report of an Inquiry by HM Chief Inspector of Prisons for England and Wales, into the Disturbances in Prison Service Establishments between 29 April and 2 May 1986*, London: HMSO.

Hobbes, T., *Leviathan*, R. Tuck (Ed.), Cambridge: Cambridge University Press, 1991.

Hobbes, T., *Of Liberty and Necessity*, Vere Chappell (Ed.), Cambridge: Cambridge University Press, 1999.

Home Office, 'Report of the Departmental Committee on Prisons', [The Gladstone Report], *Parliamentary Papers*, Vol.lvi, 25, London: Home Office, 1895.

Home Office, *People in Prison: England and Wales*, Cmnd.4714, London: HMSO, 1969.

Home Office, *The Adult Offender*, Cmnd.2852, London: HMSO, 1965.

Home Office, *Committee of Inquiry into the United Kingdom Prison Services – Report*, Cmnd. 7673, [The May Report], London: HMSO, 1979.

Home Office, *Crime, Justice and Protecting the Public*, [White Paper]. Cm. 965, London: HMSO, 1990.

Home Office, *The Victim's Charter*, London: Home Office, 1990, [Now obsolete].

Home Office. *Custody, Care and Justice: The Way Ahead for the Prison Service in England and Wales*, Cm 1647, London: HMSO, 1991.

Home Office, *Victim's Charter: A Statement of Standards for Victims of Crime*, London: HMSO, 1996.

Home Office, *Making Punishments Work*, [The Halliday Report], London: Home Office, 2001.

Home Office, *A New Deal for Victims and Witnesses: National Strategy to Deliver Improved Services*, London: Home Office, 2003.

Home Office, *Victim's Rights*, London: Home Office, 2005a.

Home Office, *The Code of Practice for Victims of Crime*, London: HMSO, 2005b.

Home Office, *Re-building Lives – Supporting Victims of Crime*, CM 6705, London: HMSO, 2005c.

Home Office, *Have You Got What It Takes: Your Role as Police and Crime Commissioner (PCC)*, London: Home Office, 2012.

Honderich, T., *Punishment: The Supposed Justifications*, [Revised Edition], Harmondsworth: Peregrine Books, 1976.

Hood, R. (Ed.), *Crime, Criminology and Public Policy: Essays in Honour of Sir Leon Radzinowicz*, London: Heinemann, 1974.

House of Commons Library, *Prison Population Statistics [England and Wales]*, Standard Note SN/SG/4334, G Berman (Author), 28 June 2013, London: House of Commons, 2013.

House of Commons, *Prison Safety and Reform*, Hansard Online, 03 November 2016, Volume 616-7, London: House of Commons, 2016.

Howard, J., *The State of the Prisons in England and Wales*, Warrington, UK: William Eyres, 1777, and Appendix 1780.

Hudson, B., *Justice Through Punishment: A Critique of the 'Justice' Model of Corrections*, Basingstoke: Macmillan Education Limited, 1981.

Hűning, D. 'Souveränität und Strafgewalt: Die Begrűnding das *Jus Puniedi* bei Samuel Pufendorf', in *Naturrecht und Staatstheorie bei Samuel Pufendorf*, Baden-Baden: Nomos, 2009.

Husak, D., *A Framework for Punishment: What is the Insight of Hart's Prolegomenon?* Rutgers State University NJ: Department of Philosophy, 2015.

Ignatieff, M., *A Just Measure of Pain: The Penitentiary in the Industrial Revolution 1750-1850*, New York: Pantheon Books, 1978.

Jeffery, C.R., 'Criminal Behaviour and Learning Theory', in *Journal of Criminal Law, Criminology and Police Science*, 56, 1965 (September), pp.294-300.

Kant, I., 'Groundwork of the Metaphysics of Morals', in *Practical Philosophy*, [Tr. M. McGregor], Cambridge: Cambridge University Press, 1996.

Kant, I., *Critique of Practical Reason: A Critical Guide*, [Tr. A. Reath & J. Timmermann], Cambridge: Cambridge University Press, 2010.

Karr, J-B., *Les Guêpes*, Paris: Calmann Lévy, 1863 Edition.

King, R. & McDermott, K., 'Security, Control and Humane Containment in the Prison System of England and Wales', in D. Downs (Ed.), *Unravelling Criminal Justice*, London: Palgrave Macmillan, 1992, pp. 96-118.

Kynaston, D., *Tales of New Jerusalem 1945-1979*, [Four Volumes], London: Bloomsbury Press, 2007.

Lacey, N., *The Prisoners' Dilemma: Political Economy and Punishment in Contemporary Democracies*, Cambridge: Cambridge University Press, 2008.

Lappi-Seppälä, T., 'Downsizing the Use of Imprisonment in Finland', in D.J. Cornwell, J.R. Blad & M. Wright (Eds.), *Civilising Criminal Justice: An International Restorative Agenda for Penal Reform*, Hook, Hampshire: Waterside Press, 2013, pp.501-524.

Learmont, Gen. Sir J., *Review of Prison Service Security in England and Wales and the Escape from Parkhurst Prison on Tuesday 3rd January 1995*, Cm 3020, London: HMSO, 1995 (September).

Lewis, D., *Hidden Agendas: Politics, Law and Disorder*, London: Hamish Hamilton, 1997.

Locke, J., *Two Treatises Concerning Government*, [Volumes 1 & 2], 1689, P. Laslett (Ed.), Cambridge: Cambridge University Press, 1988.

Lipton, D., Martinson, R. & Wilks, J., *The Effectiveness of Correctional Treatment*, London and New York, Praeger Publications, 1975.

Lukes, S. (Ed.), *Ēmile Durkheim: His Life and Works*, Harmondsworth, Middlesex: Penguin Books, 1973.

Mabbott, J.D., 'Professor Flew on Punishment', in H.B. Acton (Ed.), *The Philosophy of Punishment*, London: Macmillan, 1969, pp.115-129.

Martinson, R., 'What Works? Questions and Answers About Prison Reform', in *The Public Interest*, 1974 (Spring), and also in J.A. Gardiner & M.A. Mulkey (Eds.), *Crime and Criminal Justice*, London and Lexington: D.C. Heath and Company, 1975, pp.155-87.

Maruna, S., 'Desistence and Restorative Justice: It's Now or Never', in *Restorative Justice: An International Journal*, 4 (3), 2017, pp. 289-381.

Marwick, A., *British Society Since 1945*, [Fourth Edition], London: Penguin Books, 2003.

Mastrobuoni, G. & Rivers, D.A., *Criminal Discount Factors and Deterrence*, [Discussion Paper No. 9769], Bonn, Germany: IZA, 2016.

Mc.Elrea, F.W.M. (J), 'Restorative Justice as a Procedural Revolution: Some Lessons from the Adversary System', in D.J. Cornwell, J.R.Blad & M. Wright (Eds.), *Civilising Criminal Justice: An International Restorative Agenda for Penal Reform*, Hook, Hampshire: Waterside Press, 2013, pp.81-114.

Merton, R.K., 'Social Structure and Anomie', in *American Sociological Review*, 3, 677-682, 1938 (October).

Mill, J.S., *The Principles of Political Economy*, London: J.W. Parker, West Strand, 1848.

Mill, J.S., *Considerations on Representative Government*, London: Parker, Son & Bourn, West Strand, 1861.

Mill, J.S., *On Liberty*, London: J.W. Parker & Son, West Strand, 1859.

Mill, J.S., *Utilitarianism*, London: Parker, Son & Bourn, West Strand, 1863, and see also: E. Warnock (Ed.), London: Collins Fontana, 1964 at Chapter 5.

Ministry of Justice, *Organisations Awarded Funding from the Victim and Witness General Fund 2011-14*, London: Ministry of Justice, 2011 (June).

Ministry of Justice, *Getting it Right for Victims and Witnesses*, [Consultation Paper], CM 8288, London: Ministry of Justice, 2012a.

Ministry of Justice, *Post-consultation Report for the Consultation Paper (CP3/2012)*, London: Ministry of Justice, 2012b.

Ministry of Justice, *2013 Compendium of Re-Offending Statistics and Analysis*, London: Ministry of Justice, 2013.

Ministry of Justice, *Offender Management Statistics Annual Tables 2014*, London: Ministry of Justice, 2014a.

Ministry of Justice, *Prison Performance Digest 2012-13*, London: Ministry of Justice, 2014b.

Ministry of Justice, *Prison Annual Performance Ratings 2014-15*, London: Ministry of Justice, 2015a.

Ministry of Justice, *National Offender Management Service Annual Report 2014/15: Management Addendum*, London: Ministry of Justice, 2015b.

Ministry of Justice, *Prison Population Statistics – Population Bulletin 16 December 2016*, London: National Offender Management Service, 2016a.

Ministry of Justice, *Story of the Prison Population 1993-2016 England and Wales*, London: Ministry of Justice, 2016b, (July).

Ministry of Justice, *Proven Reoffending Statistics Quarterly: July 2013 to June 2014*, Tables C1a and C2a, 2016c, London: Ministry of Justice, 2016c.

Ministry of Justice, *Monthly Population Bulletin May 2016*, London: Ministry of Justice, 2016d.

Ministry of Justice, *Offender Management Statistics Prison Releases 2015*, London: Ministry of Justice, 2016e.

Ministry of Justice, *Offender Management Statistics*, London: Ministry of Justice, 2016f., Table 1.9 and Annual Table A2.6.

Mirsky, L., *The Nanaimo Community Justice Forum: A Restorative Justice Partnership in British Columbia, Canada*, Bethlehem, Pennsylvania: International Institute for Restorative Practices, 2005.

Monahan, J., 'The Prediction of Violence', in D. Chappell & J. Monahan (Eds.), *Violence and Criminal Justice*, Lexington, MA: D.C. Heath & Company, 1975.

Mumola, C., '*Substance Abuse and Treatment, State and Federal Prisoners 1997*', [US Bureau of Justice Special Report], Washington, DC: Bureau of Justice, 1999.

Nagin, D.S., 'Criminal Deterrence Research at the Outset of the Twenty-First Century', in M. Tonry (Ed.), *Crime and Justice: A Review of Research*, Vol.23, Chicago, ILL: University of Chicago Press, 1998, pp.1-42.

Nagin, D.S. & Pogarsky,G., 'Integrating Celerity, Impulsivity, and Extralegal Sanction Threats into a Model of General Deterrence Theory and Evidence', *Criminology*, 39(4), 2001, pp.865-892.

National Audit Office (NAO), *Managing Offenders on Short Custodial Sentences*, London: The Stationery Office, 2010.

Newburn, T., "Tough on Crime": Penal Policy in England and Wales', in M. Tonry (Ed.), *Crime and Justice: A Review of Research*, Chicago, ILL: University of Chicago Press, 2007.

Paine, T., The *Age of Reason*, Paris: Barrois & London: D.I. Eaton, 1794

Parliamentary All-Party Penal Affairs Group (PA-PPAG), *Too Many Prisoners: An Examination of Ways of Reducing the Prison Population*, [R. Kilroy-Silk, Chair], Chichester and London: Barry Rose Publishers, 1980, (June).

Parmelee, M.F., *The Principles of Anthropology and Sociology in Their Relations to Criminal Procedure*, New York: Macmillan, 1908.

Parsons, P., *Responsibility for Crime*, New York: Columbia University Press, 1909.

Parsons, T., *The Social System*, New York: Free Press, 1951.

Paternoster, R., 'The Deterrent Effect of the Perceived Certainty and Severity of Punishment: A Review of the Evidence and Issues', 4 *Justice Quarterly* 173, 1987.

Paternoster, R., 'How Much Do We Really Know About Deterrence Research?' in *Journal of Criminal Law and Criminology*, Volume 100, Issue 3, 2010, pp.765-824.

Prison Reform Trust, *Submission to Phase 2 of the Woolf Inquiry into Prison Disturbances*, London: Prison Reform Trust, 1990.

Prison Reform Trust, *Bromley Briefing 2015*, London: Prison Reform Trust.

Prison Reform Trust, *Prison: The Facts*, [Bromley Briefings Summer 2016], London: Prison Reform Trust, 2016a., available at: <www.prisonreformtrust.org.uk/Publications/Factfile> [accessed on 2 August 2016].

Prison Reform Trust, *Bromley Briefings Prison Factfile Autumn 2016*, London: Prison Reform Trust, 2016b.

Quinton, A.M., 'On Punishment', in H.B. Acton (Ed.), *The Philosophy of Punishment*, London: Macmillan, 1969, pp.55-64.

Rawls, J., 'Two Concepts of Rules', in H.B. Acton (Ed.), *The Philosophy of Punishment*, London: Macmillan, 1969, pp.105-114.

Rosenberg, J., 'Victim Surcharge: Unintended Consequences', *The Law Society Gazette*, 2013 (July), pp.1-2.

Ruck, S.K. (Ed.), *Paterson on Prisons: The Collected Papers of Sir Alexander Paterson*, London: Frederick Miller, 1951.

Scottish Government, *Redesigning the Community Justice System: Response to Consultation*, Edinburgh: Scottish Government, 2013.

Sentencing Council, *What is the Victim Surcharge*?, London: The Sentencing Council, 2016 (April), Available at: <www.sentencingcouncil.org.uk/about-sentencing/types-of-sentence/other-orders> [accessed on 16 February 2017].

Shakespeare, W., *Henry IV*, Pt2, III, i, 231, quoted in Cohen, J.M. & Cohen, M.J., *The Penguin Dictionary of Quotations*, [Reprinted 1977], Harmondsworth: Penguin Books Ltd, 1977.

Shaw, A.G.L., *Convicts and the Colonies*, London: Faber & Faber, 1966.

Sim, J., 'When You Ain't Got Nothing, You Got Nothing To Lose', in K. Bottomley, T. Fowles & R. Reiner (Eds.), *Criminal Justice: Theory and Practice*, London, British Society of Criminology, 1992, pp.273-300.

Simmons, A.J., *The Lockean Theory of Rights*, Princeton: Princeton University Press, 1992.

Simmons, A.J., *On the Edge of Anarchy: Locke, Consent and the Limits of Society*, Princeton: Princeton University Press, 1993.

Stephen, Sir J.F., 'Liberty, Equality, Fraternity', – [a Riposte to J.S. Mill], re-printed in L. Blom-Cooper and G. Drewry (Eds.), *Law and Morality – A Reader*, London: Duckworth, 1976, pp.13-18.

Strauss, L., *Natural Right and History*, Chicago, ILL: University of Chicago Press, 1953.

Sutherland, E.H., *Criminology*, [First Edition], Chicago, ILL: J.B. Lippincott Company, 1924.

Sutherland, E.H. & Cressey, D.R., *Principles of Criminology*, [Fifth Edition], Chicago, ILL: J.B. Lippincott Company, 1955.

Taylor, I, Walton, P. & Young, J. (Eds.), *The New Criminology*, London: Routledge & Kegan Paul, 1975.

Tolman, F.L., 'Study of Sociology in Institutions of Learning in the United States', in *The American Journal of Sociology*, 7: 797-838, 1902 (May), and 8: 85-121, 1902 (July), 8: 251-272, 1902 (July), and 8: 531-558, 1903 (January).

Tonry, M. (Ed.), *Confronting Crime: Crime Control Policies Under New Labour*, Cullompton, Devon: Willan Publishing, 2003.

Tonry, M., 'Learning From the Limitations of Deterrence Research', *Crime and Justice*, Vol.37, No.1, 2008, pp.279-311.

Tuck, R. (Ed.), *The Rights of War and Peace: Political Thought from Grotius to Kant*, Oxford: Oxford University Press, 1990.

Tuckness, A., 'Locke and Punishment', *Stanford Encyclopedia of Philosophy*, CSLI, Stanford University, 2016a, available at: <http://plato.stanford.edu/entries/locke-political> [accessed on 17 November 2016].

Tuckness, A. 'Locke's Political Philosophy', *Stanford Encyclopedia of Philosophy*, [Spring 2016 Edition] E.N. Zolta (Ed.), at: <http://plato.stanford.edu/archives/spr2016/entries/locke-political/> [accessed on 17 November 2016].

Umbreit, M.S., 'Restorative Justice Through Victim-Offender Mediation: A Multi-Site Assessment', in *Western Criminology Review*, Volume 1, Issue 1, 1998, (June), for which in an online version, see: <www.westerncriminology.org/documents/WCR/v01n1/Umbreit/umbreit.html> [22pp], [accessed on 18 February 2017].

Umbreit, M.S. & Greenwood, J., 'National Survey of Victim-Offender Mediation Programmes in the United States', in 16 *Mediation Quarterly*, 1999, pp.235-241.

Umbreit, M.S., Vos, B., Coates, R.B. & Lightfoot, E., 'Restorative Justice in the Twenty-First Century: A Social Movement Full of Opportunities and Pitfalls', in *Marquette Law Review*, Volume 89, Number 2, 2005, pp.253-304.

van Dijk, J.J.M., Manchin, R., van Kesteren, J.N. & Hideg, G., *The Burden of Crime in the EU: A Comparative Analysis of the European Survey of Crime and Safety, (2005EU ICS)*, Council of Europe, Brussels: Gallup Europe, 2007.

von Hirsch, *Doing Justice: The Choice of Punishments*, [Report of the Committee for the Study of Incarceration], New York: Hill & Wang, 1976.

von Hirsch, A., Bottoms, A.E., Burney, E. & Wikstrom, P-O., *Criminal Deterrence and Sentence Severity: An Analysis of Recent Research*, Oxford: Hart Publishing, 1999.

von Pufendorf, S., *Elementorum JurisprudentœUniversalis*, [Libri II], The Hague: A. Vlacq, 1660.

von Pufendorf, S., *De Jure Naturae et Gentium*, [Vol. Two], 1672, [Tr. C.H. Oldfather and W.A. Oldfather], J.B. Scott (Ed.), Oxford: Clarendon Press, 1934.

von Pufendorf, S., *De Officio Hominis et Civis Juxta Legem Naturalem*, [Vol.2], Lund: Junghans, 1673.

von Pufendorf, S., *De Rebus Gestis Frederici Magni, Electoris Brandenbugrici Commentariorum Libri Novendeicim*, Berlin: J. Schrey & H.J. Meyer, 1695.

von Pufendorf, S., *De Habitu Religionis Christianae ad Vitem Civilem*, 1687, Bremen: Schwerdfeger, Reprinted Stuttgart-Bad Cannstatt: Frommann-Holzboog, 1972.

Walgrave, L., *Restorative Justice, Self-Interest and Responsible Citizenship*, Cullompton, Devon: Willan Publishing, 2008.

Walker, P., *Punishment: An Illustrated History*, Newton Abbot: David & Charles Publishers, 1972.

Walsh, D., 'Parole', in D. Walsh & A. Poole (Eds.), *A Dictionary of Criminology*, London: Routledge & Kegan Paul, 1983, pp.154-5.

Williams, K.R., Gibbs, J.P. & Erickson, M.L., 'Public Knowledge of Statutory Penalties: The Extent and Basis of Accurate Perception', *Pacific Sociological Review*, 23(1), 1980, pp. 105-128.

Woodcock, Sir J., *The Escape from Whitemoor Prison on Friday 9th September 1994*, Cm 1456, London: HMSO, 1994, (December).

Woolf, H. (LJ) & Tumim, S. (J), *Prison Disturbances April 1990*, [Two Volumes], Cm 1456, London: HMSO, 1991.

Wright, C.D., *Outline of Practical Sociology*, New York: Longmans Green, 1899.

Wright, V., *Deterrence in Criminal Justice: Evaluating Certainty vs Severity of Punishment*, Washington, DC: The Sentencing Project, 2010.

Yates, A.L., *Thomas Hobbes on Punishment*, Ph.D Thesis, Canada: University of Western Ontario, 2012, available at: <http://ir.lib.uwo.ca/cgi/view.content.cgi?article=1651&context-etd> [accessed on 18 November 2016].

Zimring, F.E. & Hawkins, G.J., *Deterrence: The Legal Threat in Crime Control*, Chicago, ILL: University of Chicago Press, 1973.

Index